Samba For Dummies®

W9-BYK-238

Cheat Sheet

Linux Utilities

- ✔ **cat:** Displays, or concatenates, files
- ✔ **cd:** Changes directories
- ✔ **COAS:** Caldera OpenLinux utility for user administration
- ✔ **chgrp:** Changes the group associated with a file or directory
- ✔ **chmod:** Changes the rights of a file or directory
- ✔ **chown:** Changes the owner of a file or directory
- ✔ **cp:** Copies a file
- ✔ **emacs:** A complex text editor
- ✔ **find:** Finds a file in the directory structure
- ✔ **grep:** Searches through a file for a keyword
- ✔ **gzip:** Unzips files
- ✔ **kill:** Stops a running process on your Linux server
- ✔ **LISA:** Caldera OpenLinux utility for user administration
- ✔ **ln:** Creates a link between two files or directories
- ✔ **ls:** Lists the files and directories in a directory
- ✔ **more:** Displays a file one screen at a time
- ✔ **mount:** Mounts a file system on a Linux server, usually a removable drive
- ✔ **mv:** Moves a file
- ✔ **pico:** A friendly text editor
- ✔ **ping:** Checks network connectivity between two computers
- ✔ **ps:** Identifies the currently running processes on your Linux server
- ✔ **rpm:** Red Hat Package Manager, used to install packaged software
- ✔ **su:** Switches users, usually to the superuser (root)
- ✔ **tar:** Archives and restores files
- ✔ **telnet:** A program you use to access a remote server
- ✔ **umount:** Unmounts a file system on a Linux server
- ✔ **useradd and adduser:** Two scripts that add users to a UNIX server
- ✔ **userdel:** A script that deletes users from a UNIX server
- ✔ **vi:** A less friendly text editor, but on every UNIX server

For Dummies®: Bestselling Book Series for Beginners

Samba For Dummies®

Cheat Sheet

Samba Utilities

- **nmblookup:** Interrogates clients in the Network Neighborhood
- **smbclient:** Enables the Samba server to connect to another Windows-type (Samba or Windows) server, including itself
- **smbpasswd:** Enables you to change SMB encrypted passwords on Samba servers
- **smbstatus:** Lists current connections to the Samba server
- **testparm:** Checks the Samba configuration file, smb.conf, for validity and identifies the smb.conf file that Samba is using
- **testprns:** Enables you to test the printers defined in your printcap file

Important Samba Files

- **smb.conf:** The Samba configuration file
- *path*/**smbpasswd:** The Samba password file when you are using encrypted passwords; the location is set in your smb.conf file

Useful DOS Commands

- **ipconfig:** Identifies your Windows computer's IP address
- **ping:** Checks network connectivity between two computers
- **telnet:** Used to access a remote computer
- **winipcfg:** Identifies your Windows computer's TCP/IP configuration

Important Linux Files

- **/etc/group:** The file that lists the groups on a Linux server
- **/etc/inetd.conf:** The inetd configuration file, which controls programs launched by inetd
- **/etc/passwd:** The file that lists the users on a Linux server
- **/etc/rcd:** Contains the run control directories used to start and stop daemons including Samba
- **/etc/services:** The associating programs with port numbers for inetd

For Dummies®: Bestselling Book Series for Beginners

TM

References for the Rest of Us! ®

BESTSELLING BOOK SERIES

Are you intimidated and confused by computers? Do you find that traditional manuals are overloaded with technical details you'll never use? Do your friends and family always call you to fix simple problems on their PCs? Then the ...*For Dummies*® computer book series from IDG Books Worldwide is for you.

...*For Dummies* books are written for those frustrated computer users who know they aren't really dumb but find that PC hardware, software, and indeed the unique vocabulary of computing make them feel helpless. ...*For Dummies* books use a lighthearted approach, a down-to-earth style, and even cartoons and humorous icons to dispel computer novices' fears and build their confidence. Lighthearted but not lightweight, these books are a perfect survival guide for anyone forced to use a computer.

> *"I like my copy so much I told friends; now they bought copies."*
>
> — Irene C., Orwell, Ohio

> *"Quick, concise, nontechnical, and humorous."*
>
> — Jay A., Elburn, Illinois

> *"Thanks, I needed this book. Now I can sleep at night."*
>
> — Robin F., British Columbia, Canada

Already, millions of satisfied readers agree. They have made ...*For Dummies* books the #1 introductory level computer book series and have written asking for more. So, if you're looking for the most fun and easy way to learn about computers, look to ...*For Dummies* books to give you a helping hand.

IDG
BOOKS
WORLDWIDE

Samba

FOR

DUMMIES®

Samba
FOR
DUMMIES®

by George Haberberger and Lisa Doyle

IDG Books Worldwide, Inc.
An International Data Group Company

Foster City, CA ◆ Chicago, IL ◆ Indianapolis, IN ◆ New York, NY

Samba For Dummies®

Published by
IDG Books Worldwide, Inc.
An International Data Group Company
919 E. Hillsdale Blvd.
Suite 400
Foster City, CA 94404
www.idgbooks.com (IDG Books Worldwide Web Site)
www.dummies.com (Dummies Press Web Site)

Library of Congress Control Number: 00-103401

ISBN: 0-7645-0712-5

Printed in the United States of America

10 9 8 7 6 5 4 3 2 1

1B/SZ/QY/QQ/IN

Distributed in the United States by IDG Books Worldwide, Inc.

Distributed by CDG Books Canada Inc. for Canada; by Transworld Publishers Limited in the United Kingdom; by IDG Norge Books for Norway; by IDG Sweden Books for Sweden; by IDG Books Australia Publishing Corporation Pty. Ltd. for Australia and New Zealand; by TransQuest Publishers Pte Ltd. for Singapore, Malaysia, Thailand, Indonesia, and Hong Kong; by Gotop Information Inc. for Taiwan; by ICG Muse, Inc. for Japan; by Intersoft for South Africa; by Eyrolles for France; by International Thomson Publishing for Germany, Austria and Switzerland; by Distribuidora Cuspide for Argentina; by LR International for Brazil; by Galileo Libros for Chile; by Ediciones ZETA S.C.R. Ltda. for Peru; by WS Computer Publishing Corporation, Inc., for the Philippines; by Contemporanea de Ediciones for Venezuela; by Express Computer Distributors for the Caribbean and West Indies; by Micronesia Media Distributor, Inc. for Micronesia; by Chips Computadoras S.A. de C.V. for Mexico; by Editorial Norma de Panama S.A. for Panama; by American Bookshops for Finland.

For general information on IDG Books Worldwide's books in the U.S., please call our Consumer Customer Service department at 800-762-2974. For reseller information, including discounts and premium sales, please call our Reseller Customer Service department at 800-434-3422.

For information on where to purchase IDG Books Worldwide's books outside the U.S., please contact our International Sales department at 317-572-3993 or fax 317-572-4002.

For consumer information on foreign language translations, please contact our Customer Service department at 1-800-434-3422, fax 317-572-4002, or e-mail rights@idgbooks.com.

For information on licensing foreign or domestic rights, please phone +1-650-653-7098.

For sales inquiries and special prices for bulk quantities, please contact our Order Services department at 800-434-3422 or write to the address above.

For information on using IDG Books Worldwide's books in the classroom or for ordering examination copies, please contact our Educational Sales department at 800-434-2086 or fax 317-572-4005.

For press review copies, author interviews, or other publicity information, please contact our Public Relations department at 650-653-7000 or fax 650-653-7500.

For authorization to photocopy items for corporate, personal, or educational use, please contact Copyright Clearance Center, 222 Rosewood Drive, Danvers, MA 01923, or fax 978-750-4470.

is a registered trademark under exclusive license to IDG Books Worldwide, Inc. from International Data Group, Inc.

IDG BOOKS WORLDWIDE

About the Authors

George Haberberger has been working in the software field for ten years and in customer and technical support for the last seven years. He has provided administrative support for SunOS, Netware, and Solaris printers, and Macintosh, DOS, and Windows clients. He wrote user manuals for Sun-based printers and extensively revised the Mail Manager 2000 mailing list software and ZCR 2000 Zip code encoding software manuals. He coauthored the *Samba Administrator's Handbook* (IDG Books Worldwide, Inc.).

Lisa Doyle has been writing and editing tedious technical documentation for a long time. Clients range from two-person corporations (Recon Corp.) to $29 billion corporations (Intel) on everything from teaching your parents how to save a file on their Mac (the jury's still out on that one) to overhauling a one-ton, 7,200-volt electrical circuit breaker (NASA) to designing a complex software mapping application (Etak). Published books include *Basic Digital Electronics — 2nd Edition*, *How to Read Schematics* (both TAB/McGraw-Hill), and *Samba Administrator's Handbook* (IDG Books Worldwide, Inc.).

ABOUT IDG BOOKS WORLDWIDE

Welcome to the world of IDG Books Worldwide.

IDG Books Worldwide, Inc., is a subsidiary of International Data Group, the world's largest publisher of computer-related information and the leading global provider of information services on information technology. IDG was founded more than 30 years ago by Patrick J. McGovern and now employs more than 9,000 people worldwide. IDG publishes more than 290 computer publications in over 75 countries. More than 90 million people read one or more IDG publications each month.

Launched in 1990, IDG Books Worldwide is today the #1 publisher of best-selling computer books in the United States. We are proud to have received eight awards from the Computer Press Association in recognition of editorial excellence and three from Computer Currents' First Annual Readers' Choice Awards. Our best-selling ...For Dummies® series has more than 50 million copies in print with translations in 31 languages. IDG Books Worldwide, through a joint venture with IDG's Hi-Tech Beijing, became the first U.S. publisher to publish a computer book in the People's Republic of China. In record time, IDG Books Worldwide has become the first choice for millions of readers around the world who want to learn how to better manage their businesses.

Our mission is simple: Every one of our books is designed to bring extra value and skill-building instructions to the reader. Our books are written by experts who understand and care about our readers. The knowledge base of our editorial staff comes from years of experience in publishing, education, and journalism — experience we use to produce books to carry us into the new millennium. In short, we care about books, so we attract the best people. We devote special attention to details such as audience, interior design, use of icons, and illustrations. And because we use an efficient process of authoring, editing, and desktop publishing our books electronically, we can spend more time ensuring superior content and less time on the technicalities of making books.

You can count on our commitment to deliver high-quality books at competitive prices on topics you want to read about. At IDG Books Worldwide, we continue in the IDG tradition of delivering quality for more than 30 years. You'll find no better book on a subject than one from IDG Books Worldwide.

IDG BOOKS WORLDWIDE

John Kilcullen
Chairman and CEO
IDG Books Worldwide, Inc.

Eighth Annual Computer Press Awards ≥1992

Ninth Annual Computer Press Awards ≥1993

Tenth Annual Computer Press Awards ≥1994

Eleventh Annual Computer Press Awards ≥1995

IDG is the world's leading IT media, research and exposition company. Founded in 1964, IDG had 1997 revenues of $2.05 billion and has more than 9,000 employees worldwide. IDG offers the widest range of media options that reach IT buyers in 75 countries representing 95% of worldwide IT spending. IDG's diverse product and services portfolio spans six key areas including print publishing, online publishing, expositions and conferences, market research, education and training, and global marketing services. More than 90 million people read one or more of IDG's 290 magazines and newspapers, including IDG's leading global brands — Computerworld, PC World, Network World, Macworld and the Channel World family of publications. IDG Books Worldwide is one of the fastest-growing computer book publishers in the world, with more than 700 titles in 36 languages. The "...For Dummies®" series alone has more than 50 million copies in print. IDG offers online users the largest network of technology-specific Web sites around the world through IDG.net (http://www.idg.net), which comprises more than 225 targeted Web sites in 55 countries worldwide. International Data Corporation (IDC) is the world's largest provider of information technology data, analysis and consulting, with research centers in over 41 countries and more than 400 research analysts worldwide. IDG World Expo is a leading producer of more than 168 globally branded conferences and expositions in 35 countries including E3 (Electronic Entertainment Expo), Macworld Expo, ComNet, Windows World Expo, ICE (Internet Commerce Expo), Agenda, DEMO, and Spotlight. IDG's training subsidiary, ExecuTrain, is the world's largest computer training company, with more than 230 locations worldwide and 785 training courses. IDG Marketing Services helps industry-leading IT companies build international brand recognition by developing global integrated marketing programs via IDG's print, online and exposition products worldwide. Further information about the company can be found at www.idg.com. 1/26/00

Authors' Acknowledgments

George thanks his wife, Mary, and daughter, Allison, for tolerating his absence while writing this book. George would also like to acknowledge Ed and Jerry for their inspiration in creating this book.

Lisa acknowledges George's brain and almost disturbingly patient demeanor. And thanks to Ed for introducing George and myself (even though we've never actually met — yet another frightening demonstration of just what the Internet can do). And thanks to you for buying this book, even though people just might chuckle when they see you with it. So what? You're smarter than they.

Publisher's Acknowledgments

We're proud of this book; please register your comments through our IDG Books Worldwide Online Registration Form located at http://my2cents.dummies.com.

Some of the people who helped bring this book to market include the following:

Acquisitions, Editorial, and Media Development

Project Editor: John W. Pont

Senior Acquisitions Editor: Laura Lewin

Proof Editor: Teresa Artman

Technical Editor: John D. Blair

Permissions Editor: Carmen Krikorian

Associate Media Development Specialist: Megan Decraene

Editorial Manager: Kyle Looper

Media Development Manager: Heather Heath Dismore

Editorial Assistants: Candace Nicholson, Sarah Shupert

Production

Project Coordinator: Maridee Ennis

Layout and Graphics: Amy Adrian, Jason Guy, Erin Zeltner

Proofreaders: Laura Albert, Susan Moritz, York Production Services, Inc.

Indexer: York Production Services, Inc.

Special Help
Amanda M. Foxworth

General and Administrative

IDG Books Worldwide, Inc.: John Kilcullen, CEO

IDG Books Technology Publishing Group: Richard Swadley, Senior Vice President and Publisher; Walter R. Bruce III, Vice President and Publisher; Joseph Wikert, Vice President and Publisher; Mary Bednarek, Vice President and Director, Product Development; Andy Cummings, Publishing Director, General User Group; Mary C. Corder, Editorial Director; Barry Pruett, Publishing Director

IDG Books Consumer Publishing Group: Roland Elgey, Senior Vice President and Publisher; Kathleen A. Welton, Vice President and Publisher; Kevin Thornton, Acquisitions Manager; Kristin A. Cocks, Editorial Director

IDG Books Internet Publishing Group: Brenda McLaughlin, Senior Vice President and Publisher; Sofia Marchant, Online Marketing Manager

IDG Books Production for Branded Press: Debbie Stailey, Director of Production; Cindy L. Phipps, Manager of Project Coordination, Production Proofreading, and Indexing; Tony Augsburger, Manager of Prepress, Reprints, and Systems; Shelley Lea, Supervisor of Graphics and Design; Debbie J. Gates, Production Systems Specialist; Steve Arany, Associate Automation Supervisor; Robert Springer, Supervisor of Proofreading; Trudy Coler, Page Layout Manager; Kathie Schutte, Senior Page Layout Supervisor; Janet Seib, Associate Page Layout Supervisor; Michael Sullivan, Production Supervisor

Packaging and Book Design: Patty Page, Manager, Promotions Marketing

◆

The publisher would like to give special thanks to Patrick J. McGovern, without whom this book would not have been possible.

◆

Contents at a Glance

Cartoons at a Glance

By Rich Tennant

page 241

page 315

page 283

page 33

page 163

page 199

page 9

Fax: 978-546-7747
E-mail: richtennant@the5thwave.com
World Wide Web: www.the5thwave.com

Table of Contents

Introduction

● ●

*T*his could be you: You have your two Windows computers. You just bought a nice laser printer. You're running out of hard drive space on both computers. You need more space and more control in managing your files and resources. Oh, but how?

You need a file server. For the uninitiated, a file server, or "server," is a centrally connected computer that stores and shares (serves) commonly used files and devices (such as printers or backup devices). Without servers, each computer would need its own printer, and backup device, and eventually extra hard drives to keep up with the size of today's applications, and . . . Everyone would still be scurrying around with floppies in their hands when trading files, looking stressed because the file had to be stripped of all its graphics to fit on the disk.

You have Windows machines, so you must need a Windows server, right? You go to the Microsoft Web site, eventually find the small business server stuff, and . . . what?!? All that money just for the networking software? Ouch. Surely there's a better solution.

Here's a better solution: Get a hold of that old 486 PC that your roommate can't even give away. Max out the RAM in it. Install Linux and Samba, which are free or darn near, and presto: instant server. Then start reading this book.

Or this could be you: Your IT foreman just got sucked in to a pre-IPO dotcom, and you're next in the IT seniority ranks (well, you have been at the company more than 2 months now). You have 27 Windows computers, 3 Linux servers running Samba, 5 printers, and multiple backup devices. How are you going to manage this monster, eventually with authority? Start reading.

About This Book

This book tells you how to establish, configure, and maintain an inexpensive network that consists of a Linux/Samba server and one or more Windows clients. Handy for the home, office, or even a large corporation.

Maybe you know a lot. Or maybe you are freaked out right now because you don't have a clue and need to get one yesterday. While that's a wide range to cover, reading this book is a great way to fill in the gaps. It's designed for those doing baby steps with Samba, but techies will find something interesting, too. On the other hand, we tried to leave out as much geek fluff as possible. It's a tough line to walk with you already-smart-on-a-lot-of-stuff-but-Samba people.

Foolish Assumptions

Although the infinite galaxy of computer and network technology continues to expand exponentially, we can only tackle it one book at a time. So we need to make some assumptions about what we think you should already know before this book can be useful to you.

Computers 101

You know how to hook up, turn on, and log on to both Windows and UNIX-type computers (see more about Linux and UNIX next). Right?

We also have to assume, because it's just slightly beyond the scope of this book, that you have some knowledge of acquiring and connecting simple network hardware. "Simple" hardware includes common Plug-and-Play (often referred to as "Plug and Pray") PC network cards, cables, and simple hubs, but we also address those situations in which Plug and Play is not available. Fortunately, there's not a huge array of hardware options for what you need to be successful with this book, so you should be okay. At any rate, we include Appendix A, "Installing Network Hardware," to give some basic guidelines for the frightened.

Windows 101

At this juncture, you can't get away from the little buggers (Windows clients), so you need to be familiar with fun Windows stuff like opening control panels, opening the DOS prompt and typing simple commands, and restarting a lot.

We only address Windows 95 and later versions.

UNIX 101

You probably won't have a very smooth ride with this book, not to mention networking, unless you have a fundamental working knowledge of basic UNIX-like commands. Examples include `ls`, `cd`, `man`, `more`, `find`, `cp`, `mv`, `cat`, `grep`, `pwd`, and `telnet`. See? Simple.

`Man, man, man.` Those men sure know how to do documentation. Ask the man about any command, and you often get more than you want to know. UNIX software is typically packed full of helpful hints on all the various commands and options. For example, to find out what the command `grep` does, type this at a command prompt:

```
# man grep
```

where:

> `#` is the prompt.
>
> `man` is the command to open the man pages (manual, not manly) to get documentation, usage, options, blah blah blah about the command.
>
> `grep` is the command you want to know more about.

You'll get a complete description of what `grep` is all about.

UNIX-flavored operating systems abound, and while most of them use many of the same commands and syntax, each has its own way of doing some things. Using the `man` command to view the documentation should clarify any questions you might have on that system's usage of that command.

Linux

Because Samba embodies the virtues of open-source software, it naturally follows that we condone its most popular operating-system vehicle of the same ilk: Linux. In fact, most flavors of Linux come with Samba. Coincidence? Although we do include reference to other legitimate UNIX flavors, for simplicity, this book frequently assumes the OS is Linux. If you don't use Linux, you'll still find all the information you need to get a solid start with Samba.

Although you don't need to really know much about Linux specifically, you might find yourself struggling a bit without some knowledge of its most common commands and desktop environments. See the previous section, UNIX 101.

Bottom line

You need at the least

- ✔ A server with some version of Linux installed and working
- ✔ At least one Windows client (version 95 or later)
- ✔ A means of hooking these computers together

Further needs are dictated by your situation, so we do our best to at least mention them if not give you complete guidance to get your network up and running smoothly.

Conventions Used in This Book

We would bore you to tears if we didn't adopt some simple conventions to present the information you need in the most concise manner we can. Throughout this book, you'll see information presented using the easy-to-understand conventions that we describe here.

Typing commands

As a Samba administrator, you have to type lots of commands. After a while, you may ever prefer typing commands to using a mouse. At any rate, we use a few simple conventions for all the commands that we explain in this book.

Within a regular paragraph of text a command is displayed in this font. We set off longer commands and examples on separate lines, like this:

```
$ date
Mon Jun 26 01:25:39 EDT 2000
```

We mention a few Linux commands in this book, so you don't have to open up your copy of *Linux For Dummies*. Those Linux commands have some special conventions, too:

Any text in [ ] brackets is optional.

Any text not surrounded by {}, [], or <> must be typed as shown.

Text inside < > must be typed replaced with the appropriate text, with no <> brackets.

We use boldface text, like **this**, to tell you what exactly to type or what to do, while the regular text in a procedure offers descriptions and explanations.

Special keystrokes

We also mention the occasional special keystroke. If we want you to press more than one key at the same time, we join the key names with a + sign. For example, if we want you to press the Control, Alt, and Delete keys simultaneously, we write it like this: Ctrl+Alt+Del.

Opening Windows and menus

Many of the procedures we describe in this book involve working with windows interfaces — both Microsoft Windows and X-Window in Linux. If we want you to choose menu commands in a window, we use a special arrow to separate the individual commands. For example, if we tell you to choose File⇨Open, we mean click the word File and then choose Open from the menu that appears.

How This Book Is Organized

First, we tell you every practical thing you need to know about Samba (not to be confused with practically everything you need to know about Samba). Then, we tell you all the multiple ways you can install it on your (established and stable Linux) server. Then, we tell you all the multiple ways you can test and configure Samba and all your clients. That's the nitty-gritty.

But of course it doesn't end there. Networking isn't always so simple (surprise!), so we impart what's important about doing backups, ensuring security, configuring complex networks, and the all-important troubleshooting. Why? To keep your Samba setup healthy, wealthy, and wise.

Seven parts divide this book into neat little packages.

Part I: Getting Ready to Dance

Discover what Samba can do for you and then find out how to install it on your Linux server. Consider this part a free pass to the revolutonary world of free software.

Part II: Configuring Samba

This part covers all the basic goodies to get you going. We explain how to test the functions of Samba and how to make sure Samba runs like you want it to. You find out how to set up modern Windows clients and how to administer your Samba server from your Web browser. We also show you how to add users and printers on your Linux server and how to share the users' directories and the printers through Samba. Finally, we explain how to make your Samba server understand encrypted passwords.

Part III: Advanced Samba Techniques

The chapters in this part of the book show you how to improve the performance of your Samba server and how to add your Samba server to complex networks. You find out ways to see what is slowing your server down, and how to soup it up. You also find out how to add your Samba server to a large, complex Windows network.

Part IV: Troubleshooting Samba

When you're stuck or something is broken, turn to this part of the book. You can find out how to figure network and Samba problems, starting from the server to the client.

Part V: Maintaining Your Samba Server

This part covers backups and security — you want to read this part before you have any problems. In this part, you see how to use backup devices and choose a backup strategy. You discover how to make your server secure by checking crucial files and using software packages included on the CD.

Part VI: The Part of Tens

We pack this part of the book with handy tips and reminders. Here you can find out how to solve common Samba errors and read tips for having a better Samba server.

Part VII: Appendixes

The appendixes offer juicy info for both beginners and experts. You get a quick guide to installing hardware on both servers and client, including network wiring. We also discuss Internet resources, Linux scrupt writing, and how to upgrade Samba. Finally, we tell you all about the CD that accompanies this book.

On the CD

The *Samba For Dummies* CD-ROM has versions of Samba compiled for most versions of Linux and UNIX, plus administration and security tools.

Icons Used in This Book

Like other ...*For Dummies* books you've seen, icons appear throughout the text to identify certain types of information. You'll see the following icons throughout the pages of this book:

Neat tricks that can save you time doing a task, or just impress an observer. After you know enough tricks on Linux, you really begin to appreciate how much you can do with it.

A warning lets you know that what you are doing could cause irreparable damage to your server, either immediately, or down the road.

Basic rules that you need to file away in your brain.

Nerdy details that you don't need to know but may find interesting.

Where to Go from Here

As you might have noticed in the previous section that describes the parts of this book, the easy stuff is in the beginning and the more complex stuff is toward the end. Most books use this handy method of organization.

If you're a complete newbie and don't have much experience with Linux or other UNIX-like commands, start with an introductory text like, oh we don't know, *Linux For Dummies* or *UNIX For Dummies.* Then get your feet wet with a basic networking text like, say, *Networking For Dummies,* or *Networking Home PCs For Dummies.* By then you will be convinced you want a Linux-based server for your Windows clients, and you definitely will want to use Samba to put it all together.

Although it never hurts to read through the basics, Part II, whilst sort of near the front of the book, contains a cornucopia of secrets and info. Don't overlook the obvious on your way to stardom or you might step in something.

When you're pretty sure you have all the basics securely under your belt, feel free to flop around anywhere the index might take you. System administrators and gurus should feel free to read this book by memorizing the index and working backward while juggling obsolete hardware.

Part I
Getting Ready to Dance

The 5th Wave   By Rich Tennant

"YOU KNOW THAT GUY WHO BOUGHT ALL THAT SOFTWARE? HIS CHECK HAS A WARRANTY THAT SAYS IT'S TENDERED AS IS AND HAS NO FITNESS FOR ANY PARTICULAR PURPOSE INCLUDING, BUT NOT LIMITED TO, CASHING."

In this part . . .

*I*f you've gotten this far, you must really be ready to do something. To help you get started, Chapter 1 introduces you to what Samba is and how it came to be. What, why, when, where, and how — those sorts of incessant questions that kids always ask.

We assume you are ready to go for it, so we skip the part about acquiring and connecting your system's hardware. (If you need some helpful and handy hints on that topic, check out Appendix A.)

We also skip the part about getting Linux installed and running stably, with the exception of the fact that you can, and often do (or perhaps already did), install Samba at the same time you install Linux. Hence, Chapter 2 describes both methods of getting Samba installed on your soon-to-be new server — that is, installing Samba either during or after the Linux installation.

Chapter 1

Introducing Samba

● ●

In This Chapter

▶ Discovering the origins of Samba

▶ Finding out about free software

▶ Understanding what Samba does

▶ Examining the tools available for administering Samba

▶ Deciding where to install Samba

▶ Finding out where you can get Samba

● ●

*T*his chapter introduces you to Samba, the open-source software that enables networking between UNIX-based servers and Windows clients. We explain where Samba came from, what it can do, what sort of administration tools are available for it, and where you can obtain it.

What Is Samba?

Samba is a Brazilian dance. It is also a free software suite that enables a PC running Linux (or FreeBSD, or any other kind of UNIX) to act as a Windows network server. This sort of Samba gives you a proven, low-cost, high-performance means for providing Windows network services to PCs running Windows 95, 98, NT, or 2000 without having to buy expensive Windows networking software.

For example, you can

✔ Recycle that old 486 or slow Pentium and use it as a print server to share your new, fast laser printer with the other PCs in the office.

✔ Use that old machine as a file server so you need only one expensive tape backup device.

✔ Set it up as a Zip drive server so you need to have only one Zip drive that the entire office can share.

✔ Install it as a roaming profile server so users always log on to a familiar desktop.

This book won't teach you to glide sinuously across the dance floor, but it does show you how to add an inexpensive, reliable Windows server to your network by using a PC as old and as slow as a 486. You can easily share printers, store files, and share backup devices for little cost by using free Samba and Linux software and almost any PC to set up a server. (You can also run Samba on just about any kind of UNIX out there, and we talk about that, too.) Of course, you can install Samba on a new, fast PC and get wonderful performance. Samba isn't picky about the PC on which it runs.

Where did Samba come from?

Samba came to be during 1991 in Australia when Andrew Tridgell needed to connect three computers: a PC running DOS, a Sun running UNIX, and a DecStation running Digital UNIX. The PC and the DECstation were already talking to each other via a program called Pathworks, but Andrew didn't have a version of Pathworks for Sun. (Digital UNIX and Sun UNIX are members of the UNIX family but they cannot swap software.)

To fill this gap, he created his own version of Pathworks for the Sun, using packet sniffing to see what information the PC and the DEC exchanged over the network. This approach is almost as difficult as figuring out a chef's secret recipe by opening every can, box, and bottle that went into the chef's kitchen and comparing each with the taste of the finished dish. Pathworks used a form of SMB (Server Message Block) to communicate, and it became the first version of Samba.

From this humble beginning, Andrew and the other members of the Samba team started expanding the functionality of Samba and porting it to run on many different operating systems. Today, the Samba team is working on expanding Samba to act as a Windows NT primary domain controller and getting ready for full Windows 2000 functionality.

Samba is free, open-source software

Samba is licensed under the GNU Public License, which makes it free software. *Free* in this case refers more to the concept of free speech than that of free beer. You can read the GNU Public License in Appendix D, but in short, any software licensed by the GNU Public License must be made available with its source code included and with no restrictions on modifying or distributing the source code. In other words, anyone can download Samba, look through the source code, rewrite it if they want, and release their own version of Samba, which in turn falls under the same GNU Public License.

Although anyone can charge a fee for software released under the GNU Public License, the terms of the license mean that anyone can offer the same software for free. Consequently, almost all software licensed under the GNU

Public License is available free for downloading, or you can get it on CD for a nominal fee. Hence, companies that want to promote the open-software model are building businesses by offering value-added services such as customization and support.

In the section "Where Is Samba?," later in this chapter, we tell you where to download Samba. Refer to Appendix C for a host of Internet links to Linux resources that can show you how to do other, non-Samba things with your server.

Samba runs on Linux . . . or UNIX . . . or FreeBSD . . .

Samba runs on Linux, UNIX, FreeBSD, or any of the hundreds of UNIX variants around. Samba doesn't run on Windows software, but it provides networking services *for* Windows software. This arrangement is similar to that of Novell NetWare networks: NetWare isn't Windows, but network users can use Windows PCs and save their work on a NetWare server.

What are Linux, UNIX, and FreeBSD? They are all members of the UNIX operating-system family. In the past, UNIX had a reputation as a rather complex, expensive, high-performance operating system. Part of the reason for that reputation was that UNIX was being compared to DOS, which at the time was much cheaper and easier to use but had much lower performance than UNIX. Today, however, UNIX is only a little more complicated than Windows 95 or Windows 98 and about as complicated as Windows NT.

The Linux and FreeBSD versions of UNIX are much less expensive than comparable Windows products. In fact, with a fast Internet connection and the required know-how, you can get them for free. (We supply the know-how in this book.) And most importantly, they offer comparable performance.

The success of UNIX derives, at least in part, from its design philosophy. The original programmers aimed for a stable operating system composed of small, robust modules that do their jobs well. A UNIX server can run for months without rebooting. Typically, you only need to shut down the server to add or remove hardware. Contrast this with Windows operating systems, which you often need to reboot after adding many kinds of software or making some configuration changes.

Because Linux is much cheaper and more widely available than UNIX, we generally refer to Linux and only occasionally to FreeBSD or UNIX. For 95 percent of what we're doing here, you use the same process in Linux, FreeBSD, or UNIX, and we describe the differences when applicable.

Is Free Software any Good?

It's human nature to think that there must be a catch if something is free. The old saying "There's no such thing as a free lunch" comes to mind. (Again, the term *free* in free software refers somewhat more to free speech than free beer.)

Almost all free software is created because a programmer wanted to do something and wrote a program to handle that task. Andrew Tridgell wanted to connect several different computers, and ended up writing Samba. Linus Torvalds wanted his own clone of the UNIX operating system to study, and ended up writing Linux.

The software is provided free of charge, and the source code is included. Because the source code is included, free software undergoes lots of peer review. In other words, software developers all over the world look at the code, try to find problems, and fix them. There is a saying in the open-source, free-software world, "With enough eyes, all bugs are shallow." For a deeper view of the open-source software world, check out the source of the preceding quote, Eric Raymond's *The Cathedral and the Bazaar: Musings on Linux and Open Source by an Accidental Revolutionary* (published by O'Reilly & Associates).

Practically speaking, free software is often of higher quality than comparable commercial software. It's more stable, and it has fewer bugs and better security.

Some free software that works great

A good example of the success of free software is better than paragraphs of theory, and we can offer several well-known examples of free-software successes.

For years, the predominant mail-routing software was Sendmail: free, open-source software available with most UNIX distributions. This widely used mail-routing software still comes free with every Linux CD.

According to the networking consulting organization Netcraft, the most common Web server is Apache, which is an open-source software project. It might not be the fastest Web server on the planet, but its stability is second to none, and it's the most customizable Web server available.

Some of bigger Web sites run on open-source software. For example, Yahoo! and the Internet Movie Database both run on FreeBSD. And Google, the search engine, runs on Linux.

Who supports free software?

Who is responsible when free software goes bad? Although organizations exist to provide paid support for free software, in most cases, no one is legally responsible for problems in free software. If you carefully read the End-User License Agreement for many commercial, expensive software packages, you can see that few or no warranties are given. However, the developers of free software have their name attached to their work, and it's not unusual to have the person who originally wrote the program respond to an e-mailed report of a bug.

Developers of free software usually do an exemplary job of providing forums and mailing lists to discuss bugs and problems. Use these Web and Usenet resources first when you encounter a roadblock. You might discover that you've encountered a common problem or known bug, and you could get an answer faster than if you posted a question. Of course, if you don't find an answer, post a message. The sooner the developers know of a problem, the quicker they can fix it.

In general, the free software community responds to bugs with a patch within days. Compare this to commercial software developers that take months or more to deliver a patch.

If you or your boss require technical support, Appendix C lists some links to organizations that provide open-source software support. It can be comforting to know that an expert is only a phone call away.

What Can Samba Do?

Samba is a great way to add a new, low-cost network or print server to an existing network, or you can start the network from scratch. Using Samba, you can share printers, files, and backup hardware.

Samba can share a printer

To outfit every user in a 10-person office with an inkjet printer, you could pay more than $1,500 (before you even start to pay for inkjet refill cartridges). For a quarter of that money, you can buy one, nice laser printer and a more expensive, but cheaper-to-run inkjet. You get better print quality for a lower per-page cost by sharing the printers with a Samba print server.

Samba can share files

With Samba, you can easily share files. You can set up *shares* (designated directories or folders on a server) that certain members of a group can both read and write to, but everyone else can only read. In this way, you can easily share and control corporate documents, handbooks, and policies, and it sure beats shuffling a bunch of floppies around or slicing up trees.

Network administrators often set up shares so members of a project team can easily work with common files. You can store databases and spreadsheets on a Samba server and share them over a network so that everyone is always working with an up-to-date copy.

Samba can share Zip drives and other backup devices

Zip drives are useful for exchanging large files, but outfitting every PC in the office with its own Zip drive would get very expensive. With a Samba server, however, every user in the office can share a single Zip drive.

It's important to back up your data so computer failures or user errors do not cause data loss. What's easier: running from computer to computer with a tape drive every day, or having a tape drive attached to a central server that automatically backs up the files every night at a time you specify? Samba and Linux include lots of software for automated backups.

How Do I Use Samba?

Okay, so Samba can do lots of wonderful things. But is it incredibly hard to set up and administer? Although you can set up a Samba server through a possibly unfamiliar telnet and command-line interface, you can also set up a Samba server through a Web browser. That's right; if you can surf the Web and type, you can run a Samba server.

The most common Web tool used to administer a Samba server is the Samba Web Administration Tool (SWAT). Another well-known tool used to maintain a Samba server through a Web browser is Webmin, an all-in-one program that performs Samba maintenance and many other tasks.

Here are some other tools you can use to administer a Samba server:

- ✔ Smbedit, which runs on Windows 95/98
- ✔ Linuxconf, which runs with Linux
- ✔ The configuration file, which you edit from the command line. If you just want to change one parameter, you might find the command-line options useful.

You already know the main tool: a Web browser

SWAT and Webmin are the two most useful tools for maintaining a Samba server. They have the advantage of presenting a familiar interface for new Samba administrators because they look just like a Web page with forms. The only disadvantage is that they require a little more RAM to run. A Samba server that is strapped for memory might run better without SWAT or Webmin.

SWAT, the Samba Web Administration Tool

SWAT runs as a mini Web server on your Samba server and enables you to log on as the Samba server administrator. With SWAT, you have a graphical way to add and configure shared directories and printers and change the global Samba parameters for your server.

Webmin, the multipurpose administrative tool

Webmin is a little more complex than SWAT because it enables you to administer Samba as well as perform many other administrative tasks for a Linux server. Webmin runs as a mini server on your Samba server and enables you to do all the tasks that SWAT supports as well as many other Linux and network-specific tasks. In Chapter 5, we explain how to use Webmin to adjust the Samba part of your server. (We leave the other parts of Webmin for a different book.)

You might consider a tool for Windows

Smbedit is a tool that is being developed for administering a Samba server on a Windows 95/98 platform. It is considered alpha-stage software, which means it is still being developed and refined.

Smbedit is useful if you want to graphically administer your Samba server but you don't want to use SWAT or Webmin because your server doesn't have enough RAM to efficiently run the Web tools. Or, you might consider SWAT and Webmin to be insecure for use over a network.

Linux has a special tool

Red Hat Linux comes with a special tool for administering the server called Linuxconf. Linuxconf also can administer a Samba server. This tool is unusual because you can run it as a graphical utility in the X Window environment in Linux or as a menu interface through a telnet session.

You can use a command line, too

Occasionally, you might decide that the simplest way to fix a problem is to make a quick change to the Samba configuration via the command line. You have several ways to edit the configuration file from the command line. We include command-line examples throughout the book. Also see Chapter 6 for more about administering Samba from a command line. (After you become a Samba guru, you can easily impress a novice by fixing Samba from a command line in a telnet session.)

On What Sort of Server Do I Install Samba?

Samba has been ported to many different server types, most of which belong to the UNIX family of operating systems. If you are just beginning to explore Samba as a Windows server, you probably want a reliable, easy-to-install, easy-to-use, and inexpensive server. Linux and FreeBSD are the two leading contenders in the UNIX family for low-cost, reliable servers that run on common, PC-compatible software. Between Linux and FreeBSD, Linux is easier for a novice to use, and many more resources are available for Linux users. But if you have some UNIX experience, feel free to use FreeBSD, or you can even use both.

A Linux server is the most common type of UNIX server you will find, so this book focuses on Linux servers. Linux is the most common UNIX server because

- ✔ The price is right (free for a download, or for less than $50 at a software store).
- ✔ Many books and Web pages can help you use Linux.
- ✔ It's very common, so a large network of support exists.
- ✔ It runs on PC-compatible hardware (as well as many other types of computer hardware). If you have a spare 486 or faster PC with at least 16MB of RAM and a 500MB hard drive, you can install Linux and make a useful Samba server.

Where Is Samba?

Okay, you're ready to give Samba a try. Where do you get it? Samba is available from many sources, the most immediate of which is the CD you got with this book. But as you might guess, you can always find the most up-to-date version on the Internet at the official Samba Web pages.

On this book's CD

The CD you got with this book contains the latest version of Samba that was available at the time of writing (version 2.0.6). The CD also contains binary versions of Samba for several popular versions of UNIX, including Linux, FreeBSD, and Solaris. Appendix F goes into greater detail about the contents of the CD.

On your server's CD

The installation CDs for most server software contain Samba, and every Linux and FreeBSD CD we've seen contains Samba. This might be the easiest way to get the Samba server software. Most server installation routines give you the ability to install Samba while installing the server. (See Chapter 2 for more details.)

On the Internet

The main Samba Web page is at `www.samba.org`. Because of the demand for Samba, you can also use numerous mirrored pages. These mirrored pages range from exact copies of the main Samba Web page to smaller sites that just have the binary files available for download. Chapter 2 goes into greater detail regarding many of the mirrored Samba Web pages.

Chapter 2

Installing the Samba Server

・・・・・・・・・・・・・・・・・・・・・・・・・・・・・・・・・・・・・・

In This Chapter

▶ Finding out whether you need to install Samba

▶ Installing Samba along with Linux

▶ Checking out the variations of Linux

▶ Finding Samba

▶ Using Linux compression utilities to install Samba

▶ Installing binaries

▶ Installing source code

・・・・・・・・・・・・・・・・・・・・・・・・・・・・・・・・・・・・・・

*O*kay, so you're sold on Samba as a server for your Windows network. Now, how do you go about setting it all up?

This chapter guides you through the installation of Samba on your Linux server. Chapter 3 tells you how to test your installation, and Chapter 4 describes how to configure your Windows clients.

 To get results from many of the functions and commands we describe throughout this book, you often have to log on as the root user, or superuser. We specify those cases for which you need to log on as root. We also use the terms *root* and *superuser* interchangeably, so don't get confused by that. Also note that many operating systems use different prompts to remind you that you are in root or superuser mode, such as with a # rather than a $.

Figuring Out Whether Samba Is Already Installed

If you have inherited a running Linux server, check to see if Samba is already installed. If it isn't, you can easily install it after the fact. We show you how in subsequent sections of this chapter.

To see if Samba has been installed, first use the `find` command to search the hard drive of your Linux server for smb or smb.conf. The following command shows how to search for the smb executable to learn of its location. Try this command at the Linux command line as the superuser in a terminal in X Windows or in a telnet session to the Linux Samba server:

```
# find / -name smbd -print
/usr/local/sbin/smbd
```

The result shows that smbd, the primary Samba daemon, is in the /usr/local/ sbin directory. If you see a similar result on your machine, you can safely assume that Samba has been loaded on this computer, so you can skip this chapter. For all the details on testing Samba, see Chapter 3.

Installing Samba with Linux

The easiest way to install Samba on your Linux server is to do so when you install Linux. It's usually just a simple matter of checking an option, or it may be automatic. If you are building your network from scratch, this is an almost error-free way to make a Samba server happen. Just to make sure you don't miss a step, we describe each of the major Linux distributions individually.

With Red Hat

Red Hat Linux is possibly the most widely known distribution of Linux. When you install Red Hat Linux, you can choose one of three classes for the installation:

- **Workstation:** Does not install Samba.
- **Server:** Automatically installs Samba.
- **Custom:** Installs Samba if you choose to do so. Under Components to Install, choose SMB (Samba Connectivity). Alternatively, choose Networking⇨Individual Packages⇨Samba.

With Mandrake

The Mandrake distribution is loosely based on the Red Hat distribution but has been highly modified. During the installation routine, choose a customized installation, and select Server Class to ensure that Samba gets installed.

With Caldera OpenLinux

People new to Linux hold Caldera OpenLinux in high regard because this distribution offers an easy, well-thought-out installation process. Caldera OpenLinux even comes with a Partition Manager for repartitioning a hard drive to get space for adding Linux — a real boon if you're reluctant to totally remove Windows from your server.

The installation process has four levels. The minimal level does not install Samba, while the remaining three — Recommended, Recommended Plus Commercial, and All — install Samba.

With SuSE

SuSE is a very popular Linux distribution, particularly in Europe. To make sure that Samba gets installed when you install SuSE Linux, select the N, Network-Support series in the Series Selection screen. Then, scroll down to N and press Enter to go into the Individual Packages menu. In the Individual Packages menu, choose Samba.

With Slackware

By some accounts, Slackware is the most popular distribution of Linux out there. However, the installation method isn't quite as modern as Caldera's.

To make sure that Samba gets installed when you install Slackware, choose the N package (N is for network). Then, choose the Expert Configuration to check each package that gets installed. When you get to the Network section, scroll down until you see Samba and make sure it gets checked by pressing the spacebar.

Where Else Can You Get Samba?

If you haven't found Samba on your Linux server, first check your Linux CDs. Or if you want the absolute latest version, many Web pages exist from which you can download Samba. You can download it as compiled binaries that are ready to run, or if you are feeling adventurous, you can download the Samba source code and compile it yourself.

In the following sections, we explain where you can find Samba on your Linux CDs and on the Web. We also describe several Linux utilities that you need for working with the Samba files. For details about installing the downloaded software, see "Installing Binaries" and "Installing the Source Code," later in this chapter.

On your Linux CD

You can find Samba on almost every Linux CD. But depending on which version of Linux you have, your copy of Samba could be anywhere from three months to a year or more older than the most recent release. Even so, the version on your CD should be good enough to work for most users. Table 2-1 lists the Samba versions that come with various Linux distributions.

Table 2-1	Linux and Samba Versions	
Linux Distribution	*Version*	*Samba Version*
Red Hat	6.1	2.0.5a
Red Hat	6.0	2.0.3
Red Hat	5.2	1.9.18p10
Mandrake	6.1	2.0.5a
Mandrake	5.3	1.9
Caldera OpenLinux	2.3	2.0.5
Caldera OpenLinux	2.2	2.0.3
SuSE	6.3	2.0.6
SuSE	6.0	2.0.5A
Slackware	7.0	2.0.5a
Slackware	4.0	2.0.3

On your Red Hat CD

Whatever version of Red Hat you are using, Samba is stored as an RPM file in the /RedHat/RPMS directory. The section "Installing Binaries," later in this chapter, explains how to install an RPM package.

On your Mandrake CD

Like the Red Hat distribution on which Mandrake is based, Samba is stored as an RPM file in the /Mandrake/RPMS directory. RPM works the same in Mandrake as it does in Red Hat. To install Samba, type **rpm –i** *packagename* in the directory containing the Samba RPM file.

On your Caldera OpenLinux CD

Caldera OpenLinux also uses RPMS. Samba is stored in the /Packages/ RPMS directory.

On your SuSE CD

SuSE Linux now uses RPM to install packages, although older versions also use Slackware's installpkg. Because SuSE is packaged on from one to six CDs depending on the version, we cannot specify exactly where Samba is located, although you will find it in one of the directories labeled n. On the one-CD demo version of SuSE, it's located in /suse/n1.

On your Slackware CD

The Slackware distribution is a little different from the others. Samba is stored in the /slakware/n7 directory as a gzipped file.

Slackware provides these tools to install packages:

- ✔ **pkgtool:** A menu-based tool.

- ✔ **installpkg:** A command-line tool.

- ✔ **rpm2targz:** A tool that converts an RPM package into a tarred gz package, which is what Slackware wants. Use this tool if, for some reason, you can only get an RPM of Samba. (For more on using tar and gzip, see "Using Linux Installation and Decompression Utilities," later in this chapter.)

On the Web

If you want the latest and greatest Samba, as well as lots of other Samba resources like archived mailing lists and utilities, go to one of the mirrored sites on the Web.

The main Samba Web page is at www.samba.org. But because Samba is so popular, the Web has many mirrors of this page. It's faster to use a mirror in your own country; it's also good Internet etiquette because international Internet links tend to be slow and crowded.

The three mirrored Samba sites in the US are

- ✔ us1.samba.org/samba/samba.html
- ✔ us2.samba.org/samba/samba.html
- ✔ us3.samba.org/samba/samba.html

Figure 2-1 shows one of these sites.

After you get to the Samba page, click the download link to go to the download page. From there, you can download the Samba source or sometimes a compiled binary.

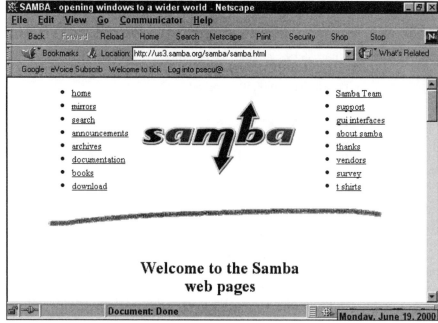

If you choose to download a binary, make sure you have the right binary for your system. Specifically, you have to know what kind of Linux or UNIX you are running because the list of binaries at the Samba Web pages is long. The Linux command uname or uname -a can tell you more about your operating system, including enough to help you download the correct binary package.

From the following examples, you can tell that terrapin is a FreeBSD server, while olorin is a Linux server.

```
terrapin$ uname
FreeBSD

[george@olorin george]$ uname -a
Linux olorin 2.2.12-20 #1 Mon Sep 27 10:25:54 EDT 1999 i586 unknown
```

Refer to the Samba Web site for more information on downloading and installing binaries and source code.

Using Linux Installation and Decompression Utilities

No matter how fast a connection you have to the Internet, downloading files always seems to take too long. You're not imagining it — as connection speeds get faster, the things you download get bigger.

Because of this inescapable rule of computer downloading, numerous utilities have been made to compress and combine files as well as to uncompress and separate files. You're probably familiar with WinZip, the Windows program used to unzip an archive of files. The Linux world has two tools that do what WinZip does:

- ✔ **gzip:** Compresses and expands files
- ✔ **tar:** Combines and separates files

You can also use GNU tar, a nifty variant of tar that enables you to decompress gzipped files in tar.

Although we could fill many pages with the options for gzip and tar, explaining how to use them to expand and separate Linux files takes only a few paragraphs.

Because most Linux distributions contain GNU tar, and this is by far the easiest, we discuss this option first. If it doesn't work for you, you can go on to the more in-depth discussion of gzip and tar.

If a file has an extension of .gz, you need gzip to uncompress it.

Using GNU tar

Most Linux distributions use GNU tar as their tar utility. To unzip the file and then untar, just use the xvfz option with tar. The following example shows the superuser unzipping and untarring the file named samba-2.0.6_tar.gz:

```
# tar -xvfz samba-2.0.6_tar.gz
```

If this doesn't work, your server probably doesn't have GNU tar loaded. You will probably need to use gzip to unzip the file and then use tar to extract it (see the following sections). Later, you might want to upgrade your tar utility to GNU tar, which saves you a step every time you download a new file.

GNU tar, where to get it, and why

GNU tar is a variety of tar that enables you to uncompress gzipped files at the command line without having to use gzip. This saves a step and is just a neat thing to have.

Just like gzip, you can download GNU tar from the GNU homepage (www.gnu.org). Once there, click the Software link to go to the page that explains how to download gzip and GNU tar.

Using gzip

You use gzip, the GNU compression utility, to compress and decompress files. In this chapter, we're interested only in decompressing downloaded files, so we'll leave the other uses of gzip to the Linux wizards.

After you have gzip working, how do you uncompress a downloaded file? You type **gzip** with a **–cd**. The following example shows the command required to decompress the file named samba-2.0.6_tar.gz.

```
# gzip -cd samba-2.0.6_tar.gz
```

A file that you uncompress with gzip usually turns into a tar file, which is a file composed of many separate files held together with the tar command. In Chapter 15, we explain how to combine files into a tar file.

Where to get gzip

Most Linux servers already have gzip installed. To see if yours does, type **gzip -h** at the Linux command prompt. If you get a small help screen about gzip, gzip has been installed.

If you get something else, such as `not found` or `no such file`, you probably do not have gzip installed. That's okay; it might be on your Linux server CD-ROM, and it's available freely from the GNU Web page.

The compressed gzip file should be on your Linux CD. For example, Red Hat stores gzip as an RPM file in the /Red Hat/RPMS directory. To install gzip on a Pentium system, type the following command:

```
# rpm -I /Red Hat/RPMS/gzip-
     1.2.415.i586.rpm
```

If for some reason you can't locate gzip on your Linux CDs or you don't have them, you can still get gzip from the GNU Web page (`http://www.gnu.org`). Once there, click the Software link to go to the page that explains how to download gzip.

Once at an FTP site, you want to download a tarred version (the filename ends in .tar). The next section on tar explains more, but in a nutshell, to untar the file gzip-1_2_4.tar, type this command:

```
# tar -xvf gzip-1_2_4.tar
```

This command separates the file into its own directory. That directory contains a file named INSTALL that explains how to compile gzip on your Linux system and install it. Usually, you type three commands to install it:

```
# ./configure
# make
# make install
```

If the installation doesn't appear to be successful, read the INSTALL file and see what recommendations it has. This can be daunting, but it is a good way to get very familiar with your Linux software.

Working with tar

Tar is the UNIX command used for combining and separating many files. This capability is useful because a simple program could require 20 or 30 separate program, library, help, and documentation files. It's much easier to type one command than to type 30, and you're much less likely to make an error.

Tar should be installed on all Linux systems. If tar isn't installed, you should probably reinstall the server from scratch. However, a variant of tar called GNU tar has a few nifty features, particularly the ability to uncompress gzipped files. You may want to download and install that tool, if you are feeling adventurous.

Using tar

Tar has many options, and listing them all and showing examples could fill many pages (we do that later in the book when we discuss backing up your server). For now, we just want to show you how to separate, or extract, the files from a tar archive. You do this by using the xvf options with tar and the filename. The following example shows the root user expanding the file named gzip-1_2_4.tar:

```
# tar xvf gzip-1_2_4.tar
```

Using gzip and tar in one line

Time for a quick Linux trick: You can use gzip and tar in the same line. You don't really save much, like having to press Enter only once, but it's more efficient (and is a good way to impress a novice Linux user). Think of it as the first step toward your Linux wizard's hat.

The one-line trick uses the pipe character: |. The pipe character is very useful because it passes the output of one command into the input of another, just like a pipe. So, to unzip a Samba file and then untar it in one line, type the following command (as superuser):

```
terrapin# gzip -cd samba-2.0.6_tar.gz | tar xvf -
```

In English, this command unzips the file named samba-2.0.6_tar.gz and then sends that unzipped file through tar to untar it.

Installing Binaries

If you can get Samba already precompiled in binary format, the installation will go quicker and with fewer errors. On the other hand, Samba might have been compiled with features you do not want, or it might be missing those you do want. Some of these features include special locations for the configuration files or logging files or special authentication features. Later in this chapter, we show you how to compile Samba and how to add those special features. For most purposes, however, almost all binary distributions of Samba should be adequate.

Examples of Samba binaries come in RPM (Red Hat Package Manager) format and tar format. RPM is easier to use, but tar is not that much more difficult. RPM files end in .rpm or .gz, while tar files end in .tar or even .gz. (As we explain in previous sections of this chapter, you unzip a file by typing **gzip –cd** *filename*, and then untar the resulting file with **tar xvf** *filename*.

With Red Hat Package Manager (RPM)

Red Hat Package Manager, RPM, is a common tool used by many Linux distributions to install and remove programs, get information about a program, check the integrity of a program, and perform many other tasks. We talk about a few of the more common uses of RPM, including installing Samba.

The first thing to do with an RPM file is get more information about it with the -qi flag. The following command shows the superuser using RPM to find out more information about the samba-2.0.5a package.

```
# rpm -qi samba-2.0.5a-12.i386.rpm
```

The next example shows the superuser installing a package using RPM; conveniently, it's Samba. The -I flag tells RPM to install the package:

```
# rpm -I samba-2.0.5a-12.i386.rpm
```

A time could come when you need to remove a package — perhaps you tried something and it wasn't what you wanted, or maybe you installed the wrong package by mistake. This is where the -e flag comes in. Type **rpm -e** and the name of the installed package (not the name of the RPM file).

With tar

If your binary Samba file was not in RPM format, it was most likely in tar format (ending in .tar or .tar.gz). If it ends in .gz, you need to use gzip to unzip it unless you have GNU tar loaded.

With a file ending in .tar, use tar with the -xvf flags to separate the files.

Installing the Source Code

You can also download the Samba source code if you want to compile it to make a custom Samba. You might need to do this in the following situations:

- ✔ Your Samba server is non-Linux.
- ✔ You need special authentication software.
- ✔ You need a feature that is only available in the latest Samba, and no pre-compiled binaries are available yet.

If none of these conditions apply, stick with the binary distributions and check out Chapter 3, which explains how to test your Samba installation.

The Samba Web page has the most recent production-level code (that is, the most stable, mostly bug-free stuff) in a file labeled samba_latest (it probably ends in .tar or .gz). Download the Samba source code into a temp directory.

In the temp directory, unzip the file if needed using gzip and then untar it. Here's an example:

```
[root@olorin /temp]# tar xvf samba-latest_tar.tar
```

If this was successful and your download was valid, you should have a directory named samba-2.0.6 (or whatever version you downloaded). Change to the source directory in the Samba directory, and you're ready to begin compiling Samba.

Choosing compile-time options

When you choose to compile Samba from the source code, you have the option of selecting special parameters at compile time. These parameters can give you special file locations or encryptions. List the current set of compile-time configuration parameters by typing **./configure --help** at the command line.

Rather than bore you with pages of configuration options, we'll just mention a few of them. The others are used in special situations that we don't cover in this book (special authentication schemes or new features that aren't fully developed yet).

Most large networks use a central database to maintain a list of users, computers, and network resources. This saves lots of time and eliminates duplication of effort for the network administrator. One type of central database common in the Linux/UNIX world is NIS, and of course, Samba works fine with NIS. To add your Samba server to a network that uses nisplus to maintain a central network database, type **./configure --with-nisplus**.

If you plan to encrypt passwords (which is the best solution for most later versions of Windows), you might use `-with-privatedir=DIR` to specify a certain location for the Samba password file. For example, to have a private password file located in /usr/local/samba/private, type **./configure –with-privatedir=/home/admin/samba/private**.

Compiling Samba

After you decide on your compile-time options, if any, you can begin to compile Samba. In the source directory as superuser, type the following command:

```
# ./configure
```

Or, if you want to compile Samba with the nisplus support option, type this command:

```
# ./configure --with-nisplus
```

These commands create a file named make. Execute the make file to install Samba by typing:

```
# ./make
```

That should complete your installation of Samba. See Chapter 3 for details about how to test your installation.

Obtaining a compiler

If for some reason you don't have a compiler on your system and you're dead set on compiling Samba, don't despair. The solution is available from the GNU homepage. The GNU compiler program is called gcc and it has its own homepage at `http://www.gnu.org/software/gcc/gcc.html`.

Downloading and installing gcc is a fairly complex undertaking and should be avoided if possible. If you encounter a Linux server without gcc installed, you might question what other important software wasn't installed. We recommend reinstalling the whole server from scratch if at all possible. If the server is being used a production server, you have to download gcc, or install it from the server CDs.

If, however, your Samba server is not Linux but some other UNIX flavor that doesn't have a compiler and you have no other option, gcc might be the answer.

Part II
Configuring Samba

"APPARENTLY MOST STUDIES INDICATE THAT WHAT PEOPLE REALLY WANT ISN'T MORE POWER OR INCREASED APPLICATIONS, BUT JUST REALLY NEAT TAIL FINS."

In this part . . .

Part II is where the fun really begins. This part is the
main course, the entrée, la pièce de résistance —
whatever. The chapters in this part tell you just about
everything you need to know to get your Samba server
serving you right. Here's the menu:

- **Appetizer:** Test and configure the installation.

- **First course:** Configure the Windows clients.

- **Second course:** Learn a gaggle of administration
  tools for configuring your Samba server, both of
  the Web-based and the other-based varieties.

- **Third course:** Add users and printers to the
  system.

- **Fourth course:** Set up device and file sharing.

- **Dessert you gotta leave room for:** Figure out that
  password encryption thing.

Hits the spot!

Chapter 3

Testing and Configuring the Installation

. . . .

In This Chapter

▶ Examining the components of Samba

▶ Testing the Samba installation

▶ Starting and stopping Samba

▶ Making Samba run automatically

. . . .

After you have Samba installed (see Chapter 2), you need to test the installation. This chapter reviews Samba's components, shows you how to test Samba to make sure it's working, and covers how to start and stop Samba.

Um, What Did I Just Install?

Samba is not a single program but rather a suite of programs. Hence, Samba has individual components that enable the following features:

✔ Making a computer or share visible in the Network Neighborhood

✔ File sharing

✔ Browsing the Network Neighborhood

✔ Logging on to other shared (Windows or Samba) directories and printers

The core components: smbd and nmbd

At the core of Samba are two daemons: smbd and nmbd. *Daemons* are UNIX programs that run in the background, waiting for tasks. Think of these daemons as software butlers waiting for their orders:

- ✔ **smbd:** The Samba smbd daemon provides file, directory, and printer sharing. Each client computer connected to the Samba server has its own smbd daemon.

- ✔ **nmbd:** The nmbd daemon provides NetBIOS name serving, WINS network address and machine name translation, and Network Neighborhood browsing support. In other words, it enables the Samba server to be visible in the right domain or workgroup.

Samba stores the configuration settings for both daemons in smb.conf.

The test tools: testparm, smbstatus, smbclient, nmblookup, and smbpasswd

Samba comes with several components that you use to test the Samba installation and configuration. By using the following tools, you can test that the Samba configuration is valid, check Samba status, or connect to the Samba server as different users:

- ✔ **testparm:** This simple program checks the Samba configuration file, smb.conf, for validity. It checks the syntax of the file to determine whether any rules are broken, but it does not guarantee that the shared files and printers are being shared as you might expect.

- ✔ **smbstatus:** This modest program reports on current connections to the Samba server.

- ✔ **smbclient:** With this program, the Samba server can connect to another Windows-type (Samba or Windows) server, including itself. This is useful for verifying that files and printers are being shared correctly because you can tell smbclient to attach as a different user.

- ✔ **nmblookup:** You use this tool to interrogate clients and servers in the Network Neighborhood, and elsewhere on your network. It is useful to test whether the Samba server can see the client computers it is supposed to see, and thus confirm or deny network problems.

- ✔ **smbpasswd:** As you might guess, you use smbpasswd to change a user's smb password. You need an smb password when working with encrypted passwords, which is usually the case. (Only the earliest Windows 95 clients use unencrypted passwords.)

The advanced utilities: smbmount, smbclient, and smbtar

Samba also comes with some advanced programs. Keep them in mind because they could solve a nagging problem some day:

- **smbmount:** A modified version of `smbclient`, `smbmount` is for mounting Samba shares. By using `smbmount`, you can attach a Samba share anywhere in the directory structure on the Samba server (it's an advanced trick). For `smbmount` to work, your server's kernel must have smbfs support.

- **smbclient:** Although `smbclient` works great as a testing tool, you can also use it to transfer files to and from a Windows-type (Samba or Windows) shared directory. Or, you can use it to print to a Windows-type (Samba or Windows) shared printer. Note that you can only use `smbclient` in this way via the command line, although it's useful in scripts.

- **smbtar:** You use this modified form of `smbclient` to back up Samba or SMB shares to a UNIX tape. For a local share, you may find it easier to use regular UNIX backup commands to back up your share. If the share is from a remote SMB server, `smbtar` may be easier to use.

Testing the Samba Installation

Finally, however you went about doing it, you have Samba installed. Now you need to test it to make sure the installation worked. Here's an overview of the steps in the process:

1. **Check the default smb.conf configuration file with** `testparm`.

2. **After you have a good configuration file, start the Samba programs smbd and nmbd. How you start Samba depends on which version of UNIX or Linux you are running.**

3. **After you have Samba running, check its status with the** `smbstatus` **command.**

4. **Check for user access with** `smbclient` **to ensure that your users can use this Samba server.**

5. **Check the Network Neighborhood with** `nmblookup`.

We describe these steps more fully in the following sections. We also show you how to stop Samba. Examples of when you need to stop Samba include keeping people from logging on or if you want to make a change to the Samba configuration.

Checking smb.conf with testparm

Use the testparm command to look for a Samba configuration file and test it for syntax rules — for example to see if it would make sense to Samba. To run testparm, type **testparm** as the superuser in a terminal window, in a telnet session, or at the console.

Write down (or print out) any error messages you get — for example:

```
Unable to open configuration file "/etc/smb.conf"!
```

This error message indicates that Samba is looking for its configuration file in the /etc directory and it expects that file to be named smb.conf. To fix this error, you need to create a Samba configuration file named smb.conf in the /etc directory. Your Samba files should include a sample smb.conf file, or you can create your own.

Here's a very simple smb.conf file copied from the Samba documentation:

```
Workgroup = MYGROUP
[home]
guest ok = no
read only = no
```

If you don't have an existing Samba configuration file, you can use this one for a start. See Chapters 5 and 6 for more information on how to create and modify configuration files.

Starting Samba

After you load Samba and use testparm to confirm that you have a good configuration file (see the preceding section), you can start Samba. The trickiest part here is determining what kind of Samba server you have — System V or BSD.

System V, also know as SVR4 (for System V, Revision 4), is a form of UNIX based on AT&T UNIX. Linux is not really a System V UNIX, but Linux can be considered a System V server when you are talking about starting programs and startup files. System V servers usually have one directory that contains programs to start and stop all the daemons; in Linux, it is usually /etc/rc.d/init.d.

The other branch of the UNIX family is called BSD, for Berkeley Standard Distribution. BSD UNIX variations use a series of startup files called *run control files*, with names that start with rc. Two typical rc files are rc.local and rc.network.

Linux and other System V servers

Okay, so how do you start Samba on a Linux or other System V server? Most System V systems have a directory containing programs to call all the daemons, usually /etc/rc.d/init.d. The smb program is a shell script that reads the command after it and then it starts, stops, or restarts Samba. For example, to start Samba in Red Hat Linux, simply type the following command as the superuser:

```
# /etc/rc.d/init.d/smb start
```

On Caldera OpenLinux, you type **/etc/rc.d/init.d/samba start**, and on Solaris, you type **/etc/init.d/smb start**. You might need to look around to find the exact file that starts Samba, but one of these three choices should come close.

Later, when you become a Samba wizard and are looking for new worlds to conquer, look at the /etc/rc.d/init.d/smb file and try to figure out the commands. You should be able to understand most of them. One of the joys of Linux is that most of the configuration files are written in ASCII, so you don't need a complex binary editor to read them.

BSD servers

Well then, how do you start Samba on a BSD server? Usually, you don't have nice scripts set up to start and stop Samba for you (although you can write your own if you ever become an elite BSD hacker). So you have to start the daemons manually. Find the directory where they are located, and launch the two Samba daemons. This can be as easy as typing the following commands as root:

```
# /usr/local/sbin/smbd -D
# /usr/local/sbin/nmbd -D
```

Those two commands take the two Samba daemons, smbd and nmbd, located in the /usr/local/sbin directory, and launch them as daemons (the -D flag).

Testing with smbstatus

After you successfully start Samba, check its status with a program called — amazingly enough — smbstatus. Just type **smbstatus**, and you should get the version of Samba that is running as well as any connected users and files they are editing.

If you get a warning message similar to Couldn't open status file /var/opt/samba/locks/STATUS..LCK when you try to run smbstatus, look for the file named STATUS..LCK with the ls command. For example, type **ls /var/opt/samba/locks**. If the STATUS..LCK file does not exist, create it with the touch command — for example, **touch /var/opt/samba/locks/STATUS..LCK**. Then restart Samba.

Testing the connection with smbclient

After checking the status of Samba with `smbstatus`, check to see if you can connect as a user with the `smbclient` utility. The `smbclient` program has many options; type **man smbclient** for a list.

In this case, you use two flags: `-L` and the server name to specify the server to which you want to connect, and `-U` and the username to specify as which user you want to connect. For example, the following line checks the server terrapin with the user allison:

```
# smbclient -L terrapin -U allison
Added interface ip=192.168.11.5 bcast=192.168.11.255 nmask=255.255.255.0
Password:password
Domain=[WORKGROUP] OS=[Unix] Server=[Samba 2.0.3]

Sharename    Type    Comment
---------    ----    -------
samba        Disk    Samba directory
testparm     Disk    run testparm
smbstatus    Disk
test         Disk
IPC$         IPC     IPC Service (Samba Server)
lp           Printer \Canon BubbleJet BJC-4300
allison      Disk    Home Directories

Server       Comment
---------    -------
LAPTOP       Samba 1.9.16p7
TERRAPIN     Samba Server

Workgroup    Master
---------    -------
WORKGROUP    TERRAPIN
```

Checking the network with nmblookup

After you successfully connect as a user to your Samba server using `smbclient` (see the preceding section), you can check your network connectivity with `nmblookup`. The `nmblookup` utility can give you a Linux/Samba view of the Network Neighborhood. First, check that the Samba server can see itself, because if it can't even see itself, it won't be able to send files elsewhere. To see if the Samba server can see itself, type **nmblookup servername**. For example, to see if the nmbd running on terrapin can see terrapin, type the following line:

```
# nmblookup terrapin
```

You should receive the IP address of your server.

You can use the `nmblookup` command to troubleshoot connectivity problems. For example, George had trouble with machines seeing his Samba server. He tried the `nmblookup` command and realized Samba was using the loopback port 127.0.0.0 instead of the IP address 192.168.11.5. He simply added an interfaces line to the smb.conf file and told Samba to use 192.168.11.5 explicitly.

Another neat `nmblookup` trick is to find out whether `nmblookup` can see a specific computer — in this case, the PC trinity:

```
# nmblookup -B trinity
```

A final trick is to see every computer in the Network Neighborhood by typing the following line:

```
# nmblookup -d 2 "*"
```

Now, everything is perfect: Samba is running, you can log on to Samba, and you can see everybody. Well now that you've accomplished all that, we're going to show you how to stop Samba. An important part of administering Samba is knowing how to stop it because any configuration changes you make only take effect when Samba starts.

Stopping Samba

In the beginning, you might discover that you are making changes to the Samba configuration file (smb.conf), but Samba doesn't seem to change. The reason is because Samba only reads the configuration file when it first starts. Thus, when you make a change, you need to restart Samba. This section describes how to stop and restart Samba so that your changes take effect.

For Linux (and other System V) only

For Linux and other System V UNIX varieties, go back to the /etc/rc.d/init.d directory and use those handy scripts. To stop Samba, just type this line:

```
# /etc/rc.d/init.d/smb stop
```

Even better, if you just want to restart Samba, for most versions of Linux, you can type this command:

```
# /etc/rc.d/init.d/smb restart
```

That command stops Samba and then restarts it, giving it a chance to reread the configuration file.

The preceding examples work for Samba on Red Hat Linux. To stop Samba on a Samba server running Caldera OpenLinux, type **/etc/rc.d/init.d/samba stop.** For Solaris, type **/etc/init.d/smb stop**. Most versions of Samba enable you to use the restart command as well, but if not, stop should always work.

Stopping by process number for all flavors

For BSD (and any version of UNIX), you can stop Samba by finding its process numbers and then killing the processes. Every program and daemon on a UNIX server has its own process number. *Killing a process* just means telling UNIX to shut down that particular program. It's kind of like pressing Ctrl+Alt+Delete in Windows, although like most other UNIX procedures, it's both harder to use and much more powerful.

To list the processes on a UNIX box, use the ps command. For our sample FreeBSD box, you would type **ps -x** at the command line as the superuser. You'd receive pages and pages of processes through which you would hunt for lines ending in smbd and nmbd. There is an easier way: Use the UNIX utility called grep.

Grep is a very useful Linux utility. In fact, it might soon become your favorite. Grep takes a stream of text and searches for a string within that stream. It then displays any lines in which the string appears.

For example, the following commands list all the processes in FreeBSD, search the list for smbd using grep, and then list all the processes and search for nmbd:

```
terrapin# ps -x | grep smbd
  205 ?? Is 0:00.25 /usr/local/sbin/smbd -D
21354 p0 R+ 0:00.03 grep smbd
terrapin# ps -x | grep nmbd
  207 ?? Ss 6:03.69 /usr/local/sbin/nmbd -D
21356 p0 R+ 0:00.10 grep nmbd
```

From this example, you can see that smbd has a process number of 205. The search for smbd (sounds like a cable TV show . . . "The Search for SMBD") returns a process number of 21354. Similarly, the process number for nmbd is 207, and the process number for the search for nmbd is 21356.

After you have the process number, you can try to kill the process, which means sending it a signal to stop. The first way to kill a process is to just type **kill *process_number*** — for example:

```
terrapin# kill 21354
terrapin# kill 21356
```

Check to make sure that smbd and nmbd are no longer running with the ps and grep commands. If they are still running, you need to use a more powerful kill command. Try kill with a -9 flag, for example:

```
terrapin# kill -9 21354
terrapin# kill -9 21356
```

The difference between the two kill commands is that the regular kill is a "nice" kill; you *ask* the application to shut itself down. The kill -9 command makes the operating system shut down the process, which is useful when a process is misbehaving or zombied and won't respond to a regular kill.

Although typing **ps -x** shows you the Samba daemons for a FreeBSD or Linux server, other UNIX systems might use slightly different syntax for ps. For example, in Sun Solaris, you type **ps -e** to list the Samba processes.

Making Samba Run Automatically

You might enjoy starting Samba manually the first time. In the real world, however, it becomes about as much fun as turning your furnace on when the weather gets too cold and off when it gets too hot. You would quickly grow tired of that and would want something like a thermostat for your Samba server. Fortunately, making Samba run automatically isn't hard to do.

The hardest part of having Samba start automatically is figuring out what kind of server you have: System V or BSD. System V servers use numbered run-control scripts. Different programs run depending on the system level. BSD servers use run-control files named after their function, like rc.local and rc.net. Linux is considered a System V system for run-control scripts, as is Sun Solaris. FreeBSD is considered a BSD style system for run-control scripts.

After you figure out what kind of server you have, you have to decide if you want Samba to start while the server is being booted or only when someone tries to connect to the server. For a dedicated Samba server, you get the best performance when you run Samba during the boot process. For an occasional Samba server (perhaps your personal workstation), it might make more sense to have Samba start only when someone attempts to connect to it.

Running Samba continually from boot time

Most Samba servers run Samba continually, so you want the Samba software to start automatically when the system starts. To do this, first determine whether your system is a System V system like Linux or a BSD system like FreeBSD because they each use different startup methods.

Linux and other System V servers

Linux and other System V servers have something called *run levels* to determine what software gets loaded. Each run level can be defined differently for each server, but usually run level 1 is the most basic system and is used for system maintenance. Run level 2 includes some network support, run level 3 has multi-user and full network support, and run level 6 is the level used to shut down a system.

The Samba startup script should then be in the run level 3 directory. For Red Hat Linux, this is /etc/rc.d/rc3.d.If you look in that directory, some files start with K and some start with S. Each file is a script that either stops (if it starts with a K) or starts (if it starts with an S) a daemon or series of daemons.

The scripts are also alphabetically and numerically executed. The script that starts with K35, K35smbd, runs before the script that starts with S10, S10network. This helps clean up the system when it changes run levels.

Therefore, you need to add a script that will get executed at the right time. Pick the highest unused number below 99 and start it with an S. For example, 98 isn't being used, so add a script called S98smb, or more accurately, add a link to a script that starts Samba.

First, if you look a little closer at the directory, the scripts are really just linked to scripts in the /etc/rc.d/init.d directory. Good! You don't have to learn script writing to have Samba start automatically. You just need to know how to make a link.

To make a link in Linux, you use the `ln` command. Someone decided that typing four letters was two letters too many, so they abbreviated it to `ln`. The following example shows how to link the file S98smb to the file smb in the /etc/rc.d/init.d directory:

```
olorin# ln -s /etc/rc.d/init.d/smb S98smb
```

Now, every time your Samba server starts, Samba starts automatically.

BSD servers

BSD servers — for example, FreeBSD — don't use run levels to configure the system. Instead, they use rc files (files that start with rc). In the case of a BSD server, you have to edit the rc files to make Samba start automatically. The rc file to edit is called rc.local, and it is located in the /etc directory. Adding the following two lines to this file causes Samba to start automatically when the FreeBSD server starts:

```
echo " smbd" && /usr/local/sbin/smbd -D
echo " nmbd" && /usr/local/sbin/nmbd -D
```

If your smbd and nmbd binaries are located in different directories, you need to specify the differing path. For more information about editing BSD configuration files, refer to the BSD manuals that came with your distribution or from the Web. For an overview of editing configuration files, see Chapter 6.

Running Samba when needed with inetd

Another option for a Samba server is to run it only when you need it. This might be a good option if you use the Samba server only occasionally, such as a Linux workstation from which users only occasionally read files.

The vehicle for this approach is to use a program called inetd. Inetd is sometimes called the Internet metadaemon. This program watches the network, and when a request comes in to the server for a program that inetd knows about, it starts the program. Thus, when you set up inetd to start Samba, you are telling inetd to watch for incoming Samba requests, and when it gets one, to start Samba. When the client is done with the Samba connection, Samba exits.

Setting up inetd takes two steps. First, check the /etc/services file to make sure that inetd will be listening for NetBIOS (Samba) calls. Then, edit the inetd configuration file /etc/inetd.conf to make sure that inetd can start Samba.

Checking /etc/services

The first step in setting up inetd to launch Samba is to check the /etc/services file to make sure that inetd is listening for NetBIOS (Samba calls). NetBIOS calls come in on ports 137 and 139. Look for the following lines in your /etc/services file:

```
netbios-ns    137/udp
netbios-ssn    139/tcp
```

If these lines are missing, use your favorite editor to add them, preferably right after the line that mentions 136. See Chapter 6 for more on using text editors to edit files, or refer to your documentation.

Checking /etc/inetd.conf

After you make sure that the /etc/services file lets inetd look for NetBIOS calls, edit the inetd.conf file to give inetd the power to start Samba. Add the following two lines (or ones resembling them, depending on your flavor of UNIX):

```
netbios-ssn stream tcp nowait root /usr/local/Samba/bin/smbd smbd
netbios-ns dgram udp wait root /usr/local/Samba/bin/nmbd nmbd
```

If you're lucky, it might be there but commented out, so you would just need to remove the commenting character (usually a #).

After you successfully change your inetd.conf file, restart inetd so it can read the configuration file when it starts. To do so, find the process number for inetd with the `ps` command and send it the `kill -HUP` signal. If the process number for inetd was 5877, you would type the following line:

```
# kill -HUP 5877
```

If all has gone well, whenever a Samba request comes in, inetd starts Samba to handle the request.

Chapter 4

Configuring the Windows Clients

● ●

In This Chapter

▶ Configuring Windows 95/98 clients

▶ Configuring Windows NT clients

▶ Configuring Windows 2000 clients

▶ Choosing between encrypted and nonencrypted passwords

● ●

*A*fter you install and test Samba on the server side (see Chapters 2 and 3), you need to configure the clients. First, ensure the client has a properly installed network interface card (NIC), also called a *network adapter card* or simply an *adapter*. Then, verify that you have the appropriate Windows drivers installed for your card. To enable networking, you then configure the client as we describe in this chapter.

What is TCP/IP?

Samba runs on a TCP/IP network. TCP/IP is a network *protocol*, which is a specific network language that computers use to talk to each other. The Internet and the World Wide Web run on TCP/IP, so it is becoming the most prevalent networking protocol out there.

TCP/IP is a rugged, routable network system designed for connecting smaller networks together into a larger internetwork. Because nearly every networked computer has Internet access, almost every network today runs TCP/IP.

Some important TCP/IP terms you will come across are *Internet address*, *domain name system*, and *network classes*:

✔ **Internet address:** The Internet address — commonly referred to as an IP address — is four numbers separated by periods — for example, 192.168.11.2. Each number ranges from 0 to 255. The Internet address is used to address each machine that is hooked up to the Internet as well as to address each Samba server hooked up on your network. Numbers are hard for humans to remember, and Internet addresses of four separate numbers are even harder. A name, such as `liberty.george.home`, is easier to remember than 192.168.11.2, but the computer finds 192.168.11.2 much easier to work with than `liberty.george.home`. Hence, the domain name system provides the translation.

(continued)

(continued)

✔ **Domain name system (DNS):** A domain name system (DNS) server is a computer that translates text-based name requests — for example, www.imdb.com — into a numerical Internet address that a computer can remember, like 208.33.219.16. Every TCP/IP network with more than a few computers should have access to a DNS server, and any network attached to the Internet must have access to a DNS server.

✔ **Network classes:** When the Internet was first growing, the range of Interet addresses was broken into several series of network classes. The idea was that a group could obtain and administer its own TCP/IP network class.

Three classes of networks are used today:

✔ **Class A networks** have a starting Internet address of 1 to 126, and each can have 16 million hosts.

✔ **Class B networks** have a starting address of 128 to 191, and each can have 65,000 hosts.

✔ **Class C networks** have a starting address of 192 to 223, and each can have 254 hosts.

When the Internet was young, it wasn't hard to get an exclusive network address. Now, until the next version of the Internet Protocol (IPv6) comes along, network addresses are getting scarce. This is really only a concern if you're going to connect directly to the Internet. If you are going to connect to the Internet through an ISP, the ISP can provide you with Internet addresses. If you're not connecting to the Internet, you can use any Internet address you want.

If your Internet connection will be through a firewall or IP masquerading device, you can probably use a reserved Internet address designed for networks not directly connected to the Internet. Each network class has reserved addresses:

✔ **Class A:** 10.0.0.0

✔ **Class B:** 172.16.0.0 through 172.31.0.0

✔ **Class C:** 192.168.0.0 through 192.168.255.0

From the example we mention earlier in this sidebar, you can see that liberty.george.net is on a private network because of the associated IP address of 192.168.11.2. If you plan to set up a network from scratch, choose one of the reserved class C networks.

Configuring Windows 95/98 Clients

After you install your network card and load the drivers, the next step is to configure your client to recognize Samba. The following sections tell you how to perform these tasks:

1. **Add theTCP/IP protocol (if necessary).**

2. **Configure TCP/IP.**

3. **Enable the SMB client.**

4. **Properly identify the client.**

5. **Connect to shares and printers.**

Adding TCP/IP

First, make sure that TCP/IP is present in the client's network protocol list. If you have been surfing the Web with this computer, you probably already have TCP/IP installed, although you might need to configure it for your Samba network.

Check in the Network control panel to see if TCP/IP is loaded. If necessary, you can install it from there. You can access the Network control panel through the Network Neighborhood or through the Control Panel:

- ✔ To open the Network control panel via the Network Neighborhood icon, right-click the Network Neighborhood icon and choose Properties from the pop-up menu.

- ✔ To open the Network control panel via the Control Panel window, choose Start➪Settings➪Control Panel and then double-click the Network icon.

As shown in Figure 4-1, the Network control panel has three tabs: Configuration, Identification, and Access Control. The Configuration tab lists the installed network components. You should see the network card listed here as well as any other installed network components. If you do not see a component that starts with TCP/IP, there is no TCP/IP adapter installed yet. If you have entries that start with TCP/IP but don't mention your network interface card (adapter), you might have TCP/IP installed but it's not connected to your network card. (It could be TCP/IP connected to a dial-up modem, for example.)

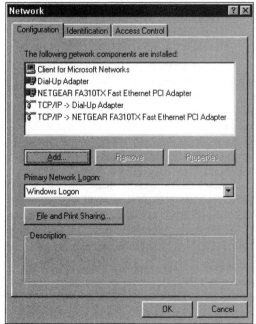

Figure 4-1:
The
Network
control
panel.

Adding the TCP/IP protocol

If you do not see any components that mention TCP/IP, you have to install it. This is a simple task:

1. **On the Network control panel's Configuration tab, click Add to open the Select Network Component Type dialog box.**

2. **In the Network Component list, select Protocol and click Add.**

3. **Select Microsoft in the left box and TCP/IP in the right box.**

4. **Click OK to load the TCP/IP protocol.**

Adding TCP/IP to a NIC

If you have TCP/IP loaded but it doesn't appear to be associated with your network card, change the bindings for the network card:

1. **On the Network control panel's Configuration tab, select your network card (it looks like a small green circuit board).**

2. **Click Properties.**

3. **In the Adapter Properties dialog box, select the Bindings tab.**

4. **On the Bindings tab, make sure that TCP/IP is checked, which binds TCP/IP to this network card.**

5. **Click OK.**

Configuring TCP/IP

After you add TCP/IP to your computer, you need to configure it for your particular network. On the Configuration tab in the Network control panel, select the TCP/IP protocol that is associated with your network card in the list and click Properties to open the TCP/IP Properties dialog box, as shown in Figure 4-2.

You might have several TCP/IP entries — for example, one for AOL, one for dialing your ISP, and one for your network interface card. Be sure to select the right one.

The TCP/IP Properties dialog box has seven tabs that help you configure the IP address, naming service properties, and network properties. We examine those tabs in the following sections.

IP Address tab

The IP Address tab is the first tab displayed in the TCP/IP Properties dialog box. This tab provides the Windows client with a unique IP address so that data flowing to and from your Samba server can get to your Windows client.

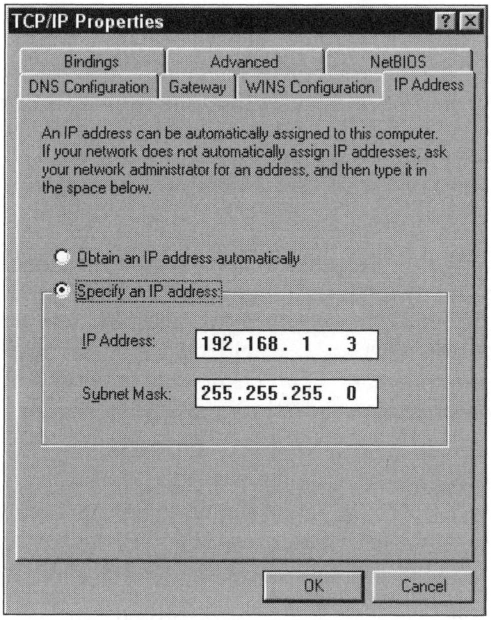

Figure 4-2:
The TCP/IP
Properties
dialog box.

First, specify whether your IP address will be assigned automatically by a DHCP server or if it will be permanently (or *statically*) assigned to this work-station. If you will be getting IP addresses from a dynamic host configuration protocol (DHCP) server, simply click the Obtain an IP Address Automatically button. Assuming your DHCP server is working as it should, every time you boot this client, it will get an IP address.

For smaller networks (for example a five-computer network), you typically assign static IP addresses. In other words, each computer has a permanently assigned IP address. Keeping track of them takes a little more bookkeeping, but you don't have to mess with a DHCP server. In this case, click the Specify an IP Address button and then enter an IP address and the subnet mask. Traditionally, small networks that are not connected to the Internet use 192.168.1.*x* for the IP address and 255.25.255.0 for the subnet mask. That provides about 250 addresses for your network (192.168.1.2 through 192.168.1.253), with 192.168.1.1 and 192.168.1.254 reserved for special purposes.

DNS Configuration tab

On the DNS Configuration tab in the TCP/IP Properties dialog box, you enable or disable DNS (domain name system). DNS is the network function that maps names to IP addresses for the entire Internet. For example, if you type `http:/slashdot.org/` in your Web browser, a DNS server translates that name into numbers a computer can understand, like http://209.207.224.41/.

If you don't have a DNS server on your network, simply select the Disable DNS button. If you do have a DNS Server on your network, select the Enable DNS button. Then complete the associated fields: the DNS Host name, the DNS Domain, one or more DNS Servers, and the Domain Suffix Search Order. (Contact a knowledgeable network administrator to find out this information, or copy the information from a PC that is already working.)

Gateway tab

The Gateway tab in the TCP/IP Properties dialog box is simple. This is where you tell your client about any gateways on your network. A *gateway* is another computer (or router) that connects two different networks. To add a gateway, just complete the New Gateway field, click Add, and then fill in the IP address of the gateway. (Contact a knowledgeable network administrator to find out this information.)

WINS Configuration tab

Windows Internet Name Service (WINS) is the Windows network way of maintaining a network-wide database of IP addresses and the associated computer names. It is similar to DNS but is smaller in scale (for your network only).

If you are not using WINS, simply select Disable WINS Resolution. If you are using WINS, select Enable WINS Resolution and complete the WINS Server Search Order field. (Contact a knowledgeable network administrator to find out this information unless you're using a Samba server as the WINS server; in that case, use the IP address of the Samba server.)

If you are using DHCP, you also have the option of using DHCP for WINS Resolution. With this option, your client gets the address for the WINS server from the DHCP server, enabling you to centrally maintain the location of your WINS server.

Finally, if you have enabled WINS resolution, you will see a field for Scope ID. The Scope ID is used to separate NetBIOS computer names in complex networks; it is tricky to use, so we recommend you don't use it.

Bindings tab

The Bindings tab shows the network programs that use the TCP/IP protocol. You should see Client for Microsoft Networks here, and the box should be checked.

Advanced tab

The Advanced tab isn't used for TCP/IP, so you have nothing to worry about here.

NetBIOS tab

You shouldn't have to worry about the NetBIOS tab either; the box to enable NetBIOS over TCP/IP, which is what Samba does, should be checked.

Enabling the SMB client

After you set up TCP/IP, configure the SMB client software (Client for Microsoft Networks) to enable Windows 95/98 to communicate with the SMB server via the TCP/IP protocol.

Follow these steps to configure the SMB client:

1. **On the Network control panel's Configuration tab, click Add to open the Select Network Component Type dialog box.**

2. **Select the Client network component and click Add.**

3. **In the left box, select Microsoft, and in the right box, select Client for Microsoft Networks.**

4. **Click OK to load the Client for Microsoft Networks software.**

Identifying the Windows 95/98 Client

After you successfully configure the SMB client software, you need to identify this client to the network. You also need to determine whether this client will be in a workgroup or a domain.

Workgroup or domain?

So what is the difference between a workgroup and a domain, and why would you choose one over the other?

A *workgroup* is the easier one of the two to implement. It's simply a collection of computers with the same workgroup name. A common way to derive a workgroup name is to name it after the department. For example, all users in the billing office might have their computers in the Billing workgroup.

A *domain* is more complex and has more features. If you have a domain, you need to have a domain server as a central repository for user-related information. (Your Samba server can do this.) Among other tasks, your domain server can centrally verify passwords for your users or centrally hold their domain profiles (customized settings for a computer). Domains and profiles are effective for users who use multiple computers for the same purposes but might move amongst more than one machine (such as in a computer lab).

If you're setting up a network from scratch, you get to choose between the easier setup of a workgroup versus the more complex but central administration of a domain. If you have an existing network, find out from a network administrator whether you have workgroups or a domain.

In Chapter 12, we explain how to make your Samba server act as a domain server.

Identifying the client

To identify the client to the network, select the Identification tab in the Network control panel. Enter a valid NetBIOS name in the Computer Name field. A valid NetBIOS name is up to 15 characters long and can include alphanumeric characters and the following punctuation characters: ~ ! @ # $ % ^ & *( ) – ` { }.

Identifying the workgroup

To have the Windows 95/98 client become a member of a workgroup, simply type the workgroup name in the Workgroup field on the Identification tab.

Identifying the domain

To have the Windows 95/98 client become a member of a domain, you have to do a little more work:

1. **On the Configuration tab in the Network control panel, select Client for Microsoft Networks and click Properties.**

   (If you do not see Client for Microsoft Networks, see the section "Enabling the SMB client," earlier in this chapter).

2. **In the Logon Validation section, check the Log on to Windows NT Domain box (yes, even if you are using a Windows 95/98 domain), and enter the domain name in the Windows NT Domain field.**

3. **In the Network Logons section, select one of the following options:**

   - Quick Logon, which doesn't check network drives until you try to use them

   - Logon and Restore Network Connections, in which Windows tries to verify each drive

   Determine which option best serves your needs depending on how many drives you want to map and how patient your users are.

 If you get an error message such as `Unable to browse the network` when trying to view shares, you might have a network adapter conflict. Use the System control panel to create a separate hardware profile in which you can disable the possibly conflicting adapter. For example, if you have a dial-up adapter that already has TCP/IP properties applied to it, that could override your TCP/IP settings for your network card and prevent you from connecting to the server. You can also try disabling the adapter directly as follows:

1. **Open the System control panel.**

2. **Click the Device Manager tab.**

3. **Click the plus box to expand the Network Adapters device list.**

4. **Select the suspected adapter and click Properties.**

5. **Check the box labeled Disable in This Hardware Profile and click OK.**

6. **Click OK to close the System Properties dialog box.**

Connecting to Samba's shared drives and printers

Okay, everything appears to be working. It's time to start using your Samba shares. To begin, you have to know how to make a permanent connection to a network drive. (Otherwise, it's frustrating to make the same connection each time you start your computer, and not doing so can lead to strange errors when your drives get misplaced.)

Also, in the end you usually need to print something. We cover two ways of connecting to a printer.

Connecting to network drives

One of the reasons you want a Samba server is to share network drives. First, we explain how to set up a permanent network connection and then how to create a temporary connection.

Making a permanent network drive connection

Permanent network connections are very useful because your users (and their applications) always know which drive contains their files. Complete these steps to set up a permanent network connection:

1. **Open the Network Neighborhood.**

2. **Select the server you want to access.**

3. **Right-click the share to which you want to make a permanent connection and then choose Map Network Drive from the pop-up menu.**

4. **Pick a drive letter for this share, check the Reconnect at Logon box to make it permanent, and then click OK.**

Making a temporary network drive connection

Sometimes, you just need temporary access to a Samba share. To create a temporary network drive connection, complete these simple steps:

1. **Open the Network Neighborhood.**

2. **Click the server you want to access.**

3. **Double-click the share you want to use.**

   Now, you can use it like any other Windows folder.

 If you have trouble connecting and you keep getting a prompt for a password even though you know you typed it correctly, you probably have a Windows client sending encrypted passwords to a nonencrypted Samba server. Chapter 9 explains how to solve this problem.

TIP

Connecting to a printer using the My Computer window

You can also connect a printer to your Windows client by using the Printers folder in the My Computer window. This method can be quicker than using the Add Printer wizard if you already know the network path name of the printer:

1. **Open My Computer.**

2. **Right-click the Printers folder.**

3. **Choose Capture Printer Port from the pop-up menu.**

4. **Select LPT1 for a Device (or LPT2 if LPT1 is being used).**

5. **Type the network path name of the printer — for example, \\terrapin\lp.**

6. **If you want to make this a permanent connection, check the Reconnect at Logon box.**

7. **Click OK.**

Connecting to printers

At some point in using a computer, you're going to need to print something. In fact, you might even be using Samba to create a printer server. You can connect a client to a Samba printer with the Printer wizard or via the My Computer window.

The best way to connect a Windows 95/98 client to a Samba printer is to use the Add Printer wizard:

1. **Open the Printers control panel by choosing Start➪ Settings➪Printers.**

2. **Double-click the Add Printer icon to start the Add Printer wizard and then click Next.**

3. **Select Network printer and click Next.**

4. **Browse through the network neighborhood to locate the printer (or type the full path if you know it — for example, \\terrapin\lp).**

5. **Select Yes if you need to print from DOS applications and then click Next.**

6. **Choose the necessary printer driver.**

   The list displays printer drivers that are on the Windows CD, with the manufacturer's name in the left window and the printer model in the right window. If you have a newer or unusual printer, you might need to get the driver from the manufacturer's disk or CD by clicking the Have Disk button. Then click Next.

7. **Type a name for the printer in the Printer Name field, and decide if this will be the default printer for this Windows client. Click Next.**

8. **Print a test page to make sure everything is working and then click Finish.**

   You might be prompted for your Windows CD.

Configuring Windows NT Clients

Windows NT is a little harder to set up for networking than Windows 95/98, particularly the network card, because Windows NT does not support Plug and Play. If you have any problems installing your network cards in Windows NT (for example, NT does not recognize them), refer to an NT manual.

After you have your card installed correctly, you need to complete a two-step process to configure your NT client for Samba. First, configure the Network control panel. Then, make your connections to the shares and printers.

Configuring the Network control panel

After you successfully install your network card in your NT client, you set up the Network control panel to use Samba.

To open the Network control panel, right-click the Network Neighborhood and choose Properties from the pop-up menu. Or, choose Start⇨Settings⇨Control Panel and then double-click the Network icon.

As shown in Figure 4-3, the Network control panel has five tabs: Identification, Services, Protocols, Adapters, and Bindings. In the following sections, we describe how to configure each tab.

Identification tab

On the Identification tab in the Network control panel, you name this NT client and specify the workgroup or domain to which it belongs. It's important that you choose the same domain or workgroup that includes the Samba server; otherwise, you might not see it.

Clicking the Change button displays a dialog box in which you specify whether you are in a workgroup or a domain. Workgroups and domains are the same for Windows NT as they are for Windows 95/98, so if you're not sure of the concept, read the sidebar titled "Workgroup or domain?"

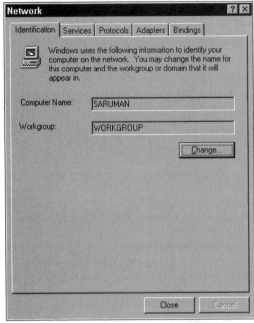

Network

Identification | Services | Protocols | Adapters | Bindings

Windows uses the following information to identify your computer on the network. You may change the name for this computer and the workgroup or domain that it will appear in.

Computer Name: SARUMAN

Workgroup: WORKGROUP

Change...

Close   Cancel

Figure 4-3:
The
Network
control
panel in
Windows NT.

If you are joining a domain for the first time, you need to check the Create a Computer Account in the Domain box and then enter the user name and domain.

Services tab

The Services tab in the Network control panel lists all the network services that NT is running. The service that acts as a Samba client is called Workstation. If Workstation is not listed, add it:

1. **To add the Samba client Workstation, click Add.**

2. **From the list of services to add, select Workstation.**

3. **Click Have Disk, and browse to your NT CD-ROM.**

4. **Click OK to finish the installation.**

Protocols tab

The Network control panel's Protocols tab lists the network protocols that are running on this machine. You can think of network protocols as languages. If two machines want to communicate directly, they must use the same protocol. Samba uses the TCP/IP network protocol, as do Web browsers, so you probably already have TCP/IP on your NT workstation.

If you don't see the TCP/IP protocol listed on the Protocols tab, you need to add TCP/IP and then configure it. For details, see the sections "Adding TCP/IP" and "Configuring TCP/IP," later in this chapter.

Adapters tab

The Network control panel's Adapters tab displays your network card and enables you to add, remove, or update network cards and change their properties.

If you need to add a network card, follow these steps:

1. **Click Add.**

2. **In the resulting Select Network Adapter dialog box, select your network card.**

3. **Click Have Disk, and browse to the CD or floppy disk that contains your network drivers.**

4. **Click OK to finish.**

Bindings tab

The Network control panel's Bindings tab displays the bindings between your network cards and your network protocols, and between your network services and your network protocols. Verify a few of these bindings to ensure that the NetBIOS Interface is using the WINS client attached to the network card.

The services for Server, Workstation, and NetBIOS Interface all have to be bound to TCP/IP to allow the Windows NT client to access a Samba server.

Adding TCP/IP

If you don't see the TCP/IP protocol listed on the Protocols tab in the Network control panel, add it by completing the following steps:

1. **Click Add.**

2. **Select TCP/IP Protocol from the list of protocols.**

3. **Click Have Disk, and browse to your NT CD-ROM.**

4. **Click OK to finish the installation.**

Configuring TCP/IP

After you load the TCP/IP protocol, you have to configure it for this client. On the Protocols tab in the Network control panel, highlight the TCP/IP Protocol and click Properties to access the Microsoft TCP/IP Properties dialog box. As shown in Figure 4-4, this dialog box has four tabs: IP Address, DNS, WINS Address, and Routing.

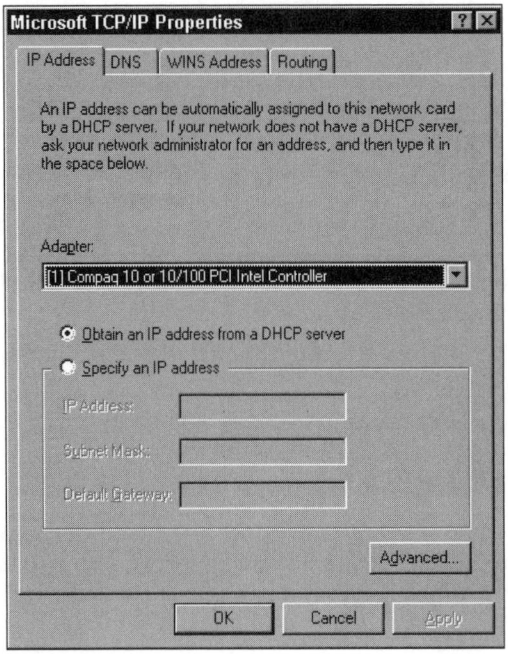

Figure 4-4:
The
Microsoft
TCP/IP
Properties
dialog box.

IP Address tab

When you open the Microsoft TCP/IP Properties dialog box, you see the IP Address tab. On this tab, you give your Windows client a unique IP address so that data flowing to and from your Samba server can get to your Windows client.

This tab is almost identical to the one you see in Windows 95/98 (see "Configuring Windows 95/98 Clients," previously in this chapter) with one exception: the Adapter choice, which enables you to specify the IP address for a particular NIC. Unless you're creating a router, which is beyond the scope of this book, leave the Adapter choice set to the default NIC.

Next, specify whether your IP address will be assigned automatically by a DHCP server or if an IP address will be permanently (statically) assigned to this workstation.

If you will be obtaining IP addresses from a DHCP server, simply check the corresponding radio button. Assuming your DHCP server is working as it should, every time you boot this client, it will get an IP address.

Smaller networks (for example a five-computer network) typically use *static IP addresses*. In other words, each computer has a permanently assigned IP address. Keeping track of the static IP addresses takes a little more book-keeping, but you don't have to mess with a DHCP server. If you're going to do this for your network, select Specify an IP Address, and complete the IP Address and Subnet Mask fields.

If you need help choosing an IP address, some have already been reserved for small networks that are not connected to the Internet. Refer to the section "Configuring Windows 95/98 Clients," earlier in this chapter — specifically, the "IP Address tab" subsection.

Finally, the Advanced button opens a dialog box with fields for Gateways, PPTP Filtering, and Security. These options really go beyond the scope of this book. If you want to know more, check out a book on Windows NT administration.

DNS tab

On the DNS tab in the Microsoft TCP/IP Properties dialog box, you enable or disable DNS (domain name system). DNS is the network function that maps names to IP addresses for the entire Internet. For example, if you type `http:/slashdot.org/` in your Web browser, a DNS server translates that address into numbers a computer can understand, like `http://209.207.224.41/`.

If you don't have a DNS server on your network, simply select Disable DNS. If you do have a DNS server on your network, select Enable DNS. Then, complete the associated fields: the DNS Host Name, the DNS Domain, one or more DNS Servers, and if you have multiple DNS servers, the Domain Suffix Search Order. (Contact a knowledgeable network administrator to find out this information.)

WINS Address tab

WINS is the Windows network way of maintaining a network-wide database of IP addresses and the associated computer names. It is similar to DNS, but is smaller in scale (for your network only).

The WINS tab in the Microsoft TCP/IP Properties dialog box is very similar to the WINS tab for Windows 95/98 (see "Configuring Windows 95/98 Clients," earlier in this chapter), with the addition of an Adapter field for setting up different WINS settings per network card.

If you are not using WINS, simply select Disable WINS Resolution. If you are using WINS, select Enable WINS Resolution and complete the primary and secondary WINS server addresses. You might need to contact a network administrator to get the addresses for your WINS server. Also, Chapter 11 describes how to set up Samba as a WINS server.

If you are using DHCP, you also have the option of using DHCP for WINS resolution. With this option, your client gets the address for the WINS server from the DHCP server, enabling you to centrally maintain the location of your WINS server.

You also have the option of using an LMHOSTS Lookup table for WINS resolution along with the ability to import a generic LMHOSTS table. You probably don't want to do this because it's one more file to be maintained per client.

Finally, if you have enabled WINS resolution, you see a field for Scope ID. The Scope ID is used to separate NetBIOS computer names in complex networks; it is tricky to use, so we recommend that you don't use it.

Routing tab

The Routing tab in the Microsoft TCP/IP Properties dialog box is for an NT machine with more than one network card in case you wanted to set it up as a router. That goes beyond the scope of this book, so don't do anything with this tab.

Connecting to shares and printers

You have several different ways to connect to network shared drives and printers. The methods are very similar to what you do for Windows 95/98 (see "Configuring Windows 95/98 Clients," earlier in this chapter), but with a few added features.

Connecting to network drives

One of the reasons you want a Samba server is to share network drives. First, we explain how to set up permanent network connection and then how to create a temporary connection.

Making a permanent network drive connection

Permanent network connections are very useful because your users (and their applications) always know which drive contains their files. Complete these steps to set up a permanent network connection:

1. **Open the Network Neighborhood.**

2. **Select the server you want to access.**

3. **Right-click the share to which you want to make a permanent connection and then choose Map Network Drive.**

4. **Optionally, you can choose to connect as a different user from the one who is logged on.**

   This feature is useful when you need to access an administrative share that the typical user would not need to access.

5. **Pick a drive letter for this share, check the Reconnect at Logon box to make the connection permanent, and then click OK.**

Making a temporary network drive connection

Sometimes, you just need temporary access to a Samba share. Complete these simple steps to make a temporary network drive connection:

1. **Open the Network Neighborhood.**

2. **Click the server you want to access.**

3. **Double-click the share you want to use.**

   Now, you can use the share like any other Windows folder.

Connecting to printers using the Add Printer wizard

At some point in using a computer, you're going to need to print something. In fact, you might even be using Samba to create a printer server. The best way to connect a Windows NT client to a Samba printer is to use the Add Printer wizard:

1. **Open the Printers control panel by choosing Start⇨ Settings⇨Printers.**

2. **Double-click the Add Printer icon to start the Add Printer wizard program. Click Next.**

3. **Select Network Printer and click Next.**

   The wizard displays the Connect to Printer dialog box.

   You can complete the first box, labeled Printer, with the name of the server and the printer. For example, to use the printer lj on the server olorin, type **olorin\lj**.

   Alternatively, you can select a displayed printer in the Shared Printers list.

4. **Select the desired option and then click OK.**

   The wizard asks whether you want your Windows-based programs to use this printer as the default printer?

5. **Click Yes or No, as appropriate, and then click Next.**

   You might be asked to install a printer driver.

6. **Scroll through the list to select your printer (the manufacturer's list is in the left window and the models are in the right window). If you have a newer printer or updated drivers, click Have Disk and browse to the drive (floppy, CD, or network drive) that has the drivers.**

   Then, you have to decide whether you want to make this a shared printer.

7. **Click No because Samba will already be sharing this printer.**

8. **Print a test page to make sure everything is working and then click Finish.**

   You might be prompted for your Windows CD.

Configuring Windows 2000 Clients

Windows 2000 is designed to be a replacement for Windows NT and include the best features of both Windows 98 and Windows NT. The screen layout and dialog boxes differ markedly from Windows 95/98 and NT. We'll alert you to the significant differences.

Windows 2000 doesn't support as many network cards or other devices as Windows 95/98 or even Windows NT. Microsoft has compiled a list of supported and tested products for Windows 2000. You should first check Microsoft's Windows 2000 Hardware Compatibility List at `http://www.microsoft.com/hcl` before you purchase any network cards or other hardware for a Windows 2000 workstation.

Windows 2000 has Plug-and-Play hardware detection. When you install a network card, Windows 2000 detects the new network card on startup and locates software drivers for the card. If that process doesn't happen automatically, use the Add/Remove Hardware control panel wizard to install the network card.

Installing the required Microsoft networking components

Windows 2000 has changed the network configuration dialog boxes from the way they are arranged in Windows 95/98 and Windows NT. The easiest way to get to the network configuration options is through the My Network Places icon:

1. **Right-click the My Network Places icon.**

2. **Choose Properties.**

3. **In the Network and Dial-Up Connections dialog box, double-click Local Area Connection.**

   As shown in Figure 4-5, the Local Area Connection Status dialog box gives you a status of the network connection, including the network speed, uptime, and packets sent and received. If your network card was installed correctly and your network is working, you should see a value for packets sent and received.

4. **Click Properties to access the properties for this Local Area Connection.**

The first field in the Local Area Connections properties should be your network card. You would click Configure to open the dialog box you use to configure the properties for this network card, but you rarely need to do so unless, for example, the computer complains of resource conflicts.

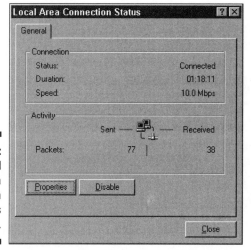

Figure 4-5:
The Local
Area
Connection
Status
dialog box.

In the Local Area Connections properties, you should have three components installed by default: Client for Microsoft Networks, File and Printer Sharing for Microsoft Networks, and Internet Protocol (TCP/IP). Samba is Microsoft networking done over TCP/IP, so you need to ensure the Client for Microsoft Networks and the Internet Protocol (TCP/IP) components are installed.

If you need to install the Client for Microsoft Networks, follow these steps:

1. **Click Install.**

2. **Select Client and click Add.**

3. **From the list of clients, select Client for Microsoft Networks and click OK.**

If you need to install File and Printer Sharing for Microsoft Networks, follow these steps:

1. **Click Install.**

2. **Select Services and click Add.**

3. **From the list of servicess, select File and Printer Sharing for Microsoft Networks and click OK.**

If you need to install the Internet Protocol (TCP/IP), follow these steps:

1. **Click Install.**

2. **Select Protocol and click Add.**

3. **From the list of Protocols, select Internet Protocol (TCP/IP) and click OK.**

Next, you need to configure the TCP/IP properties. Select the Internet Protocol (TCP/IP) component and click Properties to open the Internet Protocol (TCP/IP) Properties dialog box, shown in Figure 4-6.

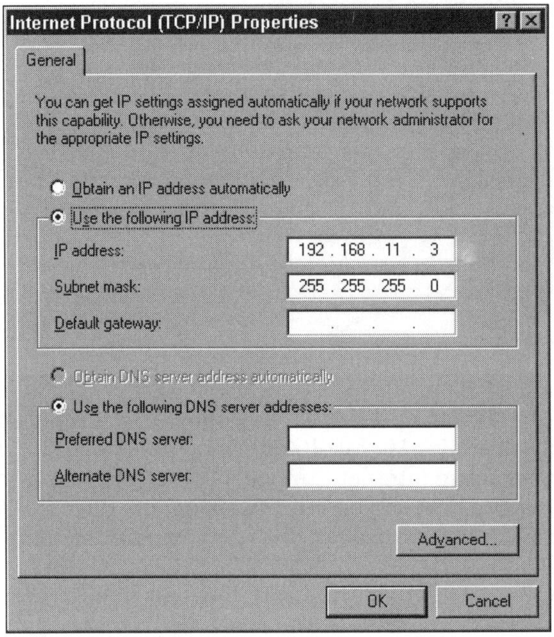

Figure 4-6:
The Internet
Protocol
(TCP/IP)
Properties
dialog box.

Configuring general TCP/IP settings

The top section of the General tab in the Internet Protocol (TCP/IP) Properties dialog box deals with the IP address for this client. The default IP addressing scheme is to use DHCP, which automatically allocates an IP address when your client boots up. Using DHCP is fine if you have DHCP services on your network. If you don't, you need to select Use the Following IP Address, and then enter the values for this client's IP address, the subnet mask, and the default gateway. (Assigning a specific IP address instead of using DHCP is called *static addressing*.)

If you're using static IP addresses and you need help choosing an IP address, some have already been reserved for small networks that are not connected to the Internet. Refer to the description of the IP Address tab in the section "Configuring Windows 95/98 Clients," earlier in this chapter.

The bottom half of the General tab in the Internet Protocol (TCP/IP) Properties dialog box deals with the DNS server setup. DNS servers provide the service that maps Internet names to IP numbers. The default choice is to get the name/number information automatically from network traffic, which you accomplish by selecting Obtain DNS Server Address Automatically. If you want to use specific DNS servers, select Use the Following DNS Server Addresses, and then complete the address for the preferred and alternate DNS servers.

Configuring advanced TCP/IP settings

Clicking the Advanced button in the Internet Protocol (TCP/IP) Properties dialog box takes you to the Advanced TCP/IP Settings dialog box. The Advanced TCP/IP Settings dialog box has four tabs: IP, DNS, WINS, and Options.

IP tab

On the IP tab, you can configure the IP address, subnet masks, and gateways for this client. You can do this on the General tab in the Internet Protocol (TCP/IP) Properties dialog box, so you do not have many reasons to go here.

DNS tab

You use the DNS tab to configure the DNS properties of this server. DNS is used to map computer names to IP addresses. For just using a DNS server, the DNS section of the General tab should be sufficient. The top part of this dialog box shows the DNS server to use, while the bottom part deals with DNS suffixes. None of this is necessary for this client to use a Samba server and it is beyond the scope of this book, so we won't talk any more about it.

WINS tab

On the WINS tab, you determine how your client deals with a WINS server. WINS is how a Microsoft network maintains a database of computer names and IP addresses. In that regard, it is similar to DNS, but on a smaller scale. In the top section of the WINS tab, you can add, edit, or remove WINS servers. You need to know the IP address of any WINS servers you want to use.

You also have the option of allowing this client to use an LMHOSTS table for IP address lookups. If you have more than a few computers on your network, you'll have many fewer headaches by using a WINS server instead of an LMHOSTS table for each client. By the way, you can set up Samba as a WINS server. See Chapter 11 for information.

At the bottom of the WINS tab, you have the option of enabling or disabling NetBIOS over TCP/IP. Because Samba uses NetBIOS over TCP/IP, you want to keep that enabled.

Options tab

You use the Options tab for network security and TCP/IP filtering. If you want to use IP security on your network, you enable it by highlighting IP Security and clicking Properties. You have the choice of three modes of network security, which all use Kerberos. (Setting up security on a network is beyond the scope of this book.)

Windows 2000 uses a version of Kerberos that conflicts with the version commonly used with UNIX and Linux servers.

You use the TCP/IP filtering option to customize the TCP/IP access your Windows 2000 client will have. To do this, highlight TCP/IP Filtering and click Properties. You don't need to do anything in this dialog box, but if you find that a client is not permitting TCP and UDP ports 137 and 139, Samba won't work.

Configuring network identification settings

With Windows 2000, the section where you identify the computer and desired workgroup or domain has been moved from the Network control panel to the System control panel. To get the Network Identification section of the System control panel, follow these steps:

1. **Click Start➪Settings➪Control Panel.**
2. **In the Control Panel, double-click System.**
3. **In System, select the Network Identification tab.**
4. **Click Properties to change or add the Network Identification.**

Windows 2000 displays the Identification Changes dialog box, as shown in Figure 4-7. The first field, labeled Computer Name, is for the NetBIOS name of this client. A NetBIOS name can be up to 15 characters long and can include alphanumeric characters and the following punctuation characters: ~ ! @ # $ % ^ & *( ) – ` { }. The More button enables you to customize the name for DNS networks, which is beyond the scope of this book.

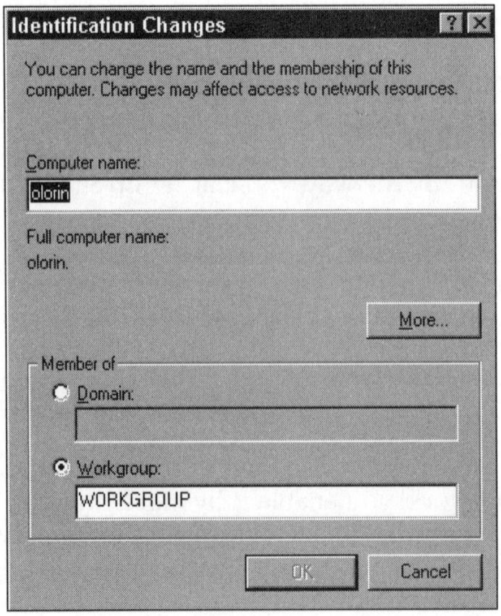

Figure 4-7:
The Identification Changes dialog box.

In the bottom section of the Identification Changes dialog box, you can choose between having this client join a domain or a workgroup and specify what domain or workgroup the client will join. If you're not sure of the difference between workgroups and domains, see the sidebar "Workgroup or domain?" previously in this chapter.

Connecting to shares

As is the case with most other tasks in Windows 2000, the steps you use for connecting to shared drives and printers differ from those in Windows 95/98 or Windows NT. The biggest change involves the elimination of the Network Neighborhood. Now, you start with the My Network Places icon. Follow these steps to make a permanent connection to a workgroup share:

1. **Click My Network Places.**

2. **Click Computers Near Me to see the computers in your workgroup.**

3. **Click the computer you want to access.**

4. **Right-click the share you want to access and choose Map Network Drive.**

5. **Choose the drive to which you want to map this share and check the Reconnect at Logon box.**

The procedure is almost the same if you want to connect to a share outside your workgroup:

1. **Click My Network Places.**

2. **Click Entire Workgroup.**

3. **Search for a resource, or view the Entire Network.**

4. **If you've viewed the Entire Network, select Microsoft Windows Network to see a list of workgroups in the network.**

5. **Click the desired workgroup to see the computers in that workgroup.**

6. **Click the computer you want to access.**

7. **Right-click the share you want to access and choose Map Network Drive.**

8. **Choose the drive to which you want to map this share and then check the Reconnect at Logon box.**

If you just want to temporarily access a share, you can just click it instead of mapping the drive.

Connecting to printers

The best way to connect to a printer is to use the Add Printer wizard:

1. **Click Start⇨Settings ⇨Printers to get to the Printers folder.**

2. **Double-click Add Printers to start the Add Printer wizard.**

3. **Click Next.**

4. **Choose Network Printer and click Next.**

5. **Click Next to browse for the printer.**

6. **Browse through your Windows network to your Samba server, select the printer on the Samba server you want to use, and click Next.**

   You might be asked to install a printer driver.

7. **If so, scroll through the list to select your printer (the manufacturer's list is in the left window and the models are in the right window). If you have a newer printer or updated drivers, click Have Disk and browse to the drive (floppy, CD, or network drive) that has the drivers.**

8. **Decide if you want to make this printer your default printer.**

9. **Click Finish to close the Add Printer wizard.**

Deciding Whether to Use Encrypted or Nonencrypted Passwords

There's one more tricky thing to configure for Windows clients: choosing between using all encrypted or all nonencrypted passwords.

The earliest versions of Windows 95 sent passwords out over the network in nonencrypted format. Therefore, they were easily viewable by anyone on the network with a packet sniffer.

Later versions of Windows 95 and subsequent versions of Windows (98, NT with Service Pack 3, and 2000) use encrypted passwords by default for increased security. Therefore, if your Samba server is not configured to use encrypted passwords, you won't be able to connect to it. For example, a Windows NT client will give you System Error 1240, which says `The Account is not authorized to log in from this workstation.`

So, for all except the earliest versions of Windows 95, if you plan to use all nonencrypted passwords, you need to edit the Registry on your Windows clients. If you plan to use all encrypted passwords, you need to do a few easy steps on your Samba server (after you have added all your users; see Chapter 7).

See Chapter 9 for all the details on passwords.

Chapter 5

Administering Samba with Web-based Tools

*I*nstalling a Samba server isn't very difficult, but the bread and butter of a Samba administrator's job is the day-to-day server maintenance. You have to make sure your users can get to their files and print their jobs. Server maintenance also means making sure the Samba server plays nicely with the other parts of the network.

Samba comes with several maintenance tools. The most commonly used tools are browser-based, which means they run as a small Web server on the Samba server and enable administration via an Internet browser interface. If you need to make a simple change, however, editing the smb.conf file from the command line is often the easiest way to get the job done.

The Samba Web Administration Tool, or *SWAT*, comes with Samba 2.0 and later. It's the most common way to administer a Samba server. The other Web-based Samba administration tool is Webmin. Webmin also includes many other functions besides its Samba maintenance tools. So if you end up doing many other kinds of maintenance on your server, Webmin might be a better choice.

Steering Samba with SWAT

SWAT enables you to maintain your Samba server via a Web browser. In essence, SWAT acts as a scaled-down Web server that runs on your Samba server, enabling you to maintain Samba from the nearest browser.

SWAT is the most common way to maintain a Samba server because everyone knows how to use a Web browser. SWAT makes modifying the server as easy as filling in a field and clicking a button.

SWAT rewrites the Samba configuration file (smb.conf). In doing so, it removes any comments you might have added to the file. If your style of administration is to add comments in the configuration file, consider using another tool.

Installing and configuring SWAT

SWAT comes with Samba 2.0 and later. It should have installed automatically with Samba. First, try to access SWAT on your Samba server:

1. **Open a Web browser.**
2. **Enter a URL with your server address and add :901, which points to port 901 on the server. For example:**

   ```
   http://192.168.11.4:901/
   ```

   If everything was installed properly, you should be prompted for a username and password.
3. **Enter the root username and root password, and the main SWAT screen should display.**

   Congratulations, you're well on your way to being a SWAT administrator!

If the SWAT page did not display, read on for instructions on how to configure your system to use SWAT.

Checking the /etc/services file

If you're using Samba Version 2.0 or later, SWAT should have been installed automatically, so you might just need to change a few configuration files. If you're using a version earlier than Samba 2.0, you should strongly consider upgrading.

First, you need to check the /etc/services file. The services file is a long list of programs with the TCP/IP *ports* to which they should be listening. To help understand ports, think of an IP address as the address of a big apartment building, and the TCP/IP port as the apartment number in the building. If you're sending an invitation to a friend who lives in apartment 30 and you send it to apartment 45 instead, it's not going to get to your friend. (Well, in real life it might, because letter carriers are much smarter than computers, but you get the idea.)

So, to reach a program (such as SWAT), you need to have both the IP address *and* the port correct, and someone must be waiting at that port. (If you send an invitation to room 300 but there is no room 300, your invitation won't get delivered.)

Now, SWAT expects TCP-type packets at port 901, so verify that your /etc/ services file contains the following line:

```
swat 901/tcp # Add swat service used via inetd
```

If you don't find this line, add it using your favorite editor. (Chapter 6 discusses some text editors.) You only really need to add the section before the # sign; everything after the # sign is a comment for the administrator's reference.

Notice that the comment in this line mentions inetd. As we explain in Chapter 3, inetd is like a butler that waits for incoming messages and starts the right programs to go with the messages. You might need to modify the inetd configuration file, conveniently named inetd.conf.

Checking the /etc/inetd.conf file

Inetd is the Internet metadaemon — a daemon that reads incoming TCP/IP packets and takes action on the packets it receives. In our example from the preceding section, if inetd gets packets on port 901, it should start SWAT and pass them to the SWAT program.

The configuration program for inetd is the /etc/inetd.conf file. Your /etc/inetd.conf file needs to include the following line:

```
swat stream tcp nowait.400 root /usr/sbin/swat swat
```

If /etc/inetd.conf does not include this line, add it with you favorite editor.

You might need to change the path field (/usr/sbin/swat) so it points to the proper location of the SWAT binary. If you're not sure where it is, you can always use the find command — for example, **find / -name swat –print**.

After you add the correct line to the /etc/inetd.conf file, inetd needs to reread its configuration file. Find the process number of the inetd program using ps -ae, and send it a kill -HUP signal to restart it. If, for example, the process ID for inetd was 421, you would type the following line:

```
# kill -HUP 421
```

You need to do this anytime you modify the inetd.conf file.

Now, go back to your browser and try to access SWAT again. Remember to log on as root so that all the configuration options are available to you.

Using SWAT

Okay, SWAT is visible in your browser, as shown in Figure 5-1. You should have a row of icons across the top of your page, and a list of links down the left-hand side of the page. The icons across the top of the page take you to different SWAT pages, while the listed links take you to the Samba man pages.

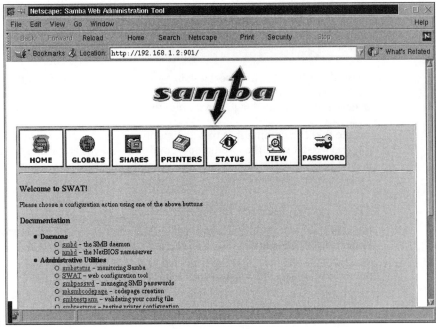

Figure 5-1:
SWAT, the
Samba Web
Administration
Tool.

The icons are as follows:

- **Home:** Open the SWAT home page.
- **Globals:** Set the Samba parameters in the Global section of the Samba configuration file.
- **Shares:** Administer each share listed in the Samba configuration file.
- **Printers:** Maintain the printers that Samba is sharing.
- **Status:** Get an overview of what your Samba server is doing and sharing.
- **View:** View the Samba configuration file.
- **Password:** Configure the Samba password file.

The Documentation links on the SWAT home page take you to the man pages for each command. The man pages are tersely written and usually offer few explanations or examples, but they can help you if you just want to remember a specific option for a command, for example.

What is on the Home page?

On the Home page, you can travel to another section by clicking the buttons across the top of the page, or you can read the Samba documentation by clicking the links.

If you have never encountered man pages before, you might be in for a surprise. The same people who decided to use cp instead of copy for a UNIX command because copy was too long also wrote the man pages. The man pages are terse and dense, and you need to have a good working knowledge of Linux. After you've been running a Samba server for a few years, you might like the brevity in the man pages. But if you're a Linux newcomer, you might find them intimidating and confusing at first, which is normal.

What are the Globals options used for?

The Globals page controls Samba configuration options that you find in the Global section of the Samba configuration file, smb.conf. Yes, it is confusing that SWAT refers to Globals while the smb.conf file refers to Global, but you just have to keep them straight:

> SWAT — Globals

> Smb.conf — Global

On the Globals page, you see the same row of buttons across the top of the page. You also see the following buttons:

- ✔ **Commit Changes:** Write your changes to the Samba configuration file, smb.conf.
- ✔ **Reset Value:** Reread the existing Samba configuration file (smb.conf) and repopulate the fields from the existing smb.conf.
- ✔ **Advanced View:** Open the Advanced View of the Globals page, which has about five times as many options as the Basic View.

You have 23 Globals options in the Basic View and 170 in the Advanced View (at the time of this writing, at least). Fortunately, you don't need to know all of these, or even most of them, so for most operations you can use the Basic View.

For the most part, you use the Globals options to determine what kind of neighbor your Samba server is in the Network Neighborhood — for example:

- ✔ What neighborhood does it try to join (with the workgroup parameter)?
- ✔ What name does it use (with the NetBIOS name and NetBIOS alias parameters)?
- ✔ What kind of locks does it have on the front door (with the security and encrypt password parameters)?
- ✔ Does it try to take over the neighborhood association (with the OS level, preferred master, and local master parameters)?

We explain these parameters throughout this book, depending on what you're trying to do. (For example, we explain encrypted passwords in Chapter 9.) Here, we just want to give you a general understanding of what the Globals page does.

What are the Shares options used for?

The Shares page enables you to administer each share in your Samba configuration file (smb.conf). To use the Shares option, you need to pick a specific share. On the Shares page, click the drop-down menu next to the Choose Share button, select the share you want to edit, and click Choose Share. If you haven't added any shares yet, you should at least see the default homes share.

When you're editing a share, you can choose the Basic View or the Advanced View. The Basic View has 9 options, while the Advanced View has about 70. You don't need to know all of these; you can set up most shares with only a few parameters specified.

Some of the things you can set on the Shares page are

- ✔ The directory that is being shared (with the path parameter)
- ✔ Users and groups that would be allowed to access this share (with the valid user option)
- ✔ Whether a user is not allowed to add things to the directory (with the read only and read list parameters)
- ✔ Any special programs that have to be run when a user connects to or disconnects from the share (with the preexec and postexec options)

We discuss these parameters in greater detail when they are being applied throughout this book. Just remember, if it has to do with a user's home directory, you probably need to access the Shares page.

What are the Printers options used for?

The Printers page is where you maintain the printers that Samba will share. For the most part, you use the Printers page to customize Samba to work with your particular operating system.

As with the Shares page, you first need to choose a printer from the drop-down menu and then click Choose Printer. If you haven't added a printer, the default printers share should be available.

After you choose a printer to modify, you see the Samba options for the printer share you've selected: 9 for the Basic View and 27 for the Advanced View.

What are the Status options used for?

The Status page provides a snapshot of what your Samba server is doing, who is connected to your Samba server, and to what they are connecting. Also, you can stop and restart Samba from the Status page, which you need to do after you make changes to your Samba configuration file, smb.conf.

The first section of the Status page is the Auto Refresh section. Here, you can turn on the option to make the Status page automatically refresh, and you can specify how often (in seconds) you want Samba to refresh. If you've chosen to auto refresh, you get a Stop Refreshing button, which — amazingly enough — stops refreshing the status view.

The second section of the Status page gives you control over the Samba daemons, smbd and nmbd. Here, you can stop or restart the daemons. You can also tell what version of Samba you are running.

The final section of the Status page shows the active connections, active shares, and open files on your Samba server. You can disconnect a user by clicking the X button next to that user's connection in the Active Connections section.

What are the View options used for?

The View page shows a text listing of your Samba configuration file, smb.conf. You first see the Normal View, which shows you the basic parameters of your Samba configuration file. To see the whole thing, click Full View.

Access the View options if you are curious about how your configuration file looks, or perhaps you want to copy a section to add to another Samba server.

What are the Password options used for?

The Password page enables you to change passwords, and add or disable Samba users. You can change user passwords on remote servers, too.

A SWAT example: Adding a share

Here is an example of how to SWAT. When you install new hardware or a new driver, you are usually prompted for the Windows 98 CD. Say you want to make all the printer drivers on the Windows 98 CD available to your users. If everyone has the drive space, you could copy an image of the Windows 98 CD to each client's hard drive. Or, if you trust your users and have lots of extra copies of that CD, you can let your users borrow the CD to install a new printer driver. For the rest of us, who don't have enough hard drive space or CDs, we can share the Windows 98 CD image.

To make the drivers available to everyone in an efficient manner, you can add a share that contains an image of the Windows 98 CD. Be sure you are logged on as root so that all the configuration options are available and then complete the following steps:

1. **Start your Web browser, enter the URL for SWAT, and enter your administrator user ID and password.**

2. **Click Shares.**

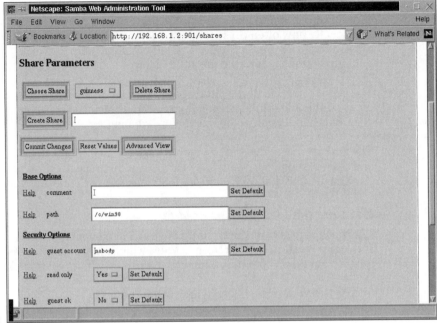

3. **In the Create Share field, enter the name of the share and click Create Share.**

   SWAT displays the Share Parameters page, as shown in Figure 5-2.

4. **Enter the details for this share.**

   For example, if you have the Windows 98 CD image stored in the /c/win98 directory, set the path option to **/c/win98**. You don't want anyone to be able to change the contents of this directory, but the read-only parameter is already set to yes for the default, so you don't have to change that. All the other default parameters look good.

5. **Click Commit Changes to make SWAT write the changes to the Samba configuration file (smb.conf).**

6. **Go to the Status page and click Restart smbd and Restart nmbd to make Samba reread the configuration file.**

Now when you connect to your server from the Network Neighborhood, you have an extra share named win98 that contains the contents of the Windows 98 CD, and none of the files can be deleted. The next time one of your users asks for the Windows 98 CD to install a printer driver, you can direct the user to that share.

A Maximum-Strength Web Tool: Webmin

Webmin is a multipurpose administration tool. It can administer Samba. It can administer jobs that need to run at scheduled times with cron. It can add users and groups. Webmin can do many other things also, but we'll just talk about the Samba-relevant parts.

Webmin is basically a simple Web server with CGI scripts that modify the Samba server's configuration files. In other words, its interface is your favorite Web browser.

Webmin and the CGI scripts are written in Perl. Perl is a common computer language used with Web servers for text processing. It's also nearly hieroglyphic in its complexity. Thankfully, you don't need to know a line of Perl to use or even install Webmin. However, you do need to have the Perl 5 package installed on your server. Fortunately, most Linux distributions load it by default.

To see if you have Perl 5 loaded, type **perl –v** at a command line. If you get something like the following, you can ignore the sidebar about downloading and installing Perl:

```
terrapin # perl -v

This is perl, version 5.005_03 built for i386-freebsd

Copyright 1987-1999, Larry Wall
```

So, you have Perl, it's version 5 or later, and you're ready to install Webmin. Now where is it?

Downloading and installing Perl

If you don't have Perl, or you have something earlier than Perl 5 loaded on your system, and your heart is set on using Webmin, don't panic. You probably have Perl close at hand, and if not, it's just a download away.

First, check your operating system CDs. Perl is likely on your Linux (or Solaris, or FreeBSD) CD awaiting an easy installation. Check the CD and if you find Perl, install it like you normally would with rpm, tar, or ports (see Chapter 2).

If you can't find Perl on your CD, you can get it on the Web. The Perl homepage is, refreshingly, `http://www.perl.com`. At the Perl homepage, you can download Perl in binary format for almost any type of server you can think of, and if you must, the source code if you want to compile it yourself.

After you download the Perl binary, you need to gunzip and untar the file. See Chapter 2 for details.

Installing and configuring Webmin

First, download Webmin from the Webmin homepage at `http://www.Webmin.com/Webmin`. The examples we describe in this chapter refer to version 0.78.

Because Webmin is written in Perl, which is an interpreted and not a compiled language, you don't need to hunt for a specific binary for your Samba server. Almost any Linux or UNIX server will work. However, you do have to run an installation script to customize Webmin for your server.

The setup script that installs Webmin asks you several questions. One of the questions is for your operating system; if you don't know it, type **uname** or **uname –a** beforehand to determine it.

Download the gzipped file (if it ends in .gz, it is gzipped) and move it to the desired directory. Then unzip and untar it. The following example shows the superuser unzipping Webmin and then sending it directly to tar:

```
# gzip -dc Webmin-0.78.tar.gz | tar xvf -
```

The result is a directory named Webmin-0.78. Inside that directory, you should have a script file named setup.sh. Run setup.sh to set up Webmin for your system. For example, if you installed Webmin in the /usr/local directory, type the following line as the root user:

```
# /usr/local/Webmin-0.78/setup.sh
```

You have to answer several questions about your system during the installation. Press Enter at each question to accept the default or if you don't know the answer or don't have a preference. At the request for a root password, we suggest using the same root password you use for your Samba server for simplicity's sake. Finally, the script asks if you want Webmin to start at boot or not; starting Webmin at boot is a good idea.

Starting Webmin

Assuming you have successfully installed Webmin, it should be listening to port 10000 on your Samba server. That means you open your Web browser and enter the IP address of your Samba server and append it with port 10000. For a Samba server with an IP address of 192.168.11.3, you'd type the following line:

```
http://192.168.11.3:10000/
```

Then a logon screen should appear. After logging on as the root user, you should see the Webmin screen. See Figure 5-3, which has the Servers tab selected. The first Webmin screen has five main tabs:

- ✓ **Webmin:** For configuring Webmin
- ✓ **System:** For controlling and modifying your operating system
- ✓ **Servers:** For maintaining the servers that run on this system (including Samba)
- ✓ **Hardware:** For controlling printers and other hardware
- ✓ **Others:** For custom commands, telnet, and a file manager

If you forget the user name you decided on for the Webmin administrator (the default choice is admin), the name and the encrypted password are stored in the miniserv.users file, which is usually in the /etc/webmin directory.

You'll do most of your Samba administration on the Servers tab, although you might end up taking a detour to the System tab to add users or schedule cron jobs, or to the Hardware section to add a printer.

The Samba Share Manager page

To access the parts of Webmin that affect Samba, select the Servers tab on the Webmin main page. *Servers* in this case refers to serving-types of programs such as Samba, Apache, or FTP (software) versus physical computers (hardware). Webmin's Servers page has 11 options — one for each of 11 different types of server programs you can run on one Linux machine.

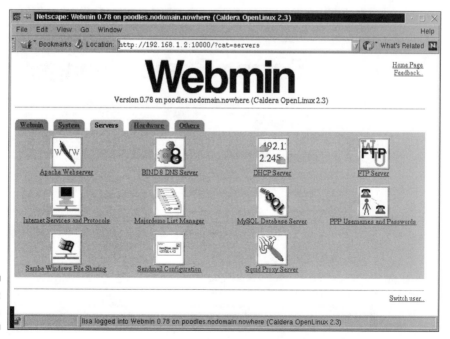

Figure 5-3:
Webmin.

The option for Samba is in the lower left; clicking it takes you to the Samba Share Manager page, as shown in Figure 5-4. Right beneath the title, you see all your defined Samba shares. Clicking a share name takes you to a page where you can modify that share.

Below the defined shares, you have four options:

- ✔ Create a New File Share
- ✔ Create a New Printer Share
- ✔ Create a New Copy
- ✔ View All Connections

Create a New File Share and Create a New Printer Share take you to pages that do exactly what their names indicate.

Create a New Copy takes you to a page where you choose a share to copy and then specify a new name for the copied share. This is useful if you need to create lots of similar new shares. You could make one, copy it as many times as you need to, and then make whatever changes are necessary to each share.

The View All Connections link takes you to a page where you can view all the Samba connections to this server along with their process IDs. That page also has a handy link to kill the process and disconnect the user. We recommend using great discretion in implementing the latter; your job is often much easier when you have the goodwill of your users.

Figure 5-4:
Webmin's
Samba
Share
Manager
page.

Global Configuration buttons

Below these links on Webmin's Samba Share Manager page, you have buttons for Samba's various Global Configuration options. Webmin arranges them logically (to the Webmin developers, at least). We'll describe what kind of option you can set via each of these buttons.

The UNIX Networking page is where you can set UNIX networking options for Samba. Most of these options are pretty specialized, and you only want to change them if you know what you're doing. The Idle Time Before Disconnect option can be useful however; it sets the `dead time` parameter to specify how long to wait before an inactive user with no open files is disconnected. That helps conserve resources that might otherwise be wasted by inactive users, and it's transparent to most users because their clients automatically reconnect when required.

Most of the options on the Windows Networking options page deal with how Samba interacts with the Windows network. In the Workgroup field, enter the workgroup in which you want the Samba server. Enter the server name and description in the respective fields. Most of the other parameters affect how Samba works with WINS servers and how Samba works with complex, sub-netted networks (which we cover in detail in Chapter 11).

The Authentication link takes you to the Password Options page. Here, you decide how Samba handles password matching and whether Samba will be using encrypted passwords. (Chapter 9 goes into detail on password encryption.)

The Windows to UNIX Printing link takes you to the Printing Options page, where you set printing options.

The Miscellaneous Options page doesn't have anything you normally need to set.

The File Share Defaults and Printer Share Defaults buttons take you to pages where you can set the default values. If you're about to add some shares, you could check here to view the current default settings.

You can also go to the SWAT (the Samba Web Administration Tool) logon page directly from Webmin via the SWAT button.

Encrypted Passwords links

Below the Global Configurations section, the Webmin's Samba Share Manager page has links for such tasks as editing Samba users and passwords, converting UNIX users to Samba users, and configuring UNIX/Samba password synchronization.

The Restart Samba Servers button

Near the bottom of Webmin's Samba Share Manager page, you have a convenient button to Restart Samba Servers, which makes Samba reread the Samba configuration file (smb.conf) so that any changes you have made take effect.

A Webmin example: Adding a share

Now that you have an idea of the layout of Webmin, we can show you how to add a share. In this example, you add a CD share that automatically mounts a CD-ROM and then shares it. This can be useful if you have computers without CD drives such as older desktops and laptops.

1. **Start your Web browser, enter the URL for Webmin, and enter your user ID and password.**

2. **Click the Servers tab and click the Samba Windows File Sharing link.**

3. **On the Samba Share Manager page, click the Create a New File Share link to go to the Create File Share page.**

4. **Enter the basic information for this share.**

   For our example, the Share name is **cdrom**, the Directory to Share field is set to **/mnt/cdrom**, and the comment is **shared cdrom**.

5. **Click Create.**

   Now, you can modify this share to make it suitable for a CD-ROM. Assume that every time users connect to this share, it's because they've loaded a new CD. So, you want the CD to mount upon connection and dismount when the user disconnects.

6. **On the Samba Share Manager page, click the new share name.**

   In this case, it is called cdrom.

7. **On the Edit File Share page, click Miscellaneous Options on the bottom right.**

   On the Miscellaneous Options page, you want to have the CD-ROM mounted and unmounted by the root user.

8. **Add the appropriate commands to the Command to Run on Connect *as Root* field and the Command to Run on Disconnect *as Root* field. These fields set the Samba root preexec and root postexec options, respectively.**

   For example, if the CD-ROM is the /dev/hdb device, and the mount point is /mnt/cdrom, enter the following command in the Command to Run on Connect *as Root* field:

```
mount -t iso9660 /dev/hdb /mnt/cdrom
```

As shown in Figure 5-5, enter the following command in the Command to Run on Disconnect *as Root* field:

```
umount /mnt/cdrom
```

9. **Click Save to return to the Edit File Share page.**

10. **Click Save to return to the Samba Share Manager page.**

11. **At the bottom of the Samba Share Manager page, click Restart Samba Servers to restart Samba so that it rereads the configuration file.**

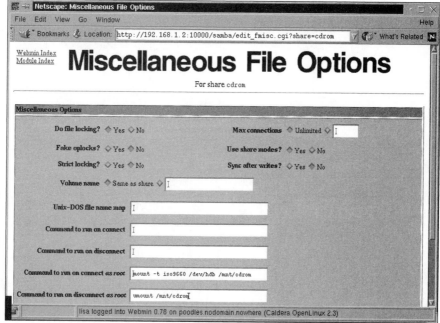

Figure 5-5:
Setting the Samba root preexec and root postexec options.

Chapter 6

Using Other Samba Administration Tools

*A*s we describe in Chapter 5, the most commonly used Samba administration tools are browser-based. This chapter describes the uses of three other administration tools: Smbedit, Linuxconf, and the reliable, old command line.

Smbedit, a Windows-Based Tool

Smbedit is a graphical tool for administering a Samba server. It's not Web-based but instead runs on Windows. It works by creating a share on the Samba server that contains the smb.conf file. It then enables you to edit that share graphically and thus change your Samba server.

Smbedit has several advantages and disadvantages compared to Web-based types of administration. One advantage is that it reduces the load on your Samba server because it doesn't have to run a Web server. Also, Smbedit is a little more secure than Web-based tools; if you are using encrypted passwords, your connection is encrypted.

One of the disadvantages is that Smbedit runs only on a Windows client. Also, when you set up Smbedit, it becomes customized for a specific type of Samba server. Consequently, you cannot easily administer a Samba server running on Linux and a Samba server running on FreeBSD from the same Smbedit. Finally, Smbedit is in the alpha stage of software development, at least at the time of this writing. Hence, some of its features might not work. However, it's being swiftly developed and therefore at least warrants a look.

Believe it or not, Microsoft Windows 2000 does not always play nicely with Samba. For example, Smbedit on Windows 2000 does not work with Samba. So, if you plan to use a Windows 2000 client to administer your Samba server, you cannot use Smbedit. Of course, that might change as Smbedit develops.

Installing and configuring Smbedit

Download Smbedit from the Samba homepage, http://www.samba.org, or your local mirror. Click the GUI Interfaces link and then scroll down to the Smbedit section. For example, in the US, one Smbedit page is http://us3.samba.org/samba/smbedit.intro.htm.

Installing Smbedit on your Windows client

You have to download and install two files on your Windows client to use Smbedit: a zipped file and an executable. As of this writing, the latest zipped file is named smbedit-1.02alpha8.zip, and the executable is named smbedit-1.02dll.exe.

First, run the executable and follow the setup instructions. After you set up Smbedit and restart your computer, unzip the Smbedit zip file in the same directory (usually C:\Program_Files\smbedit).

Making your Samba server work with Smbedit

After you install Smbedit on your Windows PC, you need to add a share on your Samba server that will contain your Samba configuration file, smb.conf. Smbedit works by accessing a share that contains the configuration file and enables you to edit it.

The following example is a share that accesses the Samba configuration file, smb.conf, located in the /etc directory. You need to add this new share by editing the Samba configuration file:

```
[Samba]
comment = smb.conf share for SMBEdit
browseable = no
path = /etc
public = no
guest only = no
writable = yes
write list = root, george, @staff
```

This example includes some interesting things that you should note. The browseable parameter is set to no, meaning the share won't show up in the Network Neighborhood. Therefore, you have to type in the address (for example, \\Liberty\Samba) instead of browsing to it. This is a minor security precaution.

Next, the path to the smb.conf file is identified as /etc. (If you forgot the path, you can find it by running the `testparm` command.)

The `public`, `guest only`, and `write list` parameters control access to this share. With `public` and `guest only` set to `no`, no guest can access this share. With the `write list` parameter set to `root`, `george`, and `@staff`, only the root user, george, and users in the staff group can access this share.

Making testparm work with Smbedit

If you intend to use Smbedit to maintain your Samba server, you must first enable the testparm button. That button enables you to test any changes you make to your Samba configuration file with the `testparm` command (always a good idea) and allows for adding more shares. To enable the testparm button, you need to add a special testparm share to your Samba server and then add a script on your server to call `testparm`. Then Smbedit can connect to the new testparm share to run `testparm` and display the results.

The following sample share enables the testparm button in Smbedit. You add this share by editing the smb.conf file:

```
[testparm]
comment = run testparm for Smbedit
path = /smbtmp
preexec = /usr/local/bin/smbtest > /smbtmp/testparm
postexec = /bin/rm -f /smbtmp/testparm
public = yes
writable = no
printable = no
write list = root, george, @staff
```

The first line of this share is a comment describing the testparm share. The next line indicates the path to the temporary directory, where files created by `testparm` will be stored. You need to create this directory with the `mkdir` command. The third line tells the Samba server to run the `smbtest` command when Smbedit first connects to this share and then store the results in a temporary file. The fourth line tells the Samba server to remove the temporary file.

The following script works with the preceding share to call `testparm` for Smbedit:

```
#!/bin/sh
#
# smbtest - script to run testparm for Smbedit
#
echo "Samba settings 'date'"
/usr/bin/testparm << EOF


EOF
```

The first line tells Linux which shell to use to execute this script. You need to do that for any script you write. The next three lines are comments to remind you about the script's purpose. The fifth line conveniently shows the date for each time you use testparm, and the sixth line is the one that actually runs testparm.

You might need to change the path to testparm for your specific system. If you're not sure where to find the testparm program for your Samba server, you can find the exact path by using the which testparm command. After you create the script in the directory referenced in the testparm share, be sure to make it executable by typing **chmod +x smbtest**.

Making smbstatus work with Smbedit

You can use the smbstatus command on your Samba server by clicking the balloon icon. Like testparm, if you want to use the smbstatus button with Smbedit, you need to add an smbstatus share on your Samba server and a shell script on your Samba server to run the smbstatus command for Smbedit.

The following sample share enables the smbstatus button to work in Smbedit:

```
[smbstatus]

comment = run smbstatus for Smbedit
path = /tmp
preexec = /usr/local/bin/smbstat > /smbtmp/smbstat
postexec = /bin/rm -f /smbtmp/smbstat
writable = no
printable = no
write list = root, george, @staff
```

The first line of this share is a comment describing the share. The next line is the path to the temporary directory, where the output from the smbstatus command will be temporarily stored. If you have not created the /smbtmp directory, you need to create it with the mkdir command. The third line is the command to be run when Smbedit connects to this share; it runs the following smbstatus script and stores the output in a file named smbstat, located in the temporary directory. The fourth line removes this file from the temporary directory. The fifth and sixth lines keep the temporary directory clean. The last line allows only the root user, george, and the members of the staff group to use the smbstatus button.

Next is the script that works with the smbstatus share. You need to create it in the /usr/local/bin directory because the preexec command in the smbstatus share expects to find it there. And, you need to name it smbstat. Here is the script:

```
#!/bin/csh
#
# smbstat - script to use smbstatus with Smbedit
#
echo "Samba status on 'date`"
echo " "
```

```
/usr/bin/smbstatus -d
echo " "
echo "Samba processes :"
foreach PID (`/usr/bin/smbstatus -p`)

echo " $PID"

end
exit 0
```

The first line tells Linux which shell to use with this script. Next, three comment lines explain this script's purpose. The fifth line conveniently adds the
date for each time smbstatus is used, and the sixth line adds a blank line for
clarity. The seventh line is the line that runs smbstatus, and the -d flag provides a verbose listing of Samba's status. The eighth and ninth lines format
the output and make it clearer. The remaining lines list all the Samba processes that are running by calling smbstatus with the -p flag.

You might need to modify this script for your particular Samba server,
depending on where smbstatus is stored. If you're not sure, you can find out
the path for smbstatus by typing **which smbstatus** or **find / -name smbstatus
-print**. If the path is not /usr/bin/smbstatus, be sure to change the seventh and
tenth lines to reflect the correct path. Finally, you have to make sure that this
script is executable. The easiest way is with the command **chmod +x smbstat**.

Using Smbedit

To use Smbedit, start it by double-clicking the globe icon in the smbedit
directory.

Next, access the share containing the Samba configuration file that you set up
earlier. To access the share containing the Samba configuration file, choose
File➪Open or click the Open Folder icon. In the resulting dialog box, enter
the path to the share — for example, \\Liberty\Samba — or browse through
the Network Neighborhood to your Samba share.

After you open the Samba configuration file smb.conf in Smbedit, as shown in
Figure 6-1, you edit a share by clicking the share name in the left pane, clicking the lock icon in Smbedit to enable editing, and then editing the share in
the right pane.

When you are done editing a share, choose File➪Save and agree to overwrite
the existing smb.conf file.

The user must have read and write rights in the directory where the Samba
configuration file (smb.conf) is kept. If you are logged on to your Windows
client as eroot and using Smbedit, eroot must have read and write rights to
the smb.conf file.

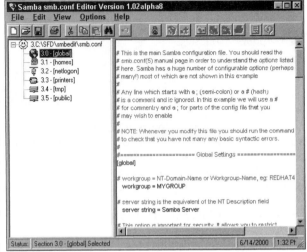

Figure 6-1:
Using
Smbedit to
view the
smb.conf
file.

Adding a share in Smbedit

To add a share to your Samba configuration file, follow these steps.

1. **Open the Samba configuration file (smb.conf) to which you want to add a share.**

2. **Highlight the global share and then click the lock icon to allow editing of the smb.conf file.**

3. **Click the + sign to open the Add New Samba Share dialog box.**

4. **In the upper-left drop-down list, select the type of share you want to add.**

5. **In the upper-right box, give this share a name.**

6. **In the parameter pane, scroll to the available parameters for this kind of share and set them as necessary. Leave the rest at the default choices.**

7. **When done, click Commit to add the share.**

8. **Choose File⇨Save to save the changes to the configuration file.**

Other useful parts of Smbedit

Earlier in this chapter, we mention using Smbedit to run `testparm` and `smbstatus`. Smbedit has other useful features. You can use Smbedit to delete a share, change your logon identity at the Samba server, and access other UNIX servers.

Deleting a share

To delete a share from your Samba configuration file, highlight the share and click the Wastebasket icon.

Changing the UNIX logon

If you want to change who you are logged on to at the Samba server, click the tabbed folder. A menu appears with the server name, desired user, and password. Just enter the desired user name and password and select Logon.

Access a different server

To access a different UNIX server, first click the two networked computer icons. This opens a page that provides several different ways to access other UNIX servers, including telnet and ftp.

Linuxconf

Many Linux systems include Linuxconf, a special tool to administer a Samba server. Red Hat Linux and other distributions include Linuxconf. Use it to configure most parts of your server, including Samba. If your version doesn't have it or you want an updated version, download it from `http://www.solucorp.qc.ca/Linuxconf`.

Using Linuxconf

Linuxconf can run in a telnet session, in an X terminal, or graphically in the Gnome X Window environment. Because Linuxconf is so powerful, you must be running with superuser access to use it.

To start Linuxconf in a command-line session (that is, in a telnet window or X terminal), simply type **Linuxconf**. To start Linuxconf in Gnome, click the Gnome program icon, then System, then LinuxConf. You use Linuxconf the same way, regardless of how you start it.

When you start Linuxconf, you see lots of options. Although you can configure many things on your Linux server with Linuxconf, this section concentrates on using Linuxconf with Samba. You can discover the rest of the options on your own.

To get to the section of Linuxconf that deals with Samba, choose Config⇨Networking⇨Server Tasks⇨Samba File Server.

The Samba File Server section has five sections. The first section, called Defaults, is used for parameters that fit into the Global section of the Samba configuration file (smb.conf). The second section, Default Setup for User's Homes, modifies the Homes section of the Samba configuration file. In the third section, Default Setup for Printers, you set up the Printers section of the Samba configuration file. The fourth section of the Samba part of Linuxconf is Netlogon Setup, where you set up a netlogon share for Windows 95/98 clients when your Samba server is acting as a domain controller. In the final section, called Disk Shares, you add a specific share to the Samba configuration file.

Defaults

The first section of the Samba section of Linuxconf is Defaults, where you define the Samba parameters that belong in the Global section of the Samba configuration file. The Defaults section has six subsections:

- ✔ **Base Config:** Specify the server description, desired workgroup, and how to synchronize Linux and Samba passwords.

- ✔ **Passwords:** Set up encrypted passwords and password server access.

- ✔ **Access:** Allow or prevent specific hosts from connecting.

- ✔ **Networking:** Define how your Samba server works with complex networks and the interfaces it will use.

- ✔ **Auto-accounts:** Set up ways to automatically add or delete users.

- ✔ **Features:** Choose options for guest accounts and a few other options.

After you make any changes, click Accept to write the changes to the Samba configuration file.

Linuxconf enables you to open several Samba configuration screens at the same time. However, that can be confusing because they're not labeled clearly, so we recommend opening only one at a time.

Default Setup for User's Homes

The second working section of the Samba part of Linuxconf is called Default Setup for User's Homes. Here, you define how Samba displays the default user's home shares (the way each user's home directory will be shared), unless you have a specific share added for that user. On the main screen, you set the comment and determine if the shares are enabled and browsable. This section of Linuxconf has three subsections:

- ✔ **Access:** Make the shares writeable or public, and allow or deny access from specific hosts.

- ✔ **Users:** Define who can connect to their home directory, who can't connect to their home directory, and how many connections are allowed.

- ✔ **Scripts:** Specify commands (or scripts) to be run when connecting to or disconnecting from a share (commonly used to mount and unmount devices).

After you make any changes, click Accept to write the changes to the Samba configuration file.

Default Setup for Printers

The Default Setup for Printers section is the third section of the Samba part of Linuxconf. Here, you manipulate the printers section of the Samba configuration file. You can turn this share off or on with the Enable button, or choose to make it public. You have to click Accept so any changes get written to the Samba configuration file.

Netlogon Setup

Use the Netlogon Setup section to set up the Netlogon share, which is required when you have Windows 95/98 clients and Samba is a domain controller. If you have no intention of making your Samba server become a domain controller, feel free to ignore the Netlogon Setup section. If you make any changes, click Accept to write the changes to the Samba configuration file.

Disk Shares

The final section of the Samba part of Linuxconf is called Disk Shares. The Disk Shares section shows all the nondefault shares added to the Samba configuration file, and you can add shares. To add a share, click Add. To edit an existing share, just click the share name in the window and then edit the share parameters in the Share Setup window.

A Linuxconf example: Adding a share

For an example of using Linuxconf to maintain a Samba server, add a share named antivirus. Every user should be able to read it, but only a few users can write to the antivirus share. The antivirus files will be kept in the /home/antivirus directory.

To add this sample share, complete the following steps:

1. **Choose Disk Shares⇨Add to open the Share Setup screen.**
2. **For the share name field, enter** antivirus.
3. **For the Comment/description field, enter data files for antivirus software.**
4. **Click This Share Is Enabled.**
5. **Click Browsable so the share appears in the Network Neighborhood.**
6. **For the Directory to Export field, enter** /home/antivirus.

7. **On the Access tab, click Public Access to allow anyone to read this share.**

8. **On the Users tab, enter the names of the administrators who will be allowed to update the antivirus files in the Write list field — for example,** root, george.

9. **Click Accept to write the changes to the Samba configuration file.**

10. **Restart Samba to make Samba reread these changes.**

The Command Line

Try as you might, you can't always avoid the command line. If it makes you feel better, think of the command line as you do a spare tire for your car. You hope that you'll never have to use it, but if you know a little bit about how to use it, you can get yourself out of a jam a lot quicker. And who knows? Someday, you might just prefer the command line.

Getting to a command line

You have several different ways to get to a command line. Your server might be running in command-line mode already, but if it is running X Window, you can bring up an X terminal. If you're not in front of your Samba server, you can telnet into it to get a command line.

If your server is in terminal mode

If your Samba server is in terminal mode, you see a black screen with an invitation to log on, or you might see a $ or # prompt. For the logon prompt, type your user name and then your password. If you see the # prompt, you might want to review your security procedures, because the server was left with the superuser logged on, and full access was available to anyone who walked up.

If your server is in X Window

If your Samba server is running X Window, you just need to open an X terminal to get to a command line. Simply right-click and choose New⇨Terminal.

If you need to telnet in

If you're not directly in front of your Samba server, you need to telnet into it to get to a command line. Fortunately, Windows 95 and all later versions have telnet built in. You can start telnet from the MS-DOS command prompt, or you can create a shortcut for it. If you plan on creating a shortcut or adding it to your Start menu, the program is named TELNET.EXE. For Windows 95/98, it resides in the Windows directory. For Windows NT, it resides in the /Winnt/ System32 directory. For Windows 2000, telnet resides in the Windows/ System32 directory.

After you start telnet, choose Connect⇨Remote System and type in your Samba server's IP address. If all goes well, you'll be prompted to log on. Be sure to log on as yourself, and then use the su command to switch to the root user. (Indeed, some Linux systems do not allow you to log on at a telnet session as root.)

Vi

Vi, the visual editor, is often the most feared text editor in the UNIX world. It is a little unforgiving, and it has hundreds of esoteric commands, but you can probably handle most file-editing emergencies by knowing just a few of them. You want to have a passing familiarity with vi because you will find it on 99.9 percent of the UNIX workstations you encounter, unlike the easier-to-use pico and emacs.

To load a file, just type **vi** *filename,* or type **vi** */path/filename* if you're not in the same directory as the file you want to edit. Vi launches in the command mode with the file loaded.

Command mode? Yes, vi has two modes: command mode (in which vi is waiting for an editing command) and input mode (in which vi is waiting for text). To go from command mode to input mode, type an editing command. To go from input mode to command mode, just press Esc. If you're not sure which mode you are in, the safest thing to do is press Esc a few times to get back into command mode.

In the command mode, you either want to start an editing command, or save the file and exit vi. With the right editing command, you can add text before or after a character, delete a character, replace one character with another, add a line, or delete a line. Whew!

You should be able to move the cursor with the arrow keys. However, if you are stuck with a strange version of UNIX or telnet, such as the telnet that comes with Windows 2000, you might have to fall back on the old-fashioned way of moving the cursor by using the keyboard keys: H moves the cursor left, J moves it down, K moves it up, and L moves the cursor right.

Refer to Table 6-1 for a list of common vi commands.

Table 6-1	Common vi Commands
To . . .	*Do This*
Delete a character	Move the cursor over the character and press **X**.
Replace a character	Move your cursor over the character, type **R**, and then type the new character.
Insert text before a character	Move the cursor to where you want to insert text and then type **I** to enable input mode. Type the text string to insert and then press Esc to get back to command mode.
Add text after a character	Move the cursor over the character and then type **a** to enable input mode. Type the text you want to add. Press Esc to get back to command mode.
Add a line	Type **O**.
Delete a line	Type **DD**.
Find a word	Type **/word**; vi scrolls to the first occurrence of that word in the file.

When you're done with your editing, save your files, and quit vi. To do that, get back into command mode by pressing Esc. You have two ways to save your changes in vi. If you want to save your work and then keep editing (for example, you're writing the great American novel in vi and you don't want to take a break), just press Esc to get back to command mode and then type **:w** and press Enter to save your work, but still stay in vi. If you want to save your work and exit vi, press Esc to get back into command mode and then type **:wq**; this stands for write and then quit.

To exit without saving changes, press Esc to get back to command mode and then type **:q!** and press Enter.

Pico

Pico is a very common text editor in Linux, although it's not as often installed on other UNIXes, which is a shame because it's easy to use. After you try pico, compared to vi, you'll probably stick with pico (unless you have a strange love of doing things the hard way). We just cover the bare minimum to use pico, but feel free to explore it to your heart's content.

To edit a file in pico, type **pico *filename***, or if you're not in that file's directory, **pico */pathname/filename***. Now just type what you want to type. It doesn't get any easier than that.

Pico has a problem with lines longer than 80 characters: It automatically tries to word-wrap them to the next line. If you have a configuration file with lines longer than 80 characters, pico can really mess it up. If you have to use pico to edit such a configuration file, you can use the line continuation character, \, to get around this 80-character limit.

When you're ready to save your file, press Ctrl+O (the WriteOut option) to save, and confirm (or change) the filename.

To exit pico, press Ctrl+X.

Emacs

Did we just say vi might be the most feared text editor in the UNIX world? According to some people, vi is a friendly little pup, while the scariest editor is something called emacs. This might have more to do with the antipathy between vi fans and emacs fans, though.

To edit a file in emacs, just type **emacs *filename***. Type whatever you want to type, or edit what you need to edit.

To save your work in emacs, press Ctrl+X and then Ctrl+S.

If you hit the wrong key, press Ctrl+G to cancel the command that you have started.

To leave emacs, press Ctrl+X and then Ctrl+C.

Chapter 7

Adding Users, Groups, and Printers at the Operating System Level

●●

●●

*B*ecause Samba runs on Linux (or UNIX, or FreeBSD), you need to do some things at the operating system (OS) level for your Samba server. For example, for each user you plan to support, you need to add a user in Linux. For each group of people you want to have in Samba, you need to add the corresponding group in Linux. For each printer you want to share, you need to add a printer in Linux.

As we explain in this chapter, you can do most of these tasks with graphical tools. However, we also mention how to do them from a command line, for those cases when you can't get in front of the server or when you want to automate a task with a script file.

About Users and Groups

You could have the best, fastest, most reliable Samba server in the world. But if you don't have properly configured users for it, it's almost useless. (But not completely useless. It can make a nice white-noise generator and space heater.) You need to know how to add, remove, and arrange users into groups for your system.

Samba doesn't have much in the way of user maintenance (except for the case of encrypted passwords; see Chapter 9 for more details). Instead, you have to dig into the operating system (Linux, or UNIX, or FreeBSD) to create and maintain users, after which Samba will know about them. So, for this section of the chapter, put on your hard hat, turn on your miner's lights, and prepare to descend deep into OS land.

What users do you have? Dissecting the /etc/passwd file

To see the list of users and the basic attributes of each, look in the user database, which Linux stores in the /etc/passwd file.

The first 19 lines or so contain users required by the system, and you usually don't need to set up Samba shares for system user IDs, so ignore them. The following is a small section of the /etc/passwd section with actual users:

```
george:uiy/Ak/UkRUNc:500:4:
    George \
    Haberberger:/home/george:/
    bin/bash
fredtest:po99st:501:501::/home/
    fredtest:/bin/bash
ghaberbe:gSSAx7IOPdz3M:502:502:
    George \
    Haberberger:/home/ghaberbe:
    /bin/bash
```

In the /etc/passwd file, each line is a record for a user, with the fields separated by colons. The first field is the user name — in this example, george, fredtest, and ghaberbe.

The second field is the password field. This field contains the encrypted password, unless your system uses shadow passwords. If your system is using shadow passwords (which gives you a little more security), it stores the encrypted passwords in a separate file, often /etc/passwd. With shadow passwords, only the root user can read the password file, so a malicious person can't retrieve the encrypted passwords and attempt to crack them.

The third field is the user ID number.

The fourth field is the user's group number, which is the primary group to which the user belongs.

The fifth field is a comment field, traditionally used for the user's full name and possibly telephone number and office location.

The sixth field is the user's home directory, where all the user's files are kept on the server. This is the home directory that Samba shares with the user by default.

The seventh field is the user's default shell.

Okay then, how do these relate to Samba? When a user connects to a Samba server, Samba checks the /etc/passwd file for matches. So, if a user has a name that's not in the /etc/passwd file, that user won't be able to connect. If the user connects but doesn't see his or her directory, make sure the user is using the right user name.

If the user has rights to a directory based on group membership but can't get to it, make sure the group information is correct.

If users don't think they are seeing their files, make sure the home directory information is correct. Samba uses that information to display the default directories.

For every user who needs to store files or print jobs on the printers attached to your Samba server, you need to have a corresponding user added to the server. If you have only five or six users to add, a graphical tool like Linuxconf or COAS (Caldera Open Administration System) might be the quickest way to add them. If you have to add many users, you might save time by using the command line, or more likely, writing a script to use the command line to add them. (You can also use Web-based tools such as SWAT and Webmin for user maintenance; see Chapter 5 for an introduction to these tools.)

After you add users to the Linux system, the time will come when you have to modify or delete their accounts. You can do so by using graphical tools or the command line.

Also, Linux gathers users into groups and assigns file and directory rights by groups and users. Organize your users in function-oriented groups so that users who do the same tasks can have shared directories.

Adding Users and Groups with GUI Tools

Because adding users is such an important part of your work as a Linux administrator, several graphical tools have been created to add users and groups.

If you're not using Linux, most other flavors of UNIX have graphical tools to help you add users and groups. For example, one Solaris-based graphical tool for adding users, groups, and printers is admintool.

Many Linux systems have a special tool to administer a Samba server named Linuxconf. Red Hat and other distributions include Linuxconf. This tool enables you to configure most parts of your server, including Samba.

Adding users and groups with Linuxconf

Linuxconf is a Linux tool that enables you to configure many aspects of your Linux server, including adding users and groups. You get Linuxconf with Red Hat and many distributions of Linux. If your Linux distribution doesn't have it, or you want an updated version, download Linuxconf from http://www.solucorp.qc.ca/Linuxconf.

Linuxconf can run in a telnet session. Start it in an X terminal or graphically in the Gnome X-Window environment. Because Linuxconf is so powerful, you must be running with superuser access to use it. If your prompt is a $ or a %, you don't have superuser access; if your prompt is a #, you do.

To start Linuxconf in a command-line session (that is, in a telnet window or an X terminal), simply type **linuxconf** as superuser. To start Linuxconf in Gnome, you must first start X Window as the superuser, then click the Gnome program icon, then System, and then Linuxconf.

Be very careful in starting X Window as the superuser; your powers are unlimited and you could easily delete your system. Starting X Window as superuser is usually discouraged.

You use Linuxconf the same way regardless of how you started it, although it's easier and less confusing to use Gnome as a graphical tool. It's probably safest and easiest to start X Window from your normal logon and then start Linuxconf from an X terminal with superuser privileges.

Adding users with Linuxconf

To add a user using Linuxconf, follow these steps:

1. **In Linuxconf, choose Config⇨User Accounts⇨Normal⇨User Accounts to open the User Accounts dialog box.**

2. **In the User Accounts dialog box, click Add.**

   The Add User section of Linuxconf has four tabs: Base Info, Params, Mail Settings, and Privileges. If you're just using this Linux server as a Samba server, you don't need to worry about the Mail Settings tab, so we don't discuss it here.

3. **The Base Info tab should open first; if not, click Base Info.**

4. **On the Base Info tab, enter the Login Name, which is the Linux user name and must match the Windows logon name for this particular user.**

5. **Enter the user's full name and any other identification information you need, such as a telephone number or office location.**

6. **Enter the user's primary group, or select it from the drop-down list for the Group field. To choose the right group, think of what this user will be doing, because you can give permission to Samba shares by user names and groups.**

7. **Enter any additional groups this user needs in the Supplementary Groups field.**

8. **Add the desired home directory to the Home Directory field. All the user's files will be stored in this directory.**

9. **Unless you have a strong need to use a different shell, accept the default Command Interpreter.**

10. **Unless you have a very good reason to pick a particular User ID, leave the User ID field blank and let the Linux server complete it.**

11. **Click the Params tab to access the Password Parameters dialog box to specify how often the password must be changed, along with other options.**

12. **In the Must Keep # Days field, specify the minimum number of days before the password can be changed.**

13. **In the Must Change After # Days field, specify a value for password aging or how often a password must be changed. Choose a value that**

changes often enough for good security, yet not so often that your users forget. Typically, administrators choose a value in the range from 60 to 90 days.

The next two fields deal with accounts that are set up to expire.

14. **Enter a value in the Warn # Days Before Expiration field if you want to give a warning that the account will expire in *x* number of days. Similarly, use the Account Expires After # Days field if you want an account to expire after a certain number of days.**

15. **Optionally, enter a date in the Expiration Date field. Set this value if you want to specify the date on which an account will expire.**

On the Privileges tab, you're concerned with two subsections when using this Linux server as a Samba server: the General System Control tab and the Services tab. Figure 7-1 shows the General System Control tab.

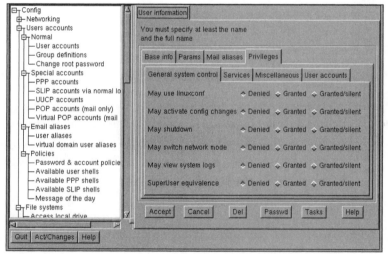

Figure 7-1:
The General
System
Control tab.

16. **On the General System Control tab, you can give a user access to certain administrative functions such as the ability to use Linuxconf, to activate configuration changes, or the ability to become the superuser.**

On the Services tab, you can give a user the ability to be a Samba administrator. Keep these options in mind when you want to create an administrator's account.

17. **When you are done, click Accept to create the user account.**

18. **Enter the new user's password, and enter it a second time when prompted.**

19. **Click Activate to activate changes before quitting Linuxconf.**

Maintaining users with Linuxconf

Much of your user administration work will probably involve maintaining your users' accounts. But if you use your Linux server mostly as a Samba server, maintaining user accounts may involve less effort than if people were using the Linux server for other tasks.

To maintain a user's account, get to the Normal Accounts section of Linuxconf by starting Linuxconf and choosing Config⇨User Accounts⇨ Normal⇨User Accounts.

Click the user's account that you want to edit, and the Linuxconf menu should appear. Make the desired changes and click Accept.

Adding groups with Linuxconf

To add a group using Linuxconf, follow these steps:

1. **In Linuxconf, choose Config⇨User Accounts⇨Normal⇨ Group Definitions.**

2. **Click Add.**

   In the User Groups dialog box, you have two tabs: Base Info and Directories.

3. **On the Base Info tab, add the desired group name to the Group Name field. Add any needed group members to the Alternate Members field.**

4. **On the Directories tab, choose whether to have different directories for each member of this group, specify the home directory for this group, and set the rights for this directory.**

5. **Click Accept to create the new group.**

6. **Remember to activate changes before quitting Linuxconf.**

Adding users with Caldera OpenLinux tools

Caldera OpenLinux has two utilities available for manipulating user, group, and printer configurations:

- **COAS:** Caldera Open Administration System
- **LISA:** Linux Installation and System Administration

COAS is a graphical tool that you use in the KDE X-Window environment. To use COAS, you have to log on as the superuser before starting KDE.

LISA is a simple system-configuration utility that comes with Caldera OpenLinux. With LISA's interface, you enter choices via the keyboard (instead of with a mouse).You start LISA from a telnet session or in an X terminal on the KDE desktop.

If you end up doing most of your user maintenance at your Caldera OpenLinux server, you might use COAS most of the time. If you do most of your user maintenance remotely by telnetting into your Caldera OpenLinux server, LISA would be a better choice.

Adding users with COAS

You can use COAS, Caldera OpenLinux's graphical tool, to maintain user accounts. You access COAS from the KDE desktop:

1. **Start the KDE graphical desktop from a command-line superuser prompt (#) by typing** kde.

2. **From the KDE Application Starter menu, choose COAS⇨System⇨ Accounts to open the User Accounts window, as shown in Figure 7-2.**

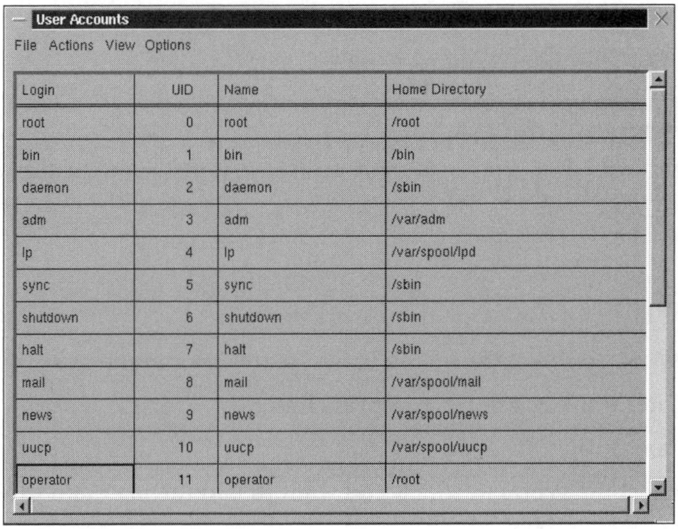

Figure 7-2:
The User
Accounts
window.

3. **Choose Actions⇨Create User.**

4. **Enter the new user's logon name.**

5. **Enter the user's full name.**

6. **If desired, change the UID, group ID (GID), default shell, and Home directory.**

7. **Click Password and then add the password.**

8. **Click Shadow Information to add the minimum number of days to change, the maximum number of days to change, the number of days to warn before expiring, the number of days to disable, and the expiration date.**

9. **Close the User Accounts window.**

COAS automatically assigns the user to either to the default group, or if using the User Private Group schema, it creates a new group with that user as the sole member.

Maintaining users with COAS

Edit user accounts with COAS as follows:

1. **Start the KDE graphical desktop from a command line by typing** kde.

2. **From the KDE Application Starter menu, choose COAS➪System➪ Accounts to open the User Accounts window.**

3. **Choose Actions➪Edit User.**

4. **Edit the user's fields that need to be changed.**

5. **Close the User Accounts window.**

Adding users with LISA

You start LISA from a telnet session or in an X terminal on the KDE desktop. To see a list of options and actions for LISA, type **lisa** at the command prompt.

To add a user with LISA, follow these steps:

1. **At the # prompt, type** lisa –useradm.

2. **Type** 2 **to select the option to add a new user and press Enter.**

3. **Enter the logon name and press Enter.**

4. **Change the UID, if desired.**

5. **Select the group to which you want to add the user and press Enter.**

6. **Change the default user's home directory, if desired.**

7. **Choose the standard shell for the user.**

8. **Enter the full name for the user.**

9. **Enter and confirm the password.**

10. **Press Esc to exit LISA.**

Adding groups with LISA

To add a group with LISA, follow these steps.

1. **At the # prompt, type** lisa –useradm.
2. **Type** 5 **to create a new group and press Enter.**
3. **Enter the new name of the group and press Enter.**
4. **Enter the new group ID and press Enter.**
5. **Confirm that you want to create the group by pressing Enter.**
6. **Press Esc to exit LISA.**

Adding Users and Groups at the Command Line

Once again, you're faced with the command line. You might just need to add one user, and you don't want to take the time to do it graphically. Or perhaps you're feeling wizardly, and you want to write a script to add a bunch of users at the same time. In any case, read on if you want to know how to add users and groups at the command line. If you're comfortable using the GUI tools that we describe in preceding sections of this chapter, feel free to pass up this section.

Useradd

In the good old days before graphical user interfaces, when you wanted to add users to your UNIX system, you had to manually edit the /etc/passwd file and manually create the user's directories. From this perspective, you can see what a boon it was when commands were created to add a user in one line. Most flavors of UNIX have a way to add users with graphical tools, and all but the most archaic flavors have a way to add users at the command line. For Linux, you use the useradd or adduser command.

Useradd and adduser are the same command. Adduser is just a link to useradd. Useradd is located in the /usr/sbin directory, so if you get a command not found error when you type **useradd**, try typing **/usr/sbin/useradd**. And yes, you must be at the superuser prompt to do so; the best way to get there is to type **su **.

At its simplest, just type **useradd *user_name***, and let useradd fill out the remaining information (home directories, shells, user and group IDs) automatically. For example, to add the user delilahj, type the following command:

```
# /usr/sbin/useradd delilahj
```

To see all the options with `useradd`, just type **useradd** with nothing following it. That displays a few lines with all the options for `useradd`.

If you were adding the user delilahj, and you wanted to add her full name, Delilah Jones, in the comments section and place her in the group 0 to allow her root access, you would type the following command:

```
# useradd -g 0 -c "Delilah Jones" delilahj
```

Deleting a user with userdel

If you made a mistake with `useradd`, use the `userdel` command to delete the user. This command is located in the /usr/sbin directory. To remove the user fred, simply type this command:

```
# userdel fred
```

If you get an error about `command not found`, try typing this command:

```
# /usr/sbin/userdel fred
```

Groupadd

The `groupadd` command., which you use to add a group, is located in the /usr/sbin directory, so if you get an error about `command not found` when you type **groupadd**, try typing **/usr/sbin/ groupadd**. And yes, you must be at the superuser prompt to use this command.

You need to give the group a unique group ID number (GID). The default is to use the lowest unused GID above 500 (GIDs between 0 and 499 are reserved for the system). For example, to add the group qa, type this command:

```
# /usr/sbin/groupadd -g 501 qa
```

To see all the options with `groupadd`, just type **groupadd** with nothing following it. That displays a few lines with all the options for `groupadd`.

To check that your group was created, display the /etc/group file with the `more` or the `cat` command. .

About Printers

Before you can make a printer available in Samba, you need to make it available in Linux or UNIX. After the printer works in Linux or UNIX, you can then share it in Samba.

In the old days, printers in UNIX were controlled and defined in the /etc/printcap file. If you wanted to add a printer, you had to manually edit the /etc/printcap file. If you had an extra space, or the wrong character, your printer would not work. It wasn't pretty.

Now, most versions of Linux and UNIX have graphical tools to help you add and administer printers. Red Hat comes with printtool, and Caldera OpenLinux comes with COAS. These graphical tools make it much easier to add or maintain a printer in Linux.

In the following sections, we show you how to add printers using these GUI tools. We also touch on ways to add a printer at the command line, either with the LISA tool, or by directly editing the /etc/printcap file.

Adding Printers Using GUI Tools

Linux has several graphical tools to add and administer printers, such as the printtool for Red Hat and similar distributions and COAS for Caldera OpenLinux servers. The procedure for adding a printer is nearly the same as modifying a printer, so we don't discuss modifying printers in any great detail.

Most other UNIX flavors and Linux distributions have similar graphical tools for adding printers to the server. For example, Solaris uses a graphical tool called admintool.

Adding a local printer with printtool

Printtool is Red Hat's graphical tool for adding and maintaining printers. Printtool is an X-Window application that you must run from the root user prompt. To start printtool, simply type **printtool** in an X terminal at the root prompt.

In printtool, you can add, modify, and delete printers, restart the lpd printing daemon, and send test pages to the printers.

In most cases, the printer you want to share with Samba is attached to your Linux server, usually at the parallel port. The highly technical term for this is a *local* printer, as opposed to a *remote* printer that you access over the network. Printtool easily adds local printers.

Before you add your local printer, test it first. In Linux, you should first be able to see lp in the /proc/devices file. Display this file with the `cat` command — for example, **cat /proc/devices**.

Next, test the printer by using the `lptest` command to print directly to the printer device. The following command should print 20 lines of 5 characters each to the lpt1 port of your printer:

```
# lptest 5 20 > /dev/lp0
```

If `/dev/lp0` does not work, try `/dev/lp1` (which maps to lpt2).After you get output at your local printer, you have enough information to add the printer using printtool. Follow these steps to add a printer with printtool:

1. **In an X terminal window at the # prompt, type** printtool **to open the Red Hat Linux Print System Manager window.**

2. **Click Add to open the Add a Printer Entry dialog box, as shown in Figure 7-3.**

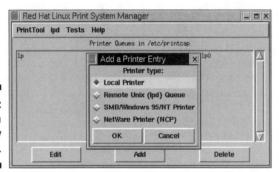

Figure 7-3:
The Add a
Printer Entry
dialog box.

3. **From the four choices in the Add a Printer Entry dialog box, Select Local Printer.**

4. **Click OK.**

   Printttool should automatically detect the port to which your printer is attached. If not, review the previous paragraphs regarding `lptest`.

5. **Choose a name for the printer.**

   Something short and descriptive works best, and 8 characters or less works best with Windows.

6. **Specify the spool directory (where the printing software stores the job until it is printed).**

7. **Specify any file-size limit for the maximum size of the job.**

8. **Specify the printer device**

9. **Click Select to open the Configure Filter dialog box, as shown in Figure 7-4. You use this dialog box to choose the Input Filter.**

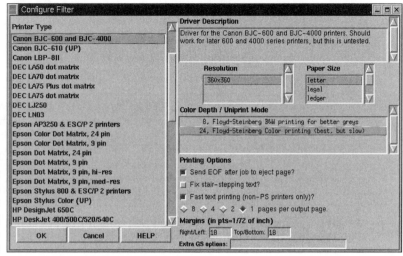

Figure 7-4:
The
Configure
Filter dialog
box.

10. In the Configure Filter dialog box, under Printer Type, select the printer model that is closest to your printer.

11. Select the preferred resolution.

12. Select the preferred paper size.

13. Select the preferred Color Depth/Uniprint mode.

14. Specify whether you want to enable such options as sending EOF after a job, fixing stair-stepping text, and fast text printing.

15. Specify the number of pages per output.

16. Set the margin.

17. Add any Ghostscript options.

18. Indicate whether you want to suppress headers.

19. Click OK to add this printer.

20. When done modifying and adding printers, restart lpd by clicking lpd and selecting Restart lpd.

Adding a remote printer with printtool

You might want to add access to a remote printer from your Samba server. For example, rather than log on to every print server they might need to print to, your users might prefer to log on to your Samba server and use it to access other printers. You can easily do this in Samba, but you must first add access to the remote printers using printtool.

You can add access to remote UNIX, SMB, and Netware printers. We don't discuss Netware printers, but we do cover how you add access to a remote UNIX printer (perhaps a UNIX server that isn't running Samba) and access to a remote SMB printer (perhaps a Windows print server in another workgroup).

Adding a remote UNIX printer with printtool

If your network has UNIX or Linux servers with special printers attached (perhaps high-speed printers), you can give your users access to these printers with a remote printer via printtool and a corresponding share in Samba. To add a remote UNIX printer, all you really need to know is the remote server's IP address or hostname (if the hostname is in your Samba server's host table) and the printer name. Follow these steps to add access to a remote printer:

1. **Start printtool from an X terminal by typing** printtool **at the # prompt to open the Red Hat Linux Print System Manager window.**

2. **Click Add to open the Add a Printer Entry dialog box.**

3. **From the four choices in the Add a Printer Entry dialog box, select Remote Unix (lpd) Queue and then click OK.**

4. **Choose a name.**

   This will be the local name for the remote printer.

5. **Specify the spool directory (where the jobs are stored until they are forwarded to the remote printer).**

6. **Specify any limit on the job size.**

7. **Specify the remote server name in the Remote Host field either by IP address or name, if the name is in the hosts table or can be resolved through DNS.**

8. **Add the remote printer name to the Remote Queue field.**

9. **Click Select for the Input Filter.**

10. **Choose to Suppress Headers.**

11. **Click OK to save to the /etc/printcap file.**

12. **When done adding and modifying printers, restart lpd by clicking lpd and selecting Restart lpd.**

Adding a remote SMB printer with printtool

Assume that you already have a printer attached to a Windows server, and you want your users to have access to that printer without having to log on to that remote Windows server. You can do this in Samba by first using printtool to add a remote SMB printer and then sharing it in Samba.

To add a remote SMB printer using printtool, follow these steps:

1. **In an X terminal at a # prompt, start printtool by typing** printtool **to open the Red Hat Linux Print System Manager window.**

2. **Click Add to open the Add a Printer Entry dialog box.**

3. **In the resulting dialog box, select SMB/Windows 95/NT Printer and click OK.**

4. **Enter the local name for this printer.**

5. **Enter the spool directory (where jobs will be stored until they are sent to the remote SMB printer).**

6. **If you want to make a limit on the job size, fill out the File Size field.**

7. **Enter the hostname of the remote server.**

   You can optionally enter the IP address of the remote server.

8. **Enter the name for the remote printer.**

   It must match the name of the printer at the remote server.

9. **Specify the name of the user that this Linux server will be connecting as.**

10. **Enter the password for this user.**

11. **Enter the desired workgroup.**

12. **Specify any desired input filters.**

13. **Check Suppress Headers, if desired.**

14. **Click OK to save these changes to the /etc/printcap file.**

15. **When done adding and modifying printers, restart lpd by clicking lpd and selecting Restart lpd.**

Using printtool to test and properly configure your printer

You can also use printtool to test and properly configure printers. Click Tests to get three options:

- ✔ Print ASCII Test Page
- ✔ Print PostScript Test Page
- ✔ Print ASCII Directly to Port

To test a printer, first select the printer in printtool, click Tests, and select the test you want to use.

Use the Print ASCII Directly to Port test if you want to bypass the /etc/printcap file and see how the printer responds to direct input. Use this test if you suspect a hardware problem with the port or printer.

Use the Print Postscript Test Page test if you want to verify whether the /etc/printcap file has been set up correctly for your printer to understand Postscript. That's a neat Linux trick — you can easily make a $100 inkjet printer output Postscript just like a $1,000 laser printer.

If you get a page with the Red Hat icon and large text (and colors, if you have a color printer), Postscript has been set up successfully. On the other hand, Postscript is not working for your printer if you get something like the following lines and lots of additional, strange text:

```
%!PS-Adobe-2.0
%%Title: testpage.fig
%%Creator: fig2dev Version 3.2 Patchlevel 1
```

Use the Print ASCII Test Page option to make sure your printer is set up correctly. Depending on the ASCII output you get, you might need to make changes in printtool to properly configure your printer.

If the text runs off the page or the exclamation points don't line up, try enabling LF->CR/LF translation by clicking the Fix Stair-Stepping Text button in the Configure Filter dialog box.

If the paper doesn't eject from the printer, you should enable Send EOF by clicking the Send EOF After Job to Eject Page button in the Configure Filter dialog box.

Adding printers with Caldera OpenLinux tools

Caldera has two utilities available for manipulating user, group, and printer configurations:

- **COAS:** Caldera Open Administration System
- **LISA:** Linux Installation and System Administration

COAS is a graphical tool that you use in the KDE X-Window environment. LISA is a simple system-configuration utility that comes with Caldera OpenLinux.

Adding a local printer with COAS

You access COAS from the KDE desktop. Log on as superuser. To add a local printer with COAS, follow these steps:

1. **Start the KDE graphical desktop from a command-line superuser prompt (#) by typing** kde.

2. **From the KDE Application Starter menu, choose COAS⇨Peripherals⇨ Printer.**

   As shown in Figure 7-5, COAS opens the Printer Configuration dialog box.

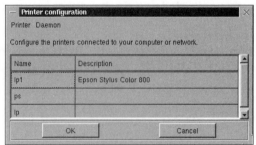

Figure 7-5:
The Printer
Configuration
dialog box.

3. **In the Printer Configuration dialog box, choose Printer⇨Add.**

4. **In the Select Printer Model dialog box, select the printer model closest to yours and click OK.**

5. **In the Printer Name dialog box, type a name for the printer and click OK.**

6. **In the Printer Attributes dialog box, choose the paper size, device, and speed, and click OK.**

7. **Click Save to save the configuration.**

8. **In the Create Printer Queue dialog box, click OK to create a printer queue.**

To make changes in the future, open the Printer Configuration dialog box, select the printer, and choose Printer⇨Edit. The Printer Attributes dialog box appears with editable fields for modifying the printer's settings.

Adding a remote printer with COAS

You access COAS from the KDE desktop. Log on as superuser. To add a remote printer with COAS, follow these steps.

1. **Start the KDE graphical desktop from a command-line superuser prompt (#) by typing** kde.

2. **From the KDE Application Starter menu, choose COAS⇨Peripherals⇨ Printer.**

3. **In the Printer Configuration dialog box, choose Printer⇨Add.**

4. **In the Select Printer Model dialog box, scroll to the bottom and select Generic Remote Printer.**

5. **In the Printer Name dialog box, enter a name for the remote printer.**

6. **In the Printer Attributes dialog box, enter the Remote Host ID and the Remote Printer name.**

7. **Click Save to save the configuration.**

8. **In the Create Printer Queue dialog box, click OK to create a printer queue.**

To make changes in the future, open the Printer Configuration window, select the printer, and choose Printer⇨Edit. The Printer Attributes dialog box appears with editable fields for modifying the printer's settings.

Adding a local printer with LISA

To see a list of options and actions for LISA, type **lisa** at the command prompt.

To add a local printer with LISA, follow these steps:

1. **At the # prompt, type** lisa –printer.

2. **Using the arrow keys, scroll to the printer driver closest to yours and press Enter.**

3. **Select the port to which the printer is connected and press Enter.**

4. **Select the default resolution for the printer and press Enter.**

5. **Select the default paper size for the printer and press Enter.**

   LISA exits and you are returned to the Terminal window.

Adding a remote printer with LISA

To add a remote printer with LISA, follow these steps.

1. **At the # prompt, type** lisa –printer.

2. **Select Use Network Printer (option 2).**

3. **Enter the hostname of the network print server and press Enter.**

4. **Enter the printer name.**

   LISA exits and you are returned to the Terminal window.

LISA can uncomment previously installed printers in the /etc/printcap file when used. It does make a backup file named /etc/printcap.lisasave.

Adding Printers at the Command Line

Think of the command line as the handsaw of the Linux world. Sure, you usually save time and effort by using a power tool, but for some jobs, the handsaw might be quicker or more convenient to use. A good carpenter might prefer a power saw, but you should also know how to use a handsaw.

Editing the printcap file

When adding or modifying a printer by editing the /etc/printcap file, you don't always work from a command line. You could do it with a graphical editor in X Window. But because editing the printcap file by hand can be hard and unforgiving, we cover this topic in the command-line section.

Make sure you have superuser privileges, and proceed to edit the /etc/printcap file. To use vi, type this command:

```
# vi /etc/printcap
```

The easiest way to add a printer when editing the /etc/printcap file is to copy an existing record and modify it to match the new printer. If you can't do that, you can use one of these sample records and modify it for your printer.

```
# local deskjet 612
lp|dj612:\
        :sp=/var/spool/lpd/dj:\
        :mx#0:\
        :lp=/dev/lp0:\
        :sh:
```

That record requires the spool directory /var/spool/lpd/dj to be created, with the proper rights, and owned by the lp group. Therefore, type these lines:

```
# mkdir /var/spool/lpd/dj
# chmod 744 dj
# chgrp lp dj
```

This printer is attached to the first parallel port — lpt1 in the Windows world, /dev/lp0 in the Linux world.

A safari through the /etc/printcap file

It's instructive to spend five minutes looking at the /etc/printcap file. If your printers are working fine and you don't have five minutes right now, just remember this section. You may find it enlightening some day.

The following is a small /etc/printcap file, generated with printtool:

```
#
# Please don't edit this file directly unless you know what you are doing!
# Be warned that the control-panel printtool requires a very strict format!
# Look at the printcap(5) man page for more info.
#
# This file can be edited with the printtool in the control-panel.

##PRINTTOOL3## LOCAL bjc600 360x360 letter {} BJC600 24 0
lp:\
        :sd=/var/spool/lpd/lp:\
        :mx#0:\
        :sh:\
        :lp=/dev/lp0:\
        :if=/var/spool/lpd/lp/filter:
##PRINTTOOL3## REMOTE POSTSCRIPT 600x600 letter {} PostScript Default {}
begonias:\
        :sd=/var/spool/lpd/lp0:\
        :mx#0:\
        :sh:\
        :rm=scarlet:\
        :rp=begonias:\
        :if=/var/spool/lpd/lp0/filter:
```

The line starting with lp starts the printer definition for the first printer, a Canon Bubblejet attached to the first parallel port. The first line after the line starting with lp is for the location of the spool directory. If your var directory is in its own partition, you want to make sure you have enough room on it for the spool directory. The next line, which starts with mx, is the maximum size for the job, with mx#0 being no maximum job size. If you are limited in size for your spool directory, you can limit the size of jobs with this line. Two lines after the mx line is the one that indicates to which device this printer prints. In this case, it's the first parallel port, l/dev/lp0, which maps to lpt1. Similarly, the second parallel port would be /dev/lp1, and so on. The fifth line after lp is for the input filter. This file looks at the job and tries to determine the best way to print it. The input filter can determine whether a job is an image, a PostScript file, or a text file. It can also fix stair-stepping and form-feed problems.

The line starting with begonias starts the printer description for the remote printer named begonias. The line after begonias, starting with sd, is the spool directory. The line after that, starting with mx, is the maximum job size. For remote printers, spool space isn't as much of an issue because the job will be transferred over to the remote machine fairly quickly. The line starting with rm is the remote machine name as it looks in your hosts table. The line starting with rp is the name of the printer on the remote machine. The last line is for the input filter. You probably don't want to do too much filtering for remote printers; it's best to let the remote machine do that.

So, what can you learn from looking at the /etc/printcap file? For a local printer, you can see which parallel port it is using, any job size limitations, and which filter is being applied. For a remote printer, you can identify the remote machine to which you should be sending the job, the remote printers you should be printing to, and any filters applied.

As always, if you want to investigate the printcap file in great depth, typing **man printcap** will give you many pages of information.

Chapter 8

Sharing Resources

After you have your Samba server populated with users, and your printers are working in Linux (see Chapter 7), you can finally make your Samba server useful.

First, verify that your users can connect to their home directories. Then, you might want to make provisions for guest users or for projects. Instead of buying a Zip drive and CD-ROMs for each computer, you might want to make those resources available to everyone through your Samba server. Finally, you have to make sure your users can connect to your printers through Samba.

Making a resource available in Samba takes two main steps:

1. **Make the resource available in Linux.**

2. **Make it available in Samba.**

Remembering this duality makes troubleshooting much easier because if something is not available in Linux, it won't be available in Samba. If something is available in Linux but not in Samba, the problem lies with Samba.

Making Directories Available in Linux

Before you can make a directory available through Samba, you have to make it available in Linux. This should happen automatically for users' home directories, but for directories that you plan to have shared by a group of users, you might need to do some work in Linux.

Linux and UNIX have a fairly simple security model. Directories (and files) have three separate security settings: one for the directory (or file) owner, one for the members of the group with which the directory is associated, and one for everyone else on the Linux system. The security level for a directory for everyone on the Linux system is referred to as *world rights*.

Inside each security level are three rights:

✔ **read:** To look at a file or directory, you need read rights for the file or directory.

✔ **write:** To save a file or save within a directory, you need write rights for the file or directory.

✔ **execute:** To run a file, you must have the execute right. To change to a directory and access files in the directory, you must have the execute right.

You can view a file or directory's security rights with the `ls -l` command. Here's an example:

```
# ls -l
total 6412
drwxr-xr-x   5 george   george      4096 Feb  6 16:31 Desktop
-rw-r--r--   1 root     root      307526 Jun 23 23:16 FG7sub
-rwxr--r--   1 george   george     71680 Apr  9 23:56 SFDC14.DOC
-rw-rw-r--   1 root     root       10240 May 19 22:26 backtest
-rwxrwxr-x   1 root     root         136 May 19 22:26 backuptest.sh
```

The leftmost column of the output details the security rights. The first character is for the type of device: d indicates a directory, and a dash (-) indicates a file. Don't worry about any other letters that appear there.

The next three characters are for the user rights. For example, `rwx` means the user has read, write, and execute rights. If you see a - there, that right is missing. For example, `r-x` means read and execute only.

The next characters refer to the rights of the group that owns the share. The final three characters show the rights for everyone else on the Linux system (the world rights).

The rights for directories are a little different. If you have read rights to a directory, you can list the files in the directories. If you have write access to a directory, you can write files to that directory. And if you have execute rights to a directory, you can access the files in that directory, use `ls -l` on the files, and change to that directory.

The two other important columns are the third and the fourth. The third column lists the file or directory owner, and the fourth column lists the group with which the file or directory is associated.

To change rights for files and directories, you use three Linux/UNIX commands:

- ✔ chown changes the owner of the file or directory.
- ✔ chgrp changes the group associated with the file or directory.
- ✔ chmod changes the rights of the file or directory.

Making directories in Linux available for a single user

When you make a directory or file in Linux available for a single user, you concentrate on the first set of rights and the file owner with the ls -l, chown, and chmod commands. You need to be logged on as the superuser to use the chown command.

1. **Move to the parent directory that contains the desired directory. Generate a long listing of the desired directory by typing** ls -l.

   The third column lists the owner. If incorrect, you need to use the chown command to change the ownership.

2. **To change the owner of the directory, use the** chown **command, with the following format:**

   ```
   chown new_owner directory _name
   ```

   Be very careful when changing the owner of system configuration files or directories — for example, anything in the /etc directory. You could prevent your Linux system from functioning if the file and directory owners are wrong. You are probably better off adding a desired user to the group associated with the directory or file and doing group-right manipulations.

3. **If you need to change the rights to make this directory available to a user, use the** su **command to switch to the superuser. Then, use the** chmod **command to assign the new rights. To give the directory owner read and write rights, type** chmod u=rw *directory_name*. **To give the directory owner full rights (read, write, and execute), type** chmod u=rwx *directory_name*.

4. **With the** ls -l **command, verify that your changes were enacted and the directory has the desired rights.**

For more information on rights and the chmod command, check out *Red Hat Linux For Dummies* or *Linux For Dummies*.

Making directories in Linux available for a group of users

If you have to make a directory or file available for a group of users, you edit the second set of rights. (The first set of rights belongs to the user, the third set of rights belongs to everyone, and the second set of rights sets the group rights.) You also need to make sure that you have the users in the desired group:

1. **Make sure that each user that needs access to this directory belongs to the desired group.**

   Use the `groups` command and the user name — that is, type **groups user_name**. If you are more comfortable using a graphical tool, try Linuxconf (see Chapter 6), COAS (see Chapter 7), or admintool (refer to Solaris documentation).

   If you need to add a user to a group or change a user's primary group, use a graphical tool or edit the /etc/group file.

2. **In the parent directory, use the `ls -l` command to check the group with which the directory or file is associated.**

3. **If you need to change the group with which the directory is associated, use the `chgrp` command with the following syntax:**

   ```
   chgrp desired_group directory_name
   ```

   Again, be careful when changing the group of system configuration directories or files, particularly the ones in the /etc/directory. You can damage your Linux system, or at least make it unable to boot. Instead of changing the group associated with the directory, try to make the users fit into the existing group associated with the directory.

4. **If you need to change the rights of the directory for the group associated with it, use the `chmod` command. To give the directory read and write rights for the group that owns the directory, type** chmod g=rw *directory_name*. **To give the directory full rights (read, write, and execute) for the group associated with the directory, type** chmod g=rwx *directory_name*.

Making directories in Linux available for everyone

To make a directory or file accessible to everyone on the Linux system, you edit the rights for everyone, not the rights for the user or group. The rights for everyone are known as the *world rights*. You don't have to change the directory or file owners or groups to set the world rights. Instead, you affect the world rights with `chmod`.

To make a directory accessible to everyone, use the `chmod` command with the o option. (This may help you to remember: If you are not the user or the group, you are the other, and you use o.) To give everyone read, write, and execute access, type **chmod o=rwx *directory_name***. To give everyone on the Linux system read and write access, type **chmod o=rw *directory_name***.

Sharing Directories

A fundamental reason to have a network in the first place is so that users can store and share files on a common server. Hence, you establish shared files or directories (folders), also called *shares*, on the server(s). For example, it makes sense to give each user a home directory on the Samba server. All the user's important files can be stored there and backed up with one backup device. Or, when users collaborate on projects, they don't want to have to pass floppy disks around; instead, they can keep the files in a common directory on the network. Finally, your users can have access to their files wherever they log on, regardless of which computer they use.

A home directory for each user

The most basic use of serving files with a Samba server is to provide each user with a home directory. The homes part of the Samba configuration file facilitates user home directories.

Whenever someone connects to the server, Samba follows a short checklist to identify a share to which the user can connect. It first looks for a share with the user's name and tries to connect to that. If a share for that specific user doesn't exist, Samba looks through the /etc/passwd file. If it finds the user there together with a valid password, Samba generates a share for that user based on the contents of the homes section in the Samba configuration file and the home directory information in the /etc/passwd file. If Samba didn't automatically generate a share for each connecting user, you would have to make a specific share for each user who connects to your Samba server, which could easily become a full-time job.

To apply standard settings to every user's home directory share (except for users who have shares that are specifically mentioned in the Samba configuration file), you edit the homes section of the Samba configuration file, as we describe next.

A basic homes section

Here is a basic homes section:

```
[homes]
    comment = Home Directories
    browseable = no
    writable = yes
```

The first line tells Samba that this is the homes section, which Samba uses to generate a share for any validated user who connects to the server and does not have a specific share in the smb.conf file. The next line is a comment describing this share. The third line, browseable = no, normally tells Samba not to display the share, but for the homes section, it still displays the share for the validated user. The fourth line, writable = yes, enables the user to store files on this share, which is a very handy thing, indeed.

This basic homes section has a downside. Because of the way Linux works, anyone who knows another user's user name on the Samba server can access the other user's share and have read access to that share.

A homes section with a little more security

UNIX and Linux were developed in very trusting worlds where there was nothing wrong with allowing anyone viewing access to your home directory. For most flavors of Linux and UNIX, when a home directory is created, every user on the system has read access to that home directory.

From a Samba viewpoint, if you know the name of another user, you could get read access to that user's home directory. For example, if you knew another user on the server terrapin was named maryg, you could access maryg's home directory by opening \\terrapin\maryg in your Network Neighborhood. Normally, you would only have read access, but even that is not a good idea.

To add a little more security, you might want to use the following homes section. It adds a valid user list to restrict the share to only the validated user that owns it. You add this restriction in a tricky way, though:

```
[homes]
comment = Home Directories
browseable = no
writable = yes
valid users = %S
```

The only change from the previous homes section is the line valid users = %S. This line assigns the user's share a list of valid users, and the list of valid users is defined by the Samba macro %S.

There are lots of Samba macros. The %S macro expands to the name of the share. If maryg was connecting to this share, the %S would equal maryg. For the share we describe in this section, the only valid user would be the user the share is named after, which makes for nice security.

Something you don't want to do in the homes section

You almost certainly don't want two Samba parameters in your homes section: guest ok = yes or public = yes. If you were to put those parameters in the homes section, you would open everyone's shares to the public, so anyone could read or write to anyone else's home directory. You probably don't want that.

A homes section with a different home directory path

Samba normally uses the home directory information in the /etc/passwd file to decide which directory to share when a user connects. A time might come when you want to send users to a different directory for their shares. With the help of a macro, Samba can use a different directory for a user instead of the user's home directory listed in the /etc/passwd file. The following example does just that:

```
[homes]
comment = Home Directories
browseable = no
writable = yes
valid users = %S
path = /winusers/%s
```

In addition to all the features that we describe in previous sections of this chapter, this homes section shares the directories in the /winusers directory. For each user that successfully connects, Samba connects that user to the /winusers/*user_name* directory. For example, when the user trinity successfully logs on to this Samba server, Samba connects that user to the /winusers/trinity directory.

Editing the homes section with SWAT

In previous sections of this chapter, we explain why you might want to edit the homes section. So, how do you use SWAT to edit it? Follow these steps to use SWAT to edit the homes section of your Samba server:

1. **Start SWAT by accessing it through your Web browser (the URL is** http://IP_Address:901/**). At the logon screen, log on as the Samba administrator and use the administrator password.**

2. **Click the Shares button.**

3. **Click the drop-down list next to the Choose Share button and select Homes.**

4. **Click Choose Share to start editing the homes section of the Samba configuration file.**

5. **If you want to set any advanced options, such as the** valid users **parameter discussed earlier in this chapter, click Advanced View.**

6. **Edit the fields you want to change for the homes section.**

7. **Click Commit Changes to save your changes to the Samba configuration file.**

8. **To make the changes take effect, click the Status button to go to the SWAT Status page, and click the Restart smbd and Restart nmbd buttons.**

Some special user shares

You might want to create a few special user shares for certain situations. Perhaps you want to be able to access the Samba configuration file from Windows. You can set up Samba shares to do that. If you are running an Apache Web server on your Linux server, you can easily set up a Samba share to give your Web administrator easy access to the Web pages.

A Samba administrator's share

Say you want to separate Linux administrative duties from Samba duties and have a separate Samba administrator. If you have a separate Samba administrator, you can make a special share to share the Samba configuration file, smb.conf. For example, if your Samba configuration file is the /usr/local/etc directory, the following example should work:

```
[samba]
comment = Samba directory
path =/usr/local/etc
public = no
writable = yes
printable = no
write list = root, @wheel
```

In this share, the Samba configuration file smb.conf is located in the /usr/local/etc directory, which is why the `path` statement shares that directory. The `write list` parameter allows only the root user and those in the wheel group to write to (edit) the files in this directory. You could also control access by adding the `valid users` parameter as mentioned previously in this chapter.

Make sure that the users in the group wheel have access to the /usr/local/etc directory. The share will appear when users connect to the server, so if you want to hide it, add the `browseable = no` parameter.

A webmaster's share

Linux and UNIX can do much more than share Windows files. Linux and UNIX machines also make fine Web servers. In fact, the Apache software that comes with Linux and FreeBSD runs most Web servers on the Internet, including such famous sites as the Internet Movie Database (www.imdb.com) and the Google search engine (www.google.com).

With a Linux, UNIX, or FreeBSD Web server, you can share the Web pages via Samba so the Web page editors can edit the files from their Windows workstations without having to use FTP to transfer the files back and forth. The following example shares the Web pages for a default installation of the Apache Web server on a Linux box:

```
[webpages]
path = /home/httpd/html
browseable = no
writable = yes
public = no
valid users = root, webmaster
```

For this share, Samba is sharing the /home/httpd/html directory, which is the directory where the Apache Web server keeps its Web pages. `Browseable` and `public` are set to no to hide this share. With the `writable = yes` and the `valid users` parameters, the root user and the webmaster can connect to the directory on the Linux server that contains the Web pages and edit them from Windows without having to FTP them back and forth.

Make sure the webmaster has Linux access to the /home/httpd/html directory

Adding a special share with SWAT

In the preceding sections, we give you some ideas about special shares. So, how do you add them in SWAT? Connect to your Samba server through SWAT like you normally do, and follow these steps:

1. **Click the Shares button.**

2. **In the field next to Create Share, type the name of the new share you are adding and click Create Share.**

3. **Start editing the new share in the Basic View. Click Advanced View if you need to add any advanced share parameters such as** valid users **or** write list.

4. **Edit the fields you want to change for the homes section.**

5. **Click Commit Changes to save your changes to the Samba configuration file.**

6. **To make these new changes take effect, click the Status button to go to the SWAT Status page, and click the Restart smbd and Restart nmbd buttons.**

Guest directories

Often, you want to have a special directory for guests on your network. You can assign a common guest user ID and password for this directory. Or, you can make it a public directory that doesn't require a password.

Four Samba parameters deal with guest directories:

- ✔ `guest account`: Enables users without a currently valid user name or password to access the server.
- ✔ `guest ok`: Tells Samba that guest users can access a share.
- ✔ `map to guest`: If you are using a security level of user, server, or domain, and you want to have guest users, you must set `map to guest` to `bad user`.
- ✔ `guest only`: Means a share can be used only by a guest.

Specifying who the guest is with guest account

With Samba, you can assign people who log on without a valid user name and password to a guest account. You set which account is the guest account in Samba with, surprise, the `guest account` parameter. .

The guest account must be a valid account in the /etc/passwd file, but it should not be an account that gives guest users many rights to the Linux server. For that reason, the two most popular guest accounts are nobody and ftp. Some Samba administrators have discovered that the nobody user doesn't have the right to print, so if printing is a required feature for your guest users, you might want to set the guest account to ftp.

To change the guest account using SWAT, go to the Globals page and check under Security Options. Commit Changes when you are done, and restart smbd and nmbd from the Status page to make the changes take effect.

You can also assign a guest account for each share. To assign a guest account for a share in SWAT, go to the Share page. Using the drop-down list next to Choose Share, select the share you want to edit and click Choose Share. The guest account field for this share is listed under Security Options. Commit changes when you are done, and restart smbd and nmbd from the Status page to make the changes take effect.

A shareable transfer directory

One use of the `guest ok` function. is to create a common directory where users can store large files so that others can access them without tying up the network by using e-mail. For example, anyone can store files to or read files from the following share:

```
[bigfiles]
path = /home/guest
comment = transfer directory for large files
writable = yes
guest ok = yes
```

With this share, anyone on your network can store, change, and delete files in the bigfiles directory. This arrangement has very little security, but if it keeps people from overloading your e-mail system with 10MB movie trailers (*Phantom Menace*, anyone?), it might be useful.

For a more stable server, you would want to put this share on its own partition, or set a quota in Linux for the guest user to prevent a user from filling
the disk and possibly crashing the server.

A read-only guest share

If you have an employee manual in electronic form, you might want to make it
available from a read-only guest directory. Everyone can read the manual, but
only the user(s) with root access can change it, and then only in Linux. Here
is a read-only guest share:

```
[manuals]
path = /home/manuals
comment = Samba share for employee manuals
read only = yes
guest ok = yes
```

The read only = yes parameter here keeps anyone from writing to or
changing the documents in this share, while the guest ok = yes lets anyone browse the /home/manuals directory.

Why did we use writable in the first example and read only in the second?
Because they are opposites: writable = no means the same thing as read
only = yes. However, SWAT does not use the writable parameter, so you
need to use read only instead.

Creating a guest share with SWAT

You can easily create a guest share with SWAT. To create a read-only guest
share, follow these steps:

1. **In SWAT, click the Shares button.**

2. **In the field next to Create Share, type in the new share's name — for
   example,** manuals.

3. **Click Create Share.**

4. **From the drop-down list, select the new share.**

5. **Click Choose Share.**

6. **Under the Base Options, enter the comment and path.**

7. **Under Security Options, set** read only **to yes and set** guest ok **to yes.**

8. **Click Commit Changes to save your changes to the Samba
   configuration file.**

9. **To make these new changes take effect, click the Status button to go
   to the SWAT Status page, and click the Restart smbd and Restart
   nmbd buttons.**

A shared directory for several users

If you have a group of users working on a common project, it makes sense to establish a shared directory to make the pertinent files available to everyone concerned. You can set up such a Samba share in either of two ways: list each user, or create a group.

Sharing with a list of users

One way to make a shared directory is to list every user in the share description in the Samba configuration file. However, this method can become unwieldy if more than a few users need access to this directory. The following example shows a share that can be accessed only by moe, larry, and curly:

```
[shared]
path = /home/shared
read only = no
valid users = moe, larry, curly
```

Make sure the users (moe, larry, and curly) have Linux access to the /home/shared directory, either by putting them together in a Linux group, or by giving the /home/shared directory read, write, and execute access for the world. If you give the /home/shared directory world access, anyone who is Linux knowledgeable can access it (though not through Samba). Hence, for security purposes, it's probably better to share Samba shares by using groups.

Sharing with a group

A second way to make a shared directory is to add a group name in the share description and then add the users to that Linux group. This method is a little more secure because it relies on the security of the underlying Linux server instead of on Samba for security, which a Linux-knowledgeable user can easily bypass. The following share is accessible by users who are members of the group stooges:

```
[shared]
path = /home/shared
read only = no
valid users = @stooges
```

This share is similar to the previous example, but instead of listing the individual users for the valid users parameter, you include the group name stooges. Setting up a share this way takes a little more work in Linux. You have to make sure the users who need to access the share are all members of the group listed in the valid users parameter. Then, you have to make sure the directory listed in the path has the correct rights for the group. (See the section "Making Directories Available in Linux" at the beginning of this chapter for details on rights.)

Sharing Media Devices

You can use a Samba server to share media devices like CD-ROM or Zip drives. You save money because you don't need to buy drives for every Windows client. Administrative control of hardware devices can also provide the benefits of increased security and stability for Windows clients. If you require your users to install new software only from the shared devices, they are less likely to try to load unapproved software.

Sharing a special device in Samba involves two main steps. First, you need to be able to use and access the device in Linux. Then, you need to make it available in Samba.

Configuring devices in Linux

Before you can make a device available in Samba, you must make it available in Linux. This process is simple — in fact, it's nearly automatic for newer ATAPI CD-ROM drives and internal ATAPI Zip drives.

After Linux detects the device, the system simply needs a means for mounting and unmounting the device whenever someone wants to use it. You can have the device mount automatically when someone connects to it in Samba with the `preexec` commands, and then have the drive automatically unmount when that user disconnects with the `postexec` command.

Configuring CD-ROMs

In the old days, when a 2X CD-ROM was considered blazingly fast, most CD-ROMs had to be connected to the computer via special boards and software. Today, almost all newer internal CD-ROM drives are either ATAPI or SCSI drives.

After you determine what kind of CD-ROM you have (see the accompanying sidebar), you have to decide how you want to access it. To decide how to access your CD-ROM, you first have to know the device name. ATAPI CD-ROMs have typical device names of /dev/hdb or /dev/hdc, while SCSI CD-ROMs have typical device names of /dev/sdb or /dev/sdc. Again, if you're not sure, use `dmesg` and `grep` to look for the kernel messages.

After you know the device name for the CD-ROM, make a local mount point, which is a local directory to which you will mount the CD-ROM. The CD-ROM mount point is normally /mnt/cdrom, but it can be anything you want. Use the `mkdir` command to create the mount point.

TIP

ATAPI or SCSI?

If you have a CD-ROM that's faster than 2X, it's almost certainly an ATAPI or SCSI CD-ROM. How then, do you tell which one it is?

Watch the Linux kernel boot messages at startup. Somewhere in all those messages, you should see a reference to your CD-ROM, and it will mention ATAPI or SCSI. The following small example reveals that the kernel detected an ATAPI CD-ROM and assigned it to the /dev/hdc device:

```
SIS5513: IDE controller on PCI bus 00 dev 01
SIS5513: not 100% native mode: will probe irqs later
    ide0: BM-DMA at 0x4000-0x4007, BIOS settings: hda:pio, hdb:pio
    ide1: BM-DMA at 0x4008-0x400f, BIOS settings: hdc:pio, hdd:pio
hda: FUJITSU MPD3043AT, ATA DISK drive
hdc: LTN382, ATAPI CD-ROM drive
ide0 at 0x1f0-0x1f7,0x3f6 on irq 14
ide1 at 0x170-0x177,0x376 on irq 15
hda: FUJITSU MPD3043AT, 4125MB w/512kB Cache, CHS=525/255/63
hdc: ATAPI 40X CD-ROM drive, 120kB Cache
Uniform CD-ROM driver Revision: 2.56
```

So all you have to do is reboot your Linux server and speed-read the messages, right? Most Linux flavors offer an easier way: the dmesg command. The dmesg command displays the kernel messages, so you can pipe the output of dmesg into grep and then grep for CD. Rather than try to over-explain that, just use the following example:

```
[root@olorin george]# dmesg | grep CD
hdc: LTN382, ATAPI CD-ROM drive
hdc: ATAPI 40X CD-ROM drive, 120kB Cache
Uniform CD-ROM driver Revision: 2.56
```

As a general rule, if you bought your Linux box and it was designated as a server model, you probably have a SCSI CD-ROM. If your Linux box was advertised as a workstation, or you used an old workstation, it's probably ATAPI.

After you create the mount point and know the device name, insert the CD-ROM. The following command mounts an ATAPI CD-ROM with the device name of /dev/hdc to the /mnt/directory:

```
# mount -t iso9660 /dev/hdc /mnt/cdrom
```

The -t iso9660 part tells the mount command that this is an iso9660-formatted CD-ROM, which is the format for almost all CD-ROMs. If you're mounting a SCSI CD-ROM, you would use a different device name, perhaps /dev/sda1 or /dev/sdb2.

When you are done with the CD-ROM and want to eject it, first unmount it. This command is a little simpler, as the following example shows:

```
# umount /mnt/cdrom
```

Now you can safely eject the CD-ROM.

Although this discussion has surely been informative, if you had to mount and unmount every time one of your users wanted to use the CD-ROM , you'd soon go crazy. Fortunately, Samba enables you to automate the process (see the section "Sharing a CD drive," later in this chapter). We just suggest that you mount and unmount the CD-ROM manually a few times to make sure you have the syntax correct.

Configuring an internal or SCSI Zip drive

The Zip drive is becoming one of the more common means for transferring large files because these drives can be less expensive than a CD burner, and some people find them easier to use.

Using an internal Zip drive is a lot like using a CD-ROM: You need to find out the device name, create a mount point, and then mount the Zip drive to the mount point. Unmount the Zip drive when you are done.

You can determine the Zip drive's device name by watching the kernel messages as the Linux system boots, or use dmesg to look at boot messages for Zip. Typical device names for a Zip drive are /dev/hdb for an ATAPI Zip drive, and /dev/sda for a SCSI Zip drive.

After you identify the Zip drive's device name, create a mount point. A typical mount point might be /mnt/zip. Use the mkdir command to create this directory.

The mount command for a Zip drive differs from the one for a CD-ROM drive, primarily because for compatibility reasons you need to access the fourth partition on the Zip disk to see the files. The following command mounts an MS-DOS-formatted Zip disk on an ATAPI Zip drive with the device name of /dev/hdb to the directory /mount /zip:

```
# mount -t msdos /dev/hdb4 /mnt/zip
```

Again, when you're done with the Zip disk, you need to unmount it before you can eject it. The following command unmounts the Zip disk so you can safely eject it:

```
# umount /mnt/zip
```

Configuring a parallel port Zip drive

Compared to an internal or SCSI Zip drive, the parallel port Zip drive is a little harder to use on a Linux box (but not that much harder). The tricky part is that you have to load the parallel port modules before you can access the Zip drive. *Modules* are Linux programs the kernel loads when it needs to access less-used devices, or the kernel needs to load one specific type of device among many. By only loading the modules when you need them, you save memory and generally get better performance. For example, rather than loading every possible ethernet driver module, only the module needed for your ethernet card will be loaded. Of course, if you use a device all the time, you get better performance if the module is compiled into the kernel so you don't have to keep loading and unloading it. On the other hand, compiling a kernel is a task for an advanced user.

Most newer Linux kernels have the parallel-port modules built in. You can see what they are by using the `lsmod` command. (If you get a `command not found` error, look for the `lsmod` command in the /sbin directory.) The following output shows that the parallel-port module is not loaded:

```
[root@olorin george]# /sbin/lsmod
Module          Size    Used by
nfsd            150936  8  (autoclean)
lockd           30856   1  (autoclean) [nfsd]
sunrpc          52356   1  (autoclean) [nfsd lockd]
3c59x           18920   1  (autoclean)
opl3            11208   0
cs4232          2440    0
ad1848          15920   0  [cs4232]
uart401         5968    0  [cs4232]
sound           57208   0  [opl3 cs4232 ad1848 uart401]
soundlow        300     0  [sound]
soundcore       2372    6  [sound]
```

If the parallel-port module is not loaded, you can load it with `insmod`, the Linux command to load a kernel module. To load the parallel-port module so you can use your parallel-port Zip drive, type the following command:

```
# insmod ppa
```

You can check that the parallel-port module got loaded with the `lsmod` command again.

If typing **insmod ppa** doesn't work to load the parallel-port driver, try this command sequence:

```
# insmod parport
# insmod ppa
```

After you have the parallel-port modules loaded, you can mount and unmount the Zip drive, very similarly to how you mount and unmount an ATAPI Zip drive (see the preceding section in this chapter).

Note, however, that you access the parallel-port Zip drive as a SCSI device instead of an ATAPI device. So, the device name will resemble /dev/sda4 or /dev/sdb4. The following example mounts a parallel-port Zip drive to the /mnt/zip directory, with a DOS-formatted Zip disk loaded:

```
# mount -t vfat /dev/sda4 /mnt/zip
```

Again, when you're finished with the Zip disk, you need to unmount it before you can safely eject it. The following command unmounts the Zip disk so you can safely eject it:

```
# umount /mnt/zip
```

Allowing everyone access to a device

In most cases, you probably want all users to be able to walk up to a CD-ROM or Zip drive, insert their disk, and then access the share from their workstation. To make sure that everyone can access a device in Samba, you need to make sure that everyone can access the device in Linux.

To make sure that everyone can access a device in Linux, you need to give it universal access rights. To give universal read rights to the directory that mounts the CD-ROM, type the following command:

```
# chmod r-xr-xr-x /mnt/cdrom
```

The execute right has to be included to allow the users to access files on the CD. With only the read right allowed, you would only be able to list the contents of the directories.

To give universal read and write rights to a device such as a Zip drive, use the following command to modify the Zip drive device name:

```
# chmod rwxrwxrwx /mnt/zip
```

Limiting access to a special device

You might want to limit access to CD-ROMs and Zip drives. Perhaps you have a school computer lab where only authorized staff members need to add software or transfer files. To limit access to special devices, modify the directories that mount them.

Linux and UNIX have a simple method for granting and denying access to directories. You can grant and deny access to directories on a user, group, or world level. To make a directory available only to the staff, you set the appropriate group rights.

First, check the rights of the directory with the ls -l command. The fourth column identifies the group to which this directory belongs.

Make sure the group has any necessary read, write, and execute rights to the directory that mounts the device. The easiest way to assign group rights using chmod is to use the g= option. For example, **chmod g=rwx *directory_name*** gives all rights (read, write, and execute) to the group assigned to the directory, while **chmod g=rw *directory_name*** only gives read and write rights to the group who owns the directory.

Next, make sure the users belong to the desired group by searching the /etc/group file. If the users are not in the desired group, add them by editing the /etc/group file or using an administrative utility like Linuxconf. .

Sharing a CD drive

To share a CD-ROM drive in Samba, first make sure that you can use the CD-ROM drive in Linux. Previous sections in this chapter describe how to make sure the CD-ROM is available in Linux.

The following share uses the root preexec and root postexec commands to allow anyone to insert a CD-ROM and then access the share over the network:

```
[CD-ROM]
root preexec = mount -t iso9660 /dev/hdb & /mnt/cdrom
comment = shared CD-ROM
browseable = yes
read only = yes
path = /mnt/cdrom
root postexec = umount /mnt/cdrom
```

The root preexec line mounts the CD-ROM with the device name /dev/hdb to the /mnt/cdrom directory as the superuser. The browseable line makes sure that the CD-ROM appears in the Network Neighborhood. The read only line makes sure that any applications know they can't write to this share. The path is the path to the directory where the CD-ROM is mounted, while the root postexec line unmounts the CD-ROM when the user disconnects from this share.

For your particular server, the device name might be different, so you might need to change the root preexec line to match the CD-ROM device name. You should not need to change anything else in the share.

Sharing a Zip drive

To share a Zip drive in Samba, first be sure that the Zip drive is usable in Linux. Previous sections in this chapter explain how to make sure your Zip drive is accessible in Linux.

If the Zip drive is accessible in Linux, make a share that automatically mounts the Zip drive when a user connects to it. The following example uses the root preexec and the root postexec commands to mount and unmount a Zip drive when a user successfully connects to it:

```
[Zip]
root preexec = mount -t vfat /dev/sda4 /mnt/zip
comment = shared Zip drive
browseable = yes
path = /mnt/zip
root postexec = umount /mnt/zip
```

This share would work with a parallel-port or SCSI Zip drive. If you were using an ATAPI Zip drive, the device name might be something like /dev/hdb4.

Adding a special device with SWAT

To add a special device (in this example, a shared CD-ROM) using SWAT, follow these steps:

1. **In SWAT, click the Shares button.**

2. **In the box next to the Create Share button, type the name of the new share — for example,** cdrom.

3. **Click Create Share.**

4. **From the drop-down list, select the share.**

5. **Click Choose Share.**

6. **Enter the necessary options to create the share for this special device.**

   Under Base Options, comment describes the share, while path is the path to the directory to which the device gets mounted (that is, /mnt/cdrom).

   Under the Miscellaneous Options, add the root preexec and root postexec parameters. The root preexec field needs the command used to mount the special device (that is, **mount -t iso9660 /dev/hdb/ mnt/cdrom**), and the root postexec field is for the command to safely unmount the special device (that is, **umount /dev/cdrom**).

   Also, add any other required options such as browseable = yes to make the share appear in the Network Neighborhood, or set read only = yes for a CD-ROM.

7. **Click the Advanced View button if you want to add any advanced parameters such as** valid users.

8. **Click Commit Changes to save your changes to the Samba configuration file.**

9. **To make these new changes take effect, click the Status button to go to the SWAT Status page, and click the Restart smbd and Restart nmbd buttons.**

Sharing Printers with Samba

After you have your printer working in Linux, you have to share it in Samba. If you're lucky, you can share all the printers in your printcap file just by adding a few lines to the global section and adding a separate printers section in your smb.conf file. Or, you might need to create specific shares for your printers.

When a user connects to a Samba server, the server displays any specific shares the user can see and then it checks the /etc/passwd to display a home directory (if this user does not have a specifically defined share). Then, the server can display the printers in the /etc/printcap file. To make a specific printer available under Samba, you can give it a share of its own, or you can make all the printers available in the /etc/printcap file.

Sharing all your printers

You can share all the printers defined in your /etc/printcap file (or on your UNIX system, if it doesn't use a printcap file) with a few lines in the global section and a printers section.

The first line in your global section should be `load printers = yes`, which causes Samba to load all the printers in your /etc/printcap file. This is the default behavior, so if you don't have a `load printers` line in the global section of your smb.conf file, the printers should load. But to be sure, you might want to include the `load printers = yes` line.

The second line in your global section is the `printing` Samba parameter, which tells Samba which style of printing to use. This should have been set correctly when Samba was compiled for your operating system. If you're having trouble with your printers, double-check the `printing` value. For Linux, you would use the following line:

```
printing = bsd
```

Other types of UNIX use different printing styles. Solaris 2, for example, has System V-style printing, so you would use the following line:

```
printing = SYSV
```

After you have Samba loading all the printers in the /etc/printcap file, it uses a share called printers to define each one. Somewhat like the homes section, the printers section sets up a Samba share for each printer in the /etc/print-cap file using the parameters in the printers section to define each share. Here is the default printers section from a Red Hat Linux server:

```
[printers]
comment = All Printers
path = /tmp
create mask = 0700
print ok = Yes
browseable = No
```

This looks like a fairly standard share but with a few new parameters. The most important is print ok = yes, which tells Samba that this is a printer. The path = /tmp entry isn't really necessary, because this is the default path.

The print ok = yes parameter enables a share to receive print jobs. Printable = yes is the same as print ok = yes.

Modifying the printers with SWAT

In SWAT, the printer section has its own page:

1. **To modify the printers share or one of the individual printers in SWAT, first click the Printers button in SWAT.**

2. **Next to the Choose Printer button, select the share you want to modify from the drop-down list (select the printers share or an individual printer share).**

3. **Click Choose Printer.**

4. **Enter any necessary changes. Click the Advanced View button to view more printer parameters.**

5. **Click Commit Changes to save your changes to the Samba configuration file.**

6. **To make these new changes take effect, click the Status button to go to the SWAT Status page and then click the Restart smbd and Restart nmbd buttons.**

Sharing a specific printer

Assume that you need to set up a printer and you can't load all the printers from a line in the global section of the smb.conf file. Or, maybe your printer needs a few special parameters to set it up properly.

First, set `load printers = no` in the global section of the Samba configuration file, to make sure you don't load all the printers. Then, create a share with the name of the printer and include the special parameters you need. The following example shows a basic share for a single printer:

```
[bubblejet]
printing = bsd
print ok = yes
printer = bubblejet
```

The `printing` line tells you that the Samba server uses bsd style printing (perhaps it's a Linux server). The `printer = bubblejet` line tells Samba to use the printer named bubblejet from the /etc/printcap file.

Sharing a restricted, specific printer

You might be interested in setting up a printer with restricted rights. Perhaps it's an expensive, color proof printer, and you want to limit access to it so you can conserve expensive toner resources. It's an easy task in Samba.

You don't want to share all the printers in the /etc/printcap file, so make sure the global section of your Samba configuration file includes the line `load printers = no`.

The following example shows a restricted printer share for the printer colorjet. The share restricts the users to the group wheel and the users djones and jstraw:

```
[colorjet]
printing = SYSV
print ok = yes
print command = lp -c -d%p %s; rm %s
printer = colorjet
valid users = djones, jstraw, @wheel
```

You should note a few things about this share. The `printing` parameter is set to SYSV because this Samba server runs on Solaris 2.6 (System V). The `print command` parameter tells Samba the command syntax for printing: It uses Samba variables and expands to `lp -c -dcolorjet spool_file; rm spool_file`.

A few other printer parameters

Samba has several other printer parameters that you might find necessary or useful. If your Samba printers don't work, your UNIX system might be using custom commands or normal commands with special options. After you determine which commands are special, you can tell Samba how to use them. You can also let Samba handle low-disk-space situations and customize your printer for incoming PostScript jobs.

Several Samba parameters let you define how Samba interacts with the operating system printers. Ideally, if you set the printing command correctly (for `printing = bsd, sysv,` and so on), you won't need to change the printing-related commands. But if you still can't print after setting the print commands, try adding some of the following commands.

Printing with the print command

If your Samba printer is not printing, and you need to do something special in Linux to print, you can incorporate that special command with the `print command` option. For example, in some versions of Solaris 2.6, you need to add the `-c` flag to `lp` to print a file. So in Samba, you would add the `print command = lp -c -d%p` parameter to your printer share or to the printers section of your smb.conf file.

Pausing and resuming your printers and queues

Similarly, if you need to use special versions of the commands to pause and resume your printers and queues, use the following parameters: `lppause` and `lpresume` for your printer, and `queuepause` and `queueresume` for your printer queues.

Getting your printer status with the lpq command

If you're having trouble getting your printer status from Samba, you might need to add an `lpq` command parameter. Solaris and other System V UNIXes use `lpstat` instead of `lpq` to get printer status. The following example shows how to set this up in Samba:

```
lpq command = lpstat -o%p
```

Removing a job with lprm

If you can't remove jobs via your Samba printers, find out how to do it in UNIX. Then, add the corresponding `lprm` command parameter. For instance, Solaris uses the `cancel` command to remove a print job instead of `lprm`. The following example shows how to configure this Samba parameter for Solaris:

```
lprm command = cancel %p-%j
```

Finding your printers

If you store your printer file (usually the /etc/printcap file) in an unusual location, you can tell Samba where to find it with the `printcap name` parameter. You can also set this to `lpstat` for the System V printers that use `lpstat` to list the available printers.

Setting the minimum print space

The `min print space` Samba parameter lets you set how much disk space must be available before Samba can accept a print job. Try this if your Samba print server keeps filling up with jobs.

Specifying PostScript printing

The postscript Samba parameter tells Samba to make the printer interpret all incoming PC jobs as PostScript. If you have a PostScript printer and your PC jobs come out as pages and pages of alphanumeric gibberish instead of properly formatted documents, add postscript = yes.

Testing your Samba printer with smbclient

After you add your printer and restart Samba, you should first test the printer with smbclient. For example, the following steps test the printer named laserjet:

1. **Connect to the printer share with** smbclient.

   For example, to connect to the printer share named laserjet on the server terrapin as the user george with smbclient, you would type the following command:

   ```
   # smbclient //terrapin/laserjet -U george
   ```

   Give the password for george when prompted.

2. **Use the** lcd **command to locally change to the /etc directory:**

   ```
   smb:> lcd /etc
   ```

3. **Print the services file with the** print **command:**

   ```
   smb:> print services
   ```

4. **Exit smbclient:**

   ```
   smb:> quit
   ```

The /etc/services file should have printed at the printer named laserjet if your share was successfully created (and the printer is working).

If you have trouble with the printer working in Linux, Chapter 7 might be a good place to review more about adding printers at the OS (that is, Linux) level.

Making Windows 95/98 automatically load a printer driver

One neat printer trick is to set up your Samba printer so that a Windows 95/98 client automatically loads the driver when the Windows client first connects to the printer. Samba needs access to the drivers so it can inform the Windows clients when they connect.

First, create a directory on your Linux server to store the printer driver files. Then, make a Samba share named printer$ that references that directory. The following example is from the Samba documentation:

```
[printer$]
path = /usr/local/samba/printer
public = yes
writable = no
browseable = no
```

In this example, the directory that you created for the printer driver files is /usr/local/samba/printer.

Next, build the list of files required for the printer driver. Start by looking for your printer in the two files named msprint.inf and msprint2.inf. Usually, these two files are located in the C:\Windows\INF directory.

If your printer is listed in one of these files, copy that file to your Samba server. At the Samba server, run the Samba utility called `make_printerdef`. You run `make_printerdef` with the name of the .inf file that you copied and the name of your printer, and then redirect the output to a file named printer.def. That's a little confusing, but the following example should clear it up:

```
# make_printerdef msprint.inf "HP LaserJet 4M" >> & printer.def
```

If you have a more modern printer, it might not be listed in msprint.inf or msprint2.inf. In that case, run `make_printerdef` with the .inf file that came with your printer driver. Its name should be similar to oemsetup.inf. To create a printer.def file for a Canon Bubblejet 4300, you would type this line:

```
# make_printerdef oemsetup.inf "Canon  BJC-4300" >> & printer.def
```

When the `make_printerdef` command runs, it prints a list of files required to automatically install the printer driver. You must copy all these files into the directory on the Samba server that you created earlier. Usually, you find these files in the C:\Windows\Server directory.

Finally, you need to add three parameters to the Samba configuration file. The first is in the global section, and the next two are in each printer share. The first parameter is `printer driver file`, which must give the path to the printer.def file you created earlier. Set it in the global section of the smb.conf file.

The second parameter is `printer driver location`, and it gives the path to the printer files that were listed when you ran `make_printerdef`. The third parameter is the `printer driver` parameter, which you should set to the printer name, such as HP LaserJet 4M.

Chapter 9

Samba and Passwords

• •

In This Chapter

▶ Handling encrypted passwords from Windows clients

▶ Making your Windows clients use unencrypted passwords

▶ Making Samba use encrypted passwords

▶ Becoming an encrypted-password server with the `update encrypted` parameter

▶ Checking passwords with a password server

▶ Synchronizing Samba and Linux passwords

▶ Giving older clients access with Samba's `password levels` parameter

• •

*I*f your network server scheme did not use encrypted passwords, you could lose network security in a matter of minutes. Using common Linux and UNIX utilities that read network packets, an outsider could easily detect your user name and password, and be able to impersonate you to the Samba server. Hence, Windows clients encrypt a password-and-challenge string before sending it to a Samba server, and the server matches the encrypted password-and-challenge string. Think of it as putting a letter in a dark envelope that only the designated people can open. (On the other hand, if your work environment is safe from snooping, you don't need encrypted passwords, which is more like using postcards for your correspondence.)

Only the very first versions of Windows 95 and Windows NT before Service Pack 3 use unencrypted passwords, so getting your Samba server to use encrypted passwords from the beginning will probably save lots of time down the road. You could change a Windows client to use unencrypted passwords, but you would have to do this for all Windows clients that connect to your Samba server.

This chapter describes how to make your Samba server understand encrypted passwords that Windows 98, NT, and 2000 clients use. We also explain how to modify a client to use unencrypted passwords. This chapter also shows you how to coordinate Samba and password servers and how to synchronize Samba and UNIX passwords.

Adjusting Windows Clients for Unencrypted Passwords

You might have a mixture of clients, with only a few that use encrypted passwords — for example, one Windows NT client and ten Windows 95 clients. In such cases, you might decide to modify the one NT client so it does not use encrypted passwords.

To turn off password encryption, you have to edit the Windows registry. The registry contains all the configuration information for the computer, and if it gets corrupted, your Windows computer might not boot. Therefore, be sure to back up the registry before you edit it.

Windows 95/98

The registry is a binary database created by two files: SYSTEM.DAT and USER.DAT. These files contain all the configuration information for the system and the user for a Windows 95/98 client. Because the registry is a binary file, you cannot edit or view it with a typical text editor like Notepad. Instead, use regedit, the registry editor supplied with Windows.

Windows stores the SYSTEM.DAT file as a hidden file in the Windows directory. The USER.DAT file is often stored as a hidden file in the Windows directory, but if you use roaming profiles to give users the same desktop and setup regardless of which PC they use (see Chapter 12), the USER.DAT file may be downloaded from the profile server.

Saving (and restoring) the registry

Because the registry contains all the configuration information for the computer, a corrupt or incorrect registry can prevent your computer from booting. Again, it's very important that you back up the registry before editing it.

Fortunately, the Windows 95 CD includes a utility to back up the registry. The utility, cfgback, is located in the other/misc/cfgback directory on the Windows CD. Double-click the cfgback program to start it, follow the directions to specify your backup media, and then back up the registry. You then use cfgback to restore the registry from the backup media when needed.

Windows 95 also has two backup registry files: SYSTEM.DA0 and USER.DA0, which it stores in the Windows directory. You can use these files to replace the SYSTEM.DAT and the USER.DAT files, respectively, in the event of a corrupted registry.

Windows 98 does not come with cfgback, but it does come with a utility called Registry Checker. Use Registry Checker to back up the registry and retrieve it in the event of registry problems.

Start Registry Checker by clicking Start⇨Programs⇨Accessories⇨ System Tools⇨System Information. In the Microsoft System Information screen, choose Tools⇨Registry Checker. The Registry Checker starts up, checks your registry, and offers to back it up.

When your Windows 98 system starts up, the Registry Checker checks the registry. If the registry is corrupt, the Registry Checker automatically replaces it with the backup that was just created. If you make an uncorrectable mistake when editing your registry, a reboot should fix it.

Editing the registry to allow unencrypted passwords

To allow unencrypted passwords, you need to edit the registry of a Windows 95/98 PC. More specifically, you add a key to the registry to tell Windows to use unencrypted passwords instead of encrypted passwords.

You can add this key in either of two ways: the hard way, by directly editing the registry; or the easy way, by importing the required key. We talk about the easy way first, but both ways use a program called regedit (the Registry Editor) to edit the registry.

The easy way to add this key is by importing an existing key into the registry:

1. **To start regedit, click Start⇨Run, type** regedit **in the Open field of the Run dialog box, and then click OK.**

   On your Samba server, you have two files named Win95_PlainPassword.reg and Win98_PlainPassword.reg. Typically, you find these files in the docs directory off your main Samba directory.

2. **Copy the file you need for your client to a directory on your client, or even a floppy disk.**

3. **In the Registry Editor, choose Registry⇨Import Registry File.**

4. **Browse to the file from the Samba server (either Win95_PlainPassword.reg or Win98_PlainPassword.reg).**

5. **Click Open.**

   The Registry key should get imported, and you should get confirmation that the key was added.

The second way is a little harder — you actually add the key into the registry by typing it in. You might have to do it this way if you have trouble getting the imported Registry key to your Windows client:

1. **To start regedit, click Start⇨Run, type** regedit **in the Open field of the Run dialog box, and then click OK.**

   In the Registry Editor window, the left panel shows the registry tree, and the right panel shows the name and value of each item.

2. **By clicking the plus box next to the appropriate entries in the left panel, expand HKEY_LOCAL_MACHINE, System, CurrentControlSet, Services, VxD, and then VNETSUP.**

3. **Choose Edit⇨New⇨DWORD Value.**

4. **In place of the default name for the new entry (New Value #1) type** EnablePlainTextPassword **and then press Enter.**

5. **Double-click EnablePlainTextPassword.**

6. **In the dialog box that's displayed, set the value to 1 and then click OK.**

7. **Choose Registry⇨Exit.**

The Registry Editor can export and import a registry as a text file. With this feature, you can edit a registry in a word processor. But because you can easily make mistakes in punctuation that can corrupt the registry, you should leave this method to Windows gurus.

Windows NT

Like Windows 95/98, the registry in Windows NT is a binary file that contains the configuration information for the system. Because the registry is a binary file, you need to use a special program, called Registry Editor, to manipulate it. You must take care when editing the registry, because a corrupted registry may make your computer nonfunctional.

Adding a registry key to enable unencrypted passwords for Windows NT is similar to the process used in Windows 95/98 (see the preceding section in this chapter), but the details differ slightly.

The Windows NT registry has Registry Editors named regedit and regedt32. The one named regedit is identical to the Windows 95/98 Registry Editor.

Saving (and restoring) the registry

Before you start editing the registry, save a good copy of it with the rdisk - sto command. This saves the registry and enables you to reboot and use the last good configuration to back up any changes. This procedure also forces you to make an emergency boot disk. If you ever make irreparable changes, rebooting with the last good configuration restores your registry.

Here's how you use the `rdisk - sto` command:

1. **Access an MS-DOS command prompt by clicking Start➪Programs➪ MS-DOS Command Prompt.**

2. **At the MS-DOS command prompt, type** rdisk -sto **and press Enter. This will save a good configuration.**

3. **You may create an emergency repair disk if you want. Answer Yes to the prompt and then insert a floppy disk into the drive.**

Now if you have a problem in editing the registry, you can reboot and choose to boot with the last good configuration, by pressing the spacebar when booting. During startup, Windows NT displays a prompt that asks whether you want to reboot using the last-known good configuration

Editing the registry

To allow Windows NT to connect to a server using unencrypted passwords, you need to change the Windows NT registry. Specifically, you need to add a registry key to make the passwords get sent out as unencrypted passwords.

As in Windows 95/98, you can add this key in either of two ways. The easier way is to import the registry key from a file named NT4_PlainPassword.reg. The harder way is to add the key manually. We show the easy way first.

The easy way to add a registry key is to use the import function in the Registry Editor:

1. **Open an MS-DOS command prompt by clicking Start➪Programs➪ MS-DOS Command Prompt.**

2. **At the MS-DOS command prompt, type** regedit **and then press Enter.**

   This command starts the Windows 95-style Registry Editor.

3. **Choose Registry➪Import Registry File.**

4. **Browse to the file from the Samba server named NT4_PlainPassword.reg.**

5. **Click Open.**

   The Registry key should get imported and you should get confirmation that the key was added.

The harder way is to actually use the Registry Editor to add a key:

1. **Open an MS-DOS command prompt by clicking Start➪Programs➪ MS-DOS Command Prompt.**

   2. **At the MS-DOS command prompt, type** regedit **and then press Enter.**

     This command starts the Windows 95/98-style Registry Editor.

   3. **Click the plus sign next to HKEY_LOCAL_MACHINE, then System, CurrentControlSet, Services, Rdr, and then Parameters.**

   4. **Choose <u>E</u>dit⇨<u>N</u>ew⇨<u>D</u>WORD Value.**

   5. **In place of the default name for the new entry (New Value #1), type** EnablePlainTextPassword **and then press Enter.**

   6. **Double-click EnablePlainTextPassword.**

   7. **In the dialog box that's displayed, set the value to 1 and then click OK.**

   8. **Choose <u>R</u>egistry⇨E<u>x</u>it.**

Windows 2000

In Windows 2000, you edit the registry with a program called regedt32. To start regedt32, click Start⇨Run, type **regedt32** in the Open field of the Run dialog box, and click OK.

Saving and restoring the registry

Windows 2000 does not come with rdisk, so to save the Windows 2000 registry you need to use Windows 2000 Backup.

Editing the registry

In the Registry Editor, the left panel shows the registry tree and the right panel shows the name and value of each item.

Adding a registry key to enable unencrypted passwords for Windows 2000 is very similar to the process used in Windows NT, but the path is slightly different. Open the folder in the Registry Editor by expanding HKEY_LOCAL_ MACHINE, System, CurrentControlSet, Services, LanManWorkstation, and then Parameters. The key you need to add is EnablePlainTextPassword: REG_DWORD=1.

Making Samba Use Encrypted Passwords

Making Samba use encrypted passwords takes just a few steps, and you can check each step as you go. Using encrypted passwords can be the most time-efficient method in the long run, and it is definitely the most secure.

Creating the password file

First, you need to create the password file, typically called smbpasswd. The Samba parameter `smb passwd file` in the global section of smb.conf lets Samba know where to find the password file if it is not in the default location. For Red Hat Linux, the default location for the smbpasswd file is /etc/smbpasswd; for most other compiled versions of Samba, it is /usr/local/samba/private/smbpasswd.

The smbpasswd file contains a line for each user who connects to the Samba server. It is very similar to the format of the /etc/passwd file. Each line starts with a user name, followed by a user ID, a field for the encrypted LanManager password, a field for the encrypted NT password, a field for the account type, and a field for when the password was last changed. Colons separate the fields.

Samba comes with a utility called mksmbpasswd.sh that you can use to create an smbpasswd file from the existing /etc/passwd file, although it won't contain any encrypted passwords yet. The following line creates the smbpasswd file by displaying the /etc/passwd file and redirecting the displayed output to the mksmbpasswd utility.

```
# cat /etc/passwd | mksmbpasswd.sh > /usr/local/etc/private/smbpasswd
```

You can also create the smbpasswd file manually with your favorite editor. Initially, you should set up the two password fields with exactly 32 Xs in each field so Samba knows it is a null password.

For security, after you create the smbpasswd file, remove all accounts from it except for the users who will be connecting to the Samba server. (Delete the system accounts — that is, cron, lp, daemon, or mail.)

Verify that the smbpasswd file now has users by displaying it with the `cat` or `more` command:

```
# cat /usr/local/etc/private/smbpasswd
```

The following few lines show a newly created smbpasswd file but without the encrypted passwords added:

```
col:100:XXXXXXXXXXXXXXXXXXXXXXXXXXXXXXXX:XXXXXXXXXXXXXXXXXXXXXXXXXXXXXXXX:[U]
            :LCT-00000000:Caldera OpenLinux User
george:500:XXXXXXXXXXXXXXXXXXXXXXXXXXXXXXXX:XXXXXXXXXXXXXXXXXXXXXXXXXXXXXXXX:[U]
            :LCT-00000000:Caldera OpenLinux User
```

By viewing the contents of the smbpasswd file, an unethical person could impersonate a user by sending that user's encrypted password. This wouldn't be easy, but it is technically possible. For the best security, the directory containing the smbpasswd file should be owned by and readable only by root. Use the Linux/UNIX commands `chown` and `chmod` to establish the proper rights for the smbpasswd file with the following three commands:

```
# chown root /usr/local/etc/private/smbpasswd
# chmod 500 /usr/local/etc/private
# chmod 600 /usr/local/etc/private/smbpasswd
```

See Chapter 8 for more about setting file and directory rights.

Configuring Samba to use encrypted passwords

For Samba to use encrypted passwords, you need to modify the smb.conf file by adding the following parameters to the global section:

- ✔ security
- ✔ encrypt passwords
- ✔ smb passwd file

The following example shows part of the global section of smb.conf, with the correct settings for these three parameters:

```
security = user
encrypt passwords = yes
smb passwd file = /usr/local/etc/private/smbpasswd
```

You set the smb passwd file parameter to the location of the encrypted smbpasswd file. In this example, the smbpasswd file is located in the /usr/local/etc/private directory.

Populating the password file

After you create the smbpasswd file, you need to populate it with the encrypted passwords for each user. For a new Samba server, just use the smbpasswd command for each user.

The following sequence shows how to add an encrypted password for the existing user george by typing smbpasswd george and then typing and confirming a password for george:

```
# smbpasswd george
New SMB password:
Retype new SMB password:
```

If you have to add a new user to your smbpasswd file, you would use `smbpasswd -a`. The following example adds the new user bartlett to the smbpasswd file:

```
# smbpasswd -a bartlett
New SMB password:
Retype new SMB password:
```

If normal, nonroot users use smbpasswd, the system prompts them for the old password first before they can change the Samba password to a new password.

If you get an error message about being unable to find the user, check to see that the location of the smbpasswd file is detailed in the smb.conf file by the `smb passwd file` parameter.

The following section shows an smbpasswd file with encrypted passwords:

```
george:1001:52AE2AA5C82C72D5695109AB020E401C:2DA7ACF57CF9EDE535615A091BE2B4C3
             :[U]:LCT-38795C03:George
alli:500:0A117BD09AD0B0AFAAD3B435B51404EE:88C73EE911328FC22B811C5C1EE12555:[U]
             :LCT-38795D75:Allison
```

After you have changed and added the smb.conf encryption parameters, the smbpasswd file has a few encrypted entries, and you have tested the smb.conf file with `testparm`, you need to kill and restart your Samba daemons.

Testing encrypted passwords

It's easiest to first test the encrypted passwords by trying to connect from the Samba server to the Samba server using `smbclient`. Yes, you are trying to make a user on the server connect to the same server. We know that seems odd, but it does test Samba's encryption.

The following example shows the root user using `smbclient` to log on to Neo's directory on the server Liberty:

```
#smbclient //Liberty/homes -U neo
```

If encrypted passwords are working, you should be prompted for Neo's password. After you enter the password, you should be connected, and be able to display Neo's home directory with the `ls` command.

Next, try to connect to a share from a Windows client. Make sure the client has not had its registry edited to use plain-text passwords.

Adding Encryption with the update encrypted Parameter

You might have a Samba server that was set up using unencrypted passwords and then you decide to add password encryption at a later time. By using the `update encrypted` Samba parameter, you can have your Samba server slowly change from a server using unencrypted passwords to a server using encrypted passwords. What really happens is that Samba starts filling a file with encrypted passwords, and when you have enough encrypted passwords, you switch Samba over to an encrypted password setting.

Creating the smbpasswd file

The first step is to create an smbpasswd file and add the user names. Samba won't be referring to this file yet, but it will be adding encrypted passwords to it whenever users successfully connect using their plain-text password.

Earlier in this chapter, we describe the process for creating the smbpasswd file in greater detail. We just describe the minimum steps here; if you need more information, please see the section "Creating the password file," earlier in this chapter.

First, create the smbpasswd file and populate it with the contents of the /etc/passwd file with the following command:

```
# cat /etc/passwd | mksmbpasswd.sh > /usr/local/etc/private/smbpasswd
```

The smbpasswd file was created in the /usr/local/etc/private directory.

Be sure that the smbpasswd file is protected. The next three commands give the smbpasswd file protection against unauthorized use:

```
# chown root /usr/local/etc/private/smbpasswd
# chmod 500 /usr/local/etc/private
# chmod 600 /usr/local/etc/private/smbpasswd
```

(See Chapter 8 for more about setting file and directory rights.)

Note that you can also create the smbpasswd file manually, and you should remove any system accounts from the smbpasswd file for better security.

Modifying the smb.conf file to gather passwords

Next, you need to make changes to the smb.conf file to allow the smbpasswd file to be populated with encrypted passwords. To complete this step, you need to add or change two parameters in the global section: the `smb passwd file` setting, and the `update encrypted` setting. Add the following lines to the global section of the smb.conf to make Samba populate the smbpasswd file with encrypted passwords:

```
smb passwd file = /usr/local/etc/private/smbpasswd
update encrypted = yes
encrypted passwords = no
```

While passwords are being logged, set the `encrypted passwords` parameter to `no`.

After a suitable period of time to allow each user to log on successfully using unencrypted passwords, you can switch to encrypted passwords. If you are not sure if your users have all logged on, you can look through the smbpasswd file; any entries with all Xs for the encrypted passwords mean that the user(s) have not logged on to the server. You can look through the smbpasswd file with the `more` command, or you can use `grep` and look for the string XXXX.

Changing your network to encrypted passwords

When you are satisfied that enough time has passed and all the encrypted passwords have been logged, it's time to change to a more secure network using encrypted passwords. You might have to change the Windows clients, and the Samba server requires slight modifications.

Modifying the clients

Modifying the clients is almost the reverse of what you do to make the client use unencrypted passwords: You edit the registry and delete the key that allows unencrypted passwords. (If you need a quick refresher on starting and using the Registry Editor, see the section "Adjusting Windows Clients for Unencrypted Passwords," earlier in this chapter.)

The first versions of Windows 95 use plain-text passwords. The two files involved are called VREDIR.VXD and VNSETUP.VXD. They are located in the Windows/System directory. If they are older than 6/2/97, they use plain-text passwords. Upgrade to a newer version to use encrypted passwords.

For later versions of Windows 95 and all versions of Windows 98, encrypted passwords are the default. If your clients are not using encrypted passwords, the registry has been changed to allow plain-text passwords. Delete the associated registry key, EnablePlainTextPassword. It is in the folder HKEY_LOCAL_MACHINE\System\CurrentControlSet\Services\VxD\VNETSUP.

Before Service Pack 3, Windows NT uses plain-text passwords, so you need to upgrade to at least Service Pack 3 if you want to use encrypted passwords.

If the registry was edited to allow plain-text passwords, delete the key from the registry. The key is EnablePlainTextPassword and is located in the folder HKEY_LOCAL_MACHINE\SYSTEM\CurrentControlSet\Services\Rdr\Parameter.

Windows 2000 uses encrypted passwords by default. If the registry was edited to allow plain-text passwords, you must delete that key from the registry. The key is EnablePlainTextPassword, and is located in the folder HKEY_LOCAL_MACHINE\System\CurrentControlSet\Services\LanManWorkstation\Parameters.

Modifying the server

You should need to change only two parameters in the smb.conf file to switch from unencrypted to encrypted passwords. Change `encrypt passwords` from `no` to `yes`, and change `update encrypted` from `yes` to `no`. Restart the Samba daemons, and your network will be using encrypted passwords.

If you want, you can verify that everything is working via the `smbclient` command. The following entry checks whether the user trinity can see the homes share on the server Morpheus:

```
# smbclient //Morpheus/homes -U trinity
```

Making Samba Work with Password Servers

You might have a more complex office with multiple servers, and one master server controls the passwords. Although you could set up Samba to authenticate its own passwords, this is unwieldy and could change the passwords between your master password server and Samba, leading to very difficult-to-diagnose problems. It's simpler in the long run just to have your Samba server use the master password server.

The password server is often a Windows Primary Domain Controller (PDC), but it can be another Windows or Samba server.

You need to make two changes to the global section of the smb.conf file to make Samba use a password server. The `security` parameter must be set to `server`, and the `password server` parameter must give the NetBIOS name of the server. The following example shows a section of the smb.conf to allow Samba to use a password server named mcenroe:

```
Password = server
Password server = mcenroe
```

The password server's NetBIOS name must be given, and the NetBIOS name to IP address translation (that is, WINS or host table) must be working correctly. One way to ensure that your Samba sever can find the password server is to add the password server to the /etc/hosts files. This also improves your network security by preventing someone from impersonating the password server.

Working more closely with a Windows NT domain is more complex. We discuss that topic in Chapter 12.

Synchronizing Samba and Linux Passwords

Although Samba and UNIX passwords on the same server do not need to match, it makes for much easier administration when they do. You can do this using as few as one parameter: `unix password sync`. Or, you might need to add the `passwd chat` or `passwd program` parameters.

The `unix passwd sync` parameter specifies whether Samba will try to synchronize the UNIX passwords. If set to true, Samba tries to change the UNIX password when the Samba password is being changed. Samba calls /bin/passwd as the root user, or it calls whatever program is named in the `password program` parameter.

The `passwd chat` parameter defines the password chat string that Samba uses to change the user's password in UNIX. This sequence changes due to the type of server and the password methods being used. If the expected output is not received, the password will not change.

The string can contain the variables %o, which expands to be the old password, and %n, which expands to be the new password.

It can also contain the characters \n for line feed, \r for carriage return, \t for tab, \s for space, and *, which matches any set of characters.

You can use double quotes for strings with spaces in them to gather them into a single string.

The default is

```
passwd chat = *old*password* %o\n *new*password* %n\n *new*password* %n\n
              changed
```

Here's another example of a password chat string:

```
passwd chat = "##Enter your old password##" %o\n "##Enter your new password##"
              %n\n "##Re-enter your new password##" %n\n "## Your password has
              been changed##"
```

One Other Samba Password Parameter

Samba has one other password parameter that you should know: `password levels`. Because UNIX passwords are case-sensitive, this parameter tells Samba the maximum number of uppercase letters it can include in the password when it tries to authenticate a user. With each increase in the number of uppercase letters allowed, the number of possible passwords dramatically increases, and the time required to authenticate a user takes longer, so this can decrease performance. You only need to worry about the `password level` parameter if you have older Windows clients to support, such as Windows for Workgroups. If all your clients are Windows 95 or later, you do not need the `password level` parameter. This parameter doesn't apply when using encrypted passwords.

Part III
Advanced Samba Techniques

The 5th Wave   By Rich Tennant

@RICHTENNANT

"That reminds me – I installed Windows 2000 on my PC last week."

In this part . . .

So you've already digested Part II? Then you must be ravenous for all the adventures of the advanced practices included in this part. You're likely to be one of those folks lucky enough to have inherited a Samba/Linux network and need to figure it out now. Or maybe you're just really brainy and like to read this kind of stuff in case somebody asks you someday how to span subnets with a WINS server. Well, that's why we're here.

The chapters in this part cover

- Maximizing and measuring Samba's performance
- Working with complex networks — stuff like WINS, subnets, and browsing
- Working with domains

Chapter 10

Increasing Samba Performance

. . . .

. . . .

*B*y now, you probably have your Samba server up and running, and you should feel confident in your ability to administer Samba's performance. Take a deep breath, lean back, pat yourself on the back, and when you're ready, roll up your sleeves to get ready for some advanced Samba tricks.

This chapter describes how to measure and increase Samba performance. Keep in mind that your mileage may vary because your network and clients might differ from others, but this chapter gives you a few things to try.

Measuring Performance

The first thing you want to check out is your server's performance. With the right tools, you can identify bottlenecks on your Linux server. If your Linux server is tied up with other tasks, Samba will run slowly on that server, too.

Next, you want to measure the Samba performance on the server. After you know how fast it performs normally, you can reevaluate it after you change things to see how much faster (or possibly slower) it has become.

Measuring your server's performance

Your first concern is your server's basic performance. You can't construct an impressive building without a solid foundation; likewise, you can't have a screaming fast Samba server without a decent Linux server supporting it.

Looking for bottlenecks with top

Top is a useful but potentially overwhelming performance-measuring tool. You can use top to see

- ✔ How many processes are running
- ✔ How busy your CPUs are
- ✔ The state of your memory

In this way, you can get a better idea of where any performance bottlenecks might be. Start top by simply typing **top**. Quit top by typing **q**.

The following is a brief section of the output from top:

```
2:57pm up 53 days,  4:24,  4 users,  load average 1.82, 1.29, 0.59
87 processes: 78 sleeping, 7 running, 2 zombie, 0 stopped
CPU states: 0.7% user,  0.7% system,  0.0% nice,  98.4% idle
Mem:   63072K av,  47108K used,  15964K free,  21944K shrd,   3932K buff
Swap:  68540K av,  21412K used,  47128K free                 14084K cached

PID USER      PRI  NI  SIZE  RSS SHARE STAT  LIB %CPU %MEM   TIME COMMAND
5183 root      17   0 16008  13M  1868 R       0 91.5 21.5 12212m X
19131 root     11  10  1228 1228  1044 R N     0  7.1  1.9  0:42 kumppa
19140 george    3   0  1024 1024   824 R       0  1.3  1.6  0:00 top
```

This might look intimidating, but you can find out a few things about your system by picking it apart. The first line indicates that the server has been running without rebooting for 53 days, which is nice, but not unusual, for a Linux server. The next line shows you have 87 processes, of which seven are running and two are zombied.

Too many zombied processes can really slow your system down, so you want to kill them. List your zombie processes with ps and grep by typing **ps -al | grep Z**. Then kill them with the **kill -9 *process_ID*** command.

The next line shows the CPU states. The numbers are low, which means the CPU has lots of horsepower left. If the numbers were running consistently high, you might want to upgrade to a faster CPU, or add another one, if you have a multiprocessor machine.

The fourth and fifth lines show the memory states. If you start to run out of free memory, you might want to add more to keep your server running at its best speed.

The next section is a list of processes sorted by CPU time. Note that X Window is taking the most time, so if this server was running with high CPU activity, you could turn off X Window for a little extra performance.

Top has many more options; see the man pages for details.

Making a quick check of your server's memory with free

If you want to quickly check your server's memory, use the `free` command. To use `free`, just type **free** at the prompt. You get columns displaying your memory usage. If your free memory is low, adding memory will probably improve your server (and Samba) performance.

Measuring Samba's performance

Because Samba uses TCP packets to communicate, it's best to measure performance against other applications that use TCP. The handiest one is ftp. Time how long it takes to copy a large file from a Samba share to your hard drive. Then, time how long it takes to ftp the same file from your Samba server to your hard drive. If the times are close, your base performance is good.

Changing Your Server's Hardware

After you check out your server's performance, the next step is to see if you can change your Samba server's hardware to improve its performance. We can only offer some guidelines — an attempt to give specific solutions would make this book three feet thick, and it would be out of date in six months.

Do you have enough RAM?

The cheapest way to improve your server's performance is to add more RAM. RAM is thousands of times faster than hard-disk memory, so the less your Samba server has to use the hard drive, the better. The easy rule here is to find out the maximum amount of memory you can put in your server, and fill 'er up.

Linux and other UNIXes use the utility of *swap space*. (Windows calls it *virtual memory*.) When something in RAM (a program, or a file) isn't needed right away, it gets copied to the hard drive, so the RAM is freed up for other, more urgent uses. That way, you can run multiple applications (or open lots of files) at the same time, more than you could just using the installed RAM.

Now, what happens when a program needs something from that bit of RAM that was copied to the hard drive? Linux is smart enough to tell the program to wait for a moment while it retrieves that information from the hard drive and delivers it to the RAM. However, that can slow down the server enough for someone to notice. Now your Samba server is no longer as fast as your RAM, but as slow as your hard drive.

You can't avoid the application of swap space (you need it to run your server), but the more RAM you have, the less often active programs and files have to be written to the hard drive. In other words, the more RAM you have, the faster your Samba server appears to your users, and the happier they will be (which will make you happy).

So, if you can't afford to maximize the server's RAM, how much do you actually need? Perhaps you need justification from the purchasing department to buy RAM. For starters, your operating system manual (or box) should tell you what you need for RAM. Then, the smbd daemon takes about 700KB, the nmbd daemon takes about 300KB, and all connected users gets their own smbd daemon. So, if you figure 1MB of RAM for all users who can connect at the same time, you're doing well. Finally, you would want to add RAM for any other applications you plan on running. For example, SWAT and Webmin start at about 0.5MB of RAM.

To see how your memory is being used on your Linux server, type **free** at the prompt. The output of free tells you how much RAM you have, how much is being used, and how much is free. As long as you have free memory, RAM is not your bottleneck.

How are your hard drives?

After you verify that you have enough RAM, look at your hard drives. Here are a couple of general principals to follow.

If you have the option, SCSI drives are usually faster and much more reliable than comparable IDE drives (although they cost more). Figure out how much you would lose if your Samba server were to crash because of a hard-drive failure and then decide whether the additional cost of SCSI is worth it.

Secondly, try to arrange your hard drives so that the load is shared. If you have two busy departments (or two busy users), try to put them on separate hard drives. Or, you could put your user files on one hard drive and Linux on the other, which also provides the benefit of being able to upgrade or replace the Linux operating system without affecting user's files.

Are your network cards (NICs) up to snuff?

A final hardware consideration is your NICs (network interface cards). Choose the most efficient ones you can find. Again, any specific recommendations we could make would be out of date in 6 months, but if you stick with cards that are advertised for server use, you should be okay.

Tweaking Samba Parameters

Many Samba parameters can increase (or decrease) your performance. Unfortunately, the complete book on how every Samba performance option reacts with every other Samba performance option for every network in the world hasn't been written yet, so all we can do is offer hints and tips and let you try them to see which ones work best. In the end, to get the best performance, you need to try a few different settings.

Oplocks

Imagine what would happen if every time you needed to call someone, you had to borrow a phone book, make your call, and then return the phone book without writing down the number. Although your whiteboard might look a lot cleaner, you would spend more time running back and forth to borrow the phone book than you would calling people.

Now, if you could write the frequently-called phone numbers on your whiteboard, assuming they don't change very often, you would be *locally caching* the phone numbers. You could make calls much quicker and become much more efficient.

Samba has a way to tell clients, "Hey, take this information and write it down, and no one else is going to change it while you have it." The client then doesn't have to keep requesting the same information over and over again, and Samba doesn't have to keep sending the same information over and over again. You can do this with an *oplock,* which is short for opportunistic lock. If you enable oplocks on your server, you can improve performance significantly.

By default, oplocks are enabled. With SWAT, you can verify that oplocks are turned on by going to the Globals page and selecting Advanced View. Scroll down to the Locking Options (near the bottom of the page) and verify that oplocks are set to yes.

If you're not using SWAT, ensure that the global section of the smb.conf file includes the following line:

```
oplocks = yes
```

Level2 oplocks

Starting with Samba 2.0.5, the Samba team has added a new kind of oplock: level2 oplocks. Level2 oplocks have been designed for shares that contain mostly executable files. They work best if the files are only going to be read and never written to. A good example of this kind of share would be a network drive where you are sharing an office suite. Users read the program files from the network drive but save their work on a different drive. Because the use of level2 oplocks is a new option, it is turned off by default.

Although you can set level2 oplocks in the global section of the smb.conf file, the Samba team recommends that you set them individually for each share. (However, if you were setting up a Samba application server that people couldn't write to, you could set it globally.) Setting level2 oplocks for any shares that would benefit from them is a good compromise between performance and the need to write to a share.

To set level2 oplocks for a specific share in SWAT, go to the Shares page and choose the share you want to change. In that share, select Advanced View. You find level2 oplocks near the bottom, in the Locking Options section. Set level2 oplocks to yes to enable.

If you're not using SWAT, add the line `level2 oplocks = true` for each share on which you want to enable level2 oplocks.

Sync commands

When a Windows client sends a message, Samba uses the `sync` commands to make sure that the file in RAM matches the file on the hard drive. This command doesn't slow down a Windows client very much, so Windows clients call it often. However, because a Linux server uses `sync` differently, it can slow down a server dramatically. Samba uses the `strict sync` option to specify whether Samba does syncs when Windows clients request them.

Because of the poor performance that can result when the Samba server performs syncs at a Windows client's request, syncs are not allowed by default, so the `strict sync` parameter is set to no. If your Samba server is running slower than expected, check this setting.

To check the `strict sync` parameter in SWAT, go to the Shares page, select a share, and click Advanced View. Scroll down to Tuning Options and verify that `strict sync` is set to no.

If you're not using SWAT, add the line `strict sync = no` to the global section of your smb.conf file.

Socket options

You can also increase performance by using Samba's socket options. Socket options optimize Samba's network communication. A detailed description of all the socket options would be suitable for a TCP/IP wizard, but we can mention a few that have increased Samba performance for many people.

Here are a few default socket options: TCP_NODELAY SO_RCVBUF=8192 and SO_SNDBUF=8192. We strongly recommend that you leave these alone. In fact, the socket option TCP_NODELAY has been known to double server read performance.

If you are on a wide-area network (WAN), adding the socket option IPTOS_THROUGHPUT can increase your performance.

If you are on a more compact, smaller local-area network (LAN), you can try adding the socket option IPTOS_LOWDELAY.

Access the socket options field in SWAT by going to the Globals page and look under Tuning Options. Keep the defaults there, and add the options you want. If you are not using SWAT, you need to add any socket options to the line that starts with `socket options` = in the global section of the smb.conf file.

Chapter 11

Working with Complex Networks

S ooner or later, you may discover that your network has grown into an unwieldy beast. Or perhaps you've joined your small, cozy network to a bigger one.

After you have more than ten computers on a network, you cannot easily coordinate all the necessary information by hand. For example, trying to remember ten different IP addresses is nearly impossible, but remembering ten names is fairly easy.

For computers, the opposite is true: A computer has no trouble remembering and coordinating ten IP addresses. The Windows Internet Name Service (WINS) was designed for just this reason: This database runs on a computer that coordinates computer names and resources with IP addresses. With WINS running, you can refer to computers by names instead of IP addresses, which should make you and your users much happier. Of course, Samba works well with the WINS server, or it can even *be* a WINS server.

Another issue with larger networks is that you often need to divide them into smaller subnetworks, or *subnets*. The TCP/IP network protocol usually allows only 254 computers on a network before you have to subdivide the group into subnets. On a more practical level, the network becomes much easier to administer if you use subnets. Also, the network performance can really suffer if you don't divide your networks into smaller subnets because of frequent broadcast messages and the resulting network traffic. After you divide your network into subnets, you'll probably need to access computers in other subnets, yet another handy function of Samba.

In this chapter, we explain how to configure Samba so it plays nicely with a WINS server, as well as how to configure Samba so it functions as a WINS server. We also describe the ins and outs of setting up and using subnets in your Samba/Windows network.

Working with the Windows Internet Name Service (WINS)

If your network has more than one subnet, you need a way to let clients on the first subnet access servers on the second subnet. The Windows solution for the problem of multiple subnets is a WINS server. A WINS server helps bring order to a large network composed of many subnets. One WINS server can keep track of each client, the client's IP address, and the subnet to which that the client belongs. This is handy when you're trying to connect to a server that is on a different subnet.

With a WINS server, clients and servers on different subnets also can talk to each other. Without a WINS server, clients and servers on different subnets are isolated, unable to talk to each other. Because a WINS server also records the subnet on which each client is located, it enables intersubnet communication.

Additionally, a WINS server cuts down on network traffic. Without a WINS server, each client broadcasts its IP address and name and maintains a database of other client names and IP addresses. With enough clients and servers, the network becomes crowded just handling this routine name-broadcasting traffic. With a WINS server, each client communicates with the WINS server, letting the WINS server catalog the name and IP address. When a client wants to know about another client or server, it queries the WINS server.

You can use your Samba server as a WINS server. Windows NT Server and Windows 2000 Server also come with WINS server capability. One difference between the two, for now, is that NT allows for a backup WINS server while Samba does not have that functionality, yet. Therefore, you have a little less redundancy if you use Samba as a WINS server. But because Samba runs on very reliable operating systems, the issue of redundancy matters more in theory than in practice.

Making Samba use a WINS server

If you already have a WINS server on the network, you should make Samba use that WINS server to correlate names and IP addresses and see clients and servers on different subnets. By default, Samba does not use a WINS server, so you need to add the `wins server` parameter to the smb.conf file. The format is `wins server = IP Address`, where the IP address is that of the WINS server.

To make Samba use a WINS server with SWAT, click the Globals icon, scroll to the bottom of the page, and enter the IP address of the WINS server in the appropriate field. Click Commit Changes and you're done.

You must restart Samba for these changes to take effect. (On Red Hat Linux, type **/etc/rc.d/init.d/snb restart**.)

Configuring Samba as a WINS server

If you don't have a WINS server but want one to make sense of your network, you can turn Samba into a WINS server. First, check the `wins server` parameter to make sure Samba is not already using a WINS server. It should be set to none, or it should not be in the smb.conf file. In SWAT, you find this parameter on the Globals page. If `wins server` is set to the IP address of the Samba server, you could confuse your Samba server; this is why you set `wins server` to none.

Next, configure Samba as the WINS server by setting the `wins support` parameter to yes. In SWAT, you change the pull-down setting for wins support to yes. Or, if you are editing the smb.conf file, add the line `wins support = yes` to the global section. If you're using SWAT, Commit Changes.

Then, restart Samba to make the changes take effect. After Samba restarts, configure your clients to use Samba as your WINS server. (See Chapter 4 for details.)

Configuring Samba as a WINS proxy

One final option for Samba is to use a WINS proxy. If you cannot bear the idea of configuring all your clients to use a WINS server, or perhaps you want to change the clients over gradually while still reaping the benefits of a WINS server immediately, you can set up Samba as a WINS server proxy.

Because name queries can't get past a subnet without a WINS server, you need a Samba server in each subnet to act as a WINS proxy. Still, configuring one server per subnet is easier than configuring 20 clients per subnet.

Each Samba server that acts as a WINS proxy forwards name queries from the clients on the subnet to the WINS server. It then returns the replies to the clients. To configure a Samba server as a WINS server, you must configure the Samba server to use a WINS server (the `wins server` parameter) or be a WINS server (the `wins support` parameter).

Next, set the `wins proxy` parameter to yes, either by changing the property in the Globals section of SWAT or by editing the smb.conf file. After you make the changes and restart Samba, naming queries that can't be answered in the local subnets should forward to the WINS server.

Configuring Samba to use DNS to resolve WINS queries

One more parameter can affect the WINS server. You can configure Samba to send queries to a DNS server (the Internet-wide naming service) if the WINS server cannot resolve the naming queries.

First, you need to have DNS working on your server. It's best if you are directly connected to a DNS server; otherwise, you might be dialing up your DNS server every time someone mistypes a computer name.

If you're sure your DNS connection can handle these frequent naming queries (your network administrator can tell you, but you should be safe if you have a DSL, ISDN, cable, or T1 connection), set the `dns proxy` parameter to yes. You find the parameter to use DNS for WINS queries on the Globals page in SWAT as a toggle between yes (enabled) and no (disabled). Or, you can set `dns proxy = yes` in the smb.conf file. Commit your changes or save the file and restart Samba.

If you are using DNS proxying, Samba may stop until it gets a response from the DNS server. If you have a slow connection to your DNS server, or the DNS server is slow, your Samba performance may really suffer.

Setting up Subnets and Browsing

If a network gets too big for easy administration, you can break it down into multiple subnetworks (subnets). For example, you could create multiple subnets along organizational lines. Windows NT uses its workgroups and domains to break a network into handy, easily administered sections. Underneath a Samba network, you'll find that TCP/IP has to break computers into different networks (subnets) if you have only slightly more than 250 computers on one network, for class C networks.

Windows/Samba networking enables you to separate the network into other modules called workgroups or domains. Whether you use workgroups or domains depends on the network model you choose. Workgroups are autonomous groups of computers, while domains are more centralized and have a domain controller. For more information, see the sidebar "Workgroup or domain?" in Chapter 4.

To cut down on extra network traffic and impose a little stability, Windows networking has something called a Master Browser for each workgroup or domain. It isn't a Web browser but rather a machine that contains a list of all the computers and resources in the Network Neighborhood.

Setting subnet parameters for Samba

Many Samba options can affect how your Samba server appears in the
Network Neighborhood. You can specify the workgroup in which you want
to put the Samba server, how to display it to someone browsing the Network
Neighborhood, which shares people can see, and how those shares are
described.

What network do you want Samba to use?

Samba has the bad tendency of using the wrong network port for sharing
files, in particular the loopback port (which has an IP address of 127.0.0.1).
That means the Samba server is only sharing files and printers with itself,
which might be a toddler's definition of sharing but it sure isn't ours.

You can easily fix this baffling behavior with the `interfaces` parameter. Set the
`interfaces` parameter to the IP address of the server. The `interfaces` parameter is a global parameter, which means you find it in the Global section of the
smb.conf file. For SWAT, it's under the Globals icon, about four lines down. If you
change this setting with SWAT, don't forget to click Commit Changes.

After you add the correct interface, restart Samba to make it read the new
interfaces value.

Is Samba using the wrong network? Look for these signs:

✔ Everything appears fine in the smb.conf configuration file.

✔ You can't see the Samba server in the Network Neighborhood.

✔ You can ping and telnet to the Samba server.

You can determine which network Samba is using with `testparm` and `grep`.
The following line runs `testparm` and sends the output to `grep`, which looks
for the network interface lines in the smb.conf file. Press Enter twice (once
for each command).

```
terrapin# testparm | grep interfaces

interfaces = 127.0.0.1
bind interfaces only = No
```

Hm, the Samba server on terrapin is "sharing" through the loopback port
(which isn't sharing at all). Changing the `interfaces` line to point to the correct network interface (interfaces = 192.168.11.5) provides this result:

```
terrapin# testparm | grep interfaces

interfaces = 192.168.11.5
bind interfaces only = No
```

Ah, everything looks much better now.

In which workgroup do you want your server?

With the `workgroup` Samba parameter, you can specify the workgroup in which your Samba Server appears. Match the workgroup name with the default workgroup name of your Windows clients so your users can easily connect to the Samba server.

You set the `workgroup` parameter in the Global section of the smb.conf file. In SWAT, click Globals and then fill in the Workgroup field. Commit Changes and restart Samba for the change to take effect.

What do you want to show in the Network Neighborhood?

With your Samba server, you have lots of discretion as to what you want to show in the Network Neighborhood. You can show everything on your server, show certain things, or hide everything.

Hiding with the browsable parameter

To show a share on your server, set the `browsable` (or `browseable` — for this parameter, spelling doesn't count) parameter to yes. To hide a share (it's still there; you just can't see it), set the value to no.

The default for this parameter is yes, so if you do nothing, shares will be visible by default.

The following example shows a share that is hidden because `browsable = no`, but you can still access it by typing the whole share path:

```
[lucky]
comment = test share for Lucky
path = /home/lucky
browsable = no
```

You wouldn't want to use this for security, but you could perhaps use it to remove some shares from a view for the sake of clarity.

Set the `browsable` parameter in each service. In SWAT, click the Shares button and then select the share you want to modify from the pull-down list next to Choose Share. Clicking Choose Share displays the Samba parameters for that share. `Browsable` is about a page down, listed under Browse Options. Commit Changes and restart Samba.

Hiding all shares by default with the browsable parameter

If you want to hide all the shares on your Samba server by default, set `browsable = no` in the global section of the smb.conf file. You can then show any desired shares with `browsable = yes` in that specific share section.

Showing all the printers with Load Printers

If you have a printers section in your smb.conf file, and you have Load Printers set to yes in the Global section of smb.conf, all the printers listed in the /etc/printcap file will be listed. If you don't have a printers section, this setting does nothing.

If you set Load Printers to no, only printers specifically mentioned with their own section should appear.

Describing what you're sharing

You can have a more orderly network by clearly describing what services you're sharing. For example, your users will know that the share labeled Customer Accounts is where they would go for information about the customers, while the one labeled Printer Drivers is where they go to download printer drivers.

Clear share descriptions can make your life easier, too. If you tell your users that they need to upgrade their antivirus software, and the files are in the Antivirus directory, it's a lot easier to find if one of the shares is labeled Antivirus.

NetBIOS name

Each computer requires a name so that it appears in the Network Neighborhood. If you use DNS, Samba uses your server's DNS host name by default. If you're not using DNS, this field is blank, and Samba uses your server's host name. If you want to use a different, perhaps more descriptive, name, you can use the NetBIOS name parameter.

The NetBIOS name can be no longer than 15 alphanumeric characters, including most of the punctuation marks (except * and ?).

If you want to change this setting using SWAT, set the NetBIOS name in the Globals section of SWAT, a few lines down. If you're not using SWAT, set the NetBIOS name in the Global section of your smb.conf file.

Server string

You use the server string parameter to describe the Samba server. It appears next to the server in the list of computers in the Network Neighborhood and also in the Properties menu. The server string parameter also has three macros defined for it:

- ✔ %v: The Samba version number
- ✔ %h: The hostname of the Samba server
- ✔ %L: The NetBIOS name of the Samba server

For example, with a server string of Samba %v, running on %h, for the Samba server running on the machine named olorin, you might see Samba 2.0.5a, running on olorin in the Network Neighborhood.

Because you are limited to 15 characters in the NetBIOS name, use the `server string` to offer a description of the Samba server.

In SWAT, set the `server string` in the Globals section, a few lines down from the top. If you need to set a `server string` without using SWAT, you can find this parameter in the Global section of your smb.conf file.

NetBIOS alias

You may want to make your Samba server appear as several separate Samba servers in the Network Neighborhood. Perhaps you have one large, fast Samba server, but three different groups access it, and you want each group to have its own apparent server for administrative simplicity. Or perhaps you want a second server for testing purposes.

To set the NetBIOS alias in SWAT, use the Advanced View of the Globals page, where it will be just a few lines down. Otherwise, set this parameter in the Global section of the smb.conf file.

For example, set the NetBIOS alias to `mithrandir stormcrow` in SWAT (or use the line `netbios alias = mithrandir stormcrow` in the smb.conf file) to cause two additional Samba servers to appear in the Network Neighborhood: mithrandir and stormcrow.

Comment

You use the Comment field to describe each share when it is displayed in the Network Neighborhood. You don't see this comment until you connect to the server, though. Choose a descriptive comment for each share.

To enter a comment in SWAT, click the Shares button and then select the share you want to modify from the Choose Share pull-down list. You find the comment in the first field of the Base Options.

To set this parameter in the smb.conf file, just add a line like `comment = This is the comment` to the specific share.

Understanding browser elections

As we mention in the section "Setting up Subnets and Browsing," earlier in this chapter, for each workgroup or NT domain, one computer maintains the browse list (the list of resources available for Windows networking). Whenever a computer starts, it sends a message to the network, and the master browser picks up the message and adds the computer to the browse list it maintains. Also, the master browser sends out the browse list to a backup browser so computers in the workgroup or domain can switch to the backup browser if the master browser gets shut down.

The main reason for a master browser is to cut down on the amount of network traffic. With just one computer (and a backup) maintaining a browse list, no need exists for every computer on the network to send out a message to every other computer on the network.

Microsoft Windows networking has a complicated formula for determining which computer becomes the master browser in a workgroup or domain. This method counts the level of the operating system (newer ones count for more) and how long it has been running, among other options. Samba lets you decide whether you want your Samba server to be the master browser by enabling you to set an election value.

How to count an election

The Microsoft browser election process is very complex. You first match operating system levels and then move on to other comparisons as tie-breakers. Fortunately, Samba lets you rig the elections to win, or lose, depending on how you have your network configured.

A master browser election starts as a result of three conditions: a browsing client cannot contact a master browser, a backup browser tries to update its browse list and cannot contact a master browser, or a preferred master browser starts and forces an election.

To count an election, each operating system gets a numeric value. Windows NT Server 4.0 has a value of 33, Windows NT Workstation 4.0 has a value of 17, and Windows 95/98 has a value of 1.

The highest value wins the election, so you can win an election (and avoid the complex tie-breaking process) simply by setting your operating system value greater than 34. You might want to do this if your Samba server is going to be the fastest and most reliable server on your network and you're not running an NT domain. If you are running your Samba server in an NT domain, you can still set your Samba server to be a master browser, but you must take care that it doesn't interfere with the domain master browser (which must be the primary domain controller, also).

Rigging an election with Samba parameters

If you want your Samba server to become the master browser, just set a few Samba parameters. Put your Samba server into the running with the `local master` parameter and then force an election with `preferred master`. Finally, set the OS level to 34 (to be higher than Windows NT 4.0 Server's 33) and set `local master` to yes.

Running for office with local master

You set the `local master` parameter to yes if you want your Samba server to attempt to become a local master browser when it starts. If you set `local master` to no, Samba will not try to become a master browser, but it can start an election if it doesn't find one. The default for `local master` is yes.

Because `local master` is a global parameter, you set it in on the Globals page of SWAT, under the Browse Options section. If you're not using SWAT, set it in the Global section of the smb.conf file.

Becoming the favorite candidate with preferred master

The `preferred master` parameter is a global setting for when you want your Samba server to be the master browser for a workgroup. If you set `preferred master` to yes, when your Samba server starts, it forces a browser election.

Winning (or losing) the election with OS level

The `OS level` parameter is the Samba setting that tells what version of Windows Samba will pretend to be for browser elections. Remember, the highest value wins the election, and a value of 34 beats Windows NT 4.0 Server's value of 33, while 18 beats Windows NT 4.0 Workstation but loses to Windows NT Server. The default value is 0, which means Samba always loses if you don't change the value.

A good general-purpose value for the `OS level` is 17. With that setting, the Samba server won't interfere with NT servers (which can cause problems in an NT domain) and is equal to the Windows NT workstations.

`OS level` is a global parameter, which you set on the Globals page of SWAT or in the Global section of the smb.conf file.

Working with other subnets

In previous sections of this chapter, we describe how you can break a Windows-based network into workgroups and domains for human convenience. If a network has too many computers, TCP/IP, the protocol on which a Windows/Samba network is built, must break the network into different subnetworks (subnets). Technically speaking, the subnet assignments result from the class of TCP/IP network you use and the value of the subnet mask.

For the examples we describe in this section, we use two subnetworks: 192.168.10.0 and 192.168.11.0. The subnet masks are 255.255.255.0. Each class C subnetwork has exactly 254 valid addresses. So when you get more than 254 computers, you have to expand to a different subnet. Ideally, you put computers of similar use on the same subnet. For example, you might put Accounting on 192.168.11.10.0, and Human Resources on 192.168.11.0.

Larger class networks can have larger numbers of computers in a subnet, though it's common to set this value to 254.

For a particular subnet, the broadcast address ends in 255. For the 192.168.10.0 subnet, the broadcast address is 192.168.10.255. If a computer wants to send a message to everyone on the subnet, it sends the message to 192.168.10.255.

Why would a computer want to send out the same message to as many as 254 other computers? For the same reason a person would shout in a room of 254 people: to get attention. Typically, a computer uses a broadcast messages to tell the network what kind of computer it is or if it's looking for another computer.

Enter the router. You can think of a *router* as a computer that connects two different networks and forwards traffic to the network. If the router straddles networks 192.168.10.0 and 192.168.11.0, a computer on network 192.168.10.0 that wanted to contact a computer on the 192.168.11.0 network would send packets to the router, and the router would forward that packet to network 192.168.11.0.

To keep networks from quickly overflowing with shouts, broadcast packets typically don't get forwarded. That cuts down considerably on network traffic, but if a computer shouts "Who are you?" and only gets answers from computers on its own subnet, it will never learn anything about other nets. At this point, each subnet is cut off from every other subnet. Microsoft Windows networking gets around this via *browsers*, computers that become the designated "goto" computer for each workgroup or domain. If a workgroup or domain spans a subnetwork (the workgroup or domain has members on two or more different subnetworks), each subnetwork has its own master browser.

So how does Samba fit into this? If your Samba server won't be a local master browser for this workgroup or subnet, you don't have to worry because the master browser should handle it. However, if you're going to use your Samba server as the local master browser, you need to make sure your Samba server wins the election first. (See "Rigging an election with Samba parameters," earlier in this chapter.)

But if your Samba server is the local master browser, how does Samba help a client on one subnet see a client on another subnet? Samba can span subnets in a few different ways. You can have your Samba server use a WINS server. You can have Samba send broadcast messages to a different subnetwork. Or, you can have Samba send messages directly to a remote master browser.

Spanning subnets with a WINS server

One way of spanning subnets is to have your Samba server send and receive remote subnet information from a WINS server. The WINS server will tell each local master browser the location of the domain master browser. Then, each local master browser can query the domain master browser for information about remote subnets. To do this, set up your Samba server as the local master browser and then set the `wins server` parameter to point to the WINS server. Set `local master` and `preferred master` to yes, set `domain master` to no, and set the `OS level` high enough to win elections. Finally, set the `wins server` parameter to the IP address (or DNS name if your network runs DNS) of the WINS server. All these parameters are global parameters, so set them in the Globals section of SWAT or in the Global section of the smb.conf file.

Spanning subnets with broadcasts

Another way to send information to remote subnets is to have your Samba server send announcements or broadcasts to the remote subnets. This method might not always work because your routers connecting your subnets might not allow broadcast messages to pass.

If you want to try this method, use the `remote announce` parameter, which tells Samba to tell the remote subnet about itself. You need to include the workgroup name and the broadcast address for the network.

For example, to send broadcast announcements to network 192.168.2.0 about the workgroup named testers, you would add 192.168.2.255/testers to the remote announce field on the Globals page of SWAT, because 192.168.2.255 is the broadcast address for the 192.168.2.0 network. You find the remote announce field under the Miscellaneous Options on the Globals page.

Now, nothing is coming back from the remote subnet about the members of that subnet. To resolve that issue, you could have a Samba server in the remote subnet send the browse list to this subnet using `remote announce`. This would work if all your master browsers were Samba servers, but if all your master browsers are Samba servers, it's easier to exchange remote subnet browsing lists with the `remote browse sync` parameter, as we describe next.

Synchronizing subnets

If you have a network in which all the master browsers are Samba servers, you can use the `remote browse sync` parameter to keep browser lists synchronized across the network. You can set this parameter to the broadcast address of the remote subnets or directly to the IP addresses of the Samba servers.

In SWAT, set the `remote browse sync` parameter on the Globals page, under the Miscellaneous Options section. To synchronize browse lists with the Samba server at 192.168.2.24, you would fill in 192.168.2.24 in the remote browse sync field.

Spanning subnets directly

Finally, you can send a browse list directly to a master browser if you know the IP address. To send a browse list, use the `remote announce` parameter, but instead of using a broadcast address (which ends in 255), you would use the exact IP address of the master browser.

If you want to have your Samba server send a browse list directly to a master browser in a remote workgroup but you're not sure of the IP address, you can use `nmblookup` to identify the master browser of the workgroup. You would add the name of the workgroup, with #1B appended, to find the local master browser, or append with #1D to find the domain master browser. For example, to find the domain master browser for the domain ENGINEERS, you would type this command:

```
# nmblookup ENGINEERS#1D
```

Chapter 12

Working with Domains

*B*y using domains, you can organize and control larger numbers of Windows clients. Microsoft recommends a domain network architecture if you have more than 10 client computers. In this chapter, we show you how to use Samba as a domain controller. We also explain how to have Samba join a Windows NT domain.

What's the Difference between Domains and Workgroups?

Domains are similar to workgroups but are more complex. If you use a domain-based network, user verification at logon happens at the server, not at the client workstation, which leads to fewer errors. Also, users can *roam* in a domain, which means they can log on to the domain from any client computer and have the same network mappings and applications.

On the other hand, if your Windows clients use workgroups, logons are not authenticated. If you mistype your user name, Windows creates a new user for you with the mistyped name, and you won't have a clue as to why you can't log on to your network shares. With a domain, you would be warned that the user doesn't exist.

After you log on and are authenticated by a properly configured domain, you should be able to connect to all shares and servers for which you have permissions without having to supply another password. Compare this to a workgroup environment, where you need to supply a password for each computer you want to access. You might need a different password for each computer — a major hassle if you needed to access several different machines.

If you use workgroups and you configure your computer with customized drive mappings, they stay on that computer. If your computer breaks down and you need to use another Windows client, you cannot access your customized drive mappings. With a domain network architecture, your drive mappings stay on the server and follow you around, which can come in handy if you store applications and data files on network drives. If you support many identical Windows clients, such as in a computer lab or call center, you can use domains to ensure that users see their same desktop and applications, no matter which computer they use for logging on to the network.

Samba interacts with Windows domains with varying degrees of success. To a Windows 95/98 client, Samba looks just like a domain controller. For Windows NT clients, Samba 2.0 does not work as a domain controller, but the beta version of Samba (2.1) does. Windows 2000 does not offer domain controller functionality yet, but it is planned for future releases.

Using Samba as a Domain Controller for Windows 95/98 Clients

Samba works very well with Windows 95/98 domains and can even function as a Windows 95/98 domain controller. You don't even need to download the beta version of Samba; the regular version of Samba does this just fine.

Setting up your Samba server as a Windows 95/98 domain controller is a two-step process. First, you set up your Samba server. Then, you set up each Windows 95/98 client.

Setting up the Samba server as a Windows 95/98 domain controller

The first step in using Samba as a domain controller for Windows 95/98 clients is to set up the Samba server as a domain controller. You must configure the Samba configuration file to make your Samba server the master browser, allow domain logons, and set the security level to the user, server, or domain level. Then, you have to add a special share called *netlogon* to which the Windows 95/98 clients connect.

Removing the local password files for extra security

Windows 95/98 clients can cache passwords locally. This feature was designed as a convenience for users, enabling them to connect to different computers without having to remember each password. However, in a properly configured domain, you should need to log on to the domain only once. Thereafter, the server authenticates you when you access other computers. You really don't need the local password cache anymore.

Also, the local password cache is a (small) security hole in your network. Windows stores the password caches in a file with the extension .PWL in the C:\Windows directory, and they

are poorly encrypted. You are better off without them if you run a domain-based network.

It isn't hard to get rid of the local password caches, although you have to edit the registry. First, delete all the files with the .PWL extension in the C:\Windows directory.

After you delete the .PWL files, add the following setting to the client's registry:

```
[HKLM\Software\Microsoft\Windows\
CurrentVersion\Policies\Network]
"DisablePwdCaching"=dword:00000001
```

For details about editing the Windows registry, see Chapter 9.

Here are the steps for setting up the Samba server as a Windows 95/98 domain controller:

1. **Configure the global section of the Samba configuration file to make your Samba server a domain controller. Make sure you have the security level set to user, server, or domain, and set the** `allow domain logon` **parameter to yes.**

   In SWAT, set these options on the Globals page. The Security parameter is the first parameter under Security Options. To check `allow domain logon`, go to the Advanced View of the Globals page. In the Advanced View, near the bottom under Logon Options, set the `domain logon` field to yes. Click Commit Changes to update the Samba configuration file.

2. **Make sure the Samba server becomes the master browser for the domain.**

   This is the same as making sure the Samba server becomes the master browser for the subnet. Set the following parameters in the global section of the Samba configuration file to make Samba start and win browser elections:

   ```
   os level = 64
   domain master = yes
   local master = yes
   preferred master = yes
   ```

If you are using SWAT, set these parameters on the Globals page in the Browse Options section of the Basic (or Advanced) View.

Remember to click Commit Changes if you changed any of the values.

3. **Add a share called netlogon because Windows 95/98 clients expect to see this share when they log on to a domain controller.**

   The share does not need to have any data; the clients just need to be able to connect to it. Here is a sample netlogon share:

   ```
   [netlogon]
   path = /export/smb/net/netlogon
   read only = yes
   guest ok = yes
   ```

   If you are using SWAT to add the netlogon share, go to the Shares page, type **netlogon** in the field next to Create Share, and click Create Share.

4. **Click Commit Changes to save your work.**

5. **Save the additions and changes you made to the Samba configuration file by restarting Samba. If you are using SWAT, go to the Status page and click the Restart smbd and Restart nmbd buttons.**

Setting up the Windows 95/98 client

After your Samba server is working as a domain controller for Windows 95/98 clients, you need to set up the clients. Follow these steps to enable a Windows 95/98 client to log on to a domain controller:

1. **Open the Network control panel by right-clicking Network Neighborhood and choosing Properties from the pop-up menu.**

2. **Highlight the Client for Microsoft Networks and click Properties.**

3. **Check the Log on to Windows NT Domain box and type the name of the domain (which is the same name as the workgroup).**

4. **Save your changes and reboot the Windows 95/98 client.**

The next time you log on to this client, the logon screen will have an extra, third field for the domain.

Setting up permanent drive mappings and roaming profiles

After you get your Samba server working as a Windows domain controller, you can add some nifty features to make life easier for you and your users.

You can use the `logon script` parameter to execute a batch file that maps your drive letters a certain way so you can configure applications to always use certain shares. You can also institute roaming profiles so your users can customize their desktop, log on to a different computer, and still get their customized desktop. These two options work best when you have many identical clients and the users have similar application requirements, such as in a computer lab or a call center.

Setting up permanent drive mappings

One of the advantages of a domain-oriented network is that you can give your users permanent drive mappings. You do that by setting up a batch file to map the drives when users first connect. You can do other things in a batch file, too, such as download antivirus updates.

To start this batch file when a user connects, you use the `logon script` parameter in the netlogon share. The following batch file, named map.bat, maps the same directories for each user when a user connects, regardless of the Windows 95/98 client from which the user connects:

```
echo Welcome to the Shire domain
echo Mapping home drive
net use f: \\bilbo\homes
echo Mapping bypass drive
net use g: \\bilbo\bypass
echo Mapping ZIP drive
net use h: \\bilbo\zip
```

This batch file uses the `net` command. For more information about the `net` command, see the sidebar titled "The `net` command: DOS in a Windows network."

You call the map.bat file with the appropriate line in the netlogon share. The following netlogon share calls the map.bat batch file when a user logs on:

```
[netlogon]
path = /export/smb/net/netlogon
read only = yes
logon script = map.bat
guest ok = yes
```

To make sure that your syntax and line endings are correct (Linux and DOS/Windows use different line endings), create and test your batch file on a Windows client before adding it to the netlogon share.

Unfortunately, SWAT does not yet understand the `logon script` option, so you have to add this option with another method, such as editing the smb.conf file with a text editor.

The net command: DOS in a Windows network

Even in a Windows networking world, you can still use DOS commands. And the most versatile DOS command with respect to Windows networking is net. With the right net command, you can verify how your network is configured, how healthy your network is, and you can even connect to network drives.

Windows 95/98, NT, and 2000 all have the net command enabled, with varying amounts of subcommands. To see what net commands your system has, type **net /?**. If you want to see what options a particular command has, type **net option /?**, to see all the options for net use, type **net use /?**.

The most common uses for the net commands are to get information about the network setup while in a DOS window or to use them in a batch file.

To check your current workgroup settings, type **net config** in a DOS window.

To see what computers are available on the network, type **net view**.

To map a network share to a drive letter, apply the net use command. A simple form of this command is net use *drive_letter* *computer**share*. For example, to map the Samba share on the server named slothrop to the f: drive, you would type **net use f: \\slothrop\samba**.

To assign a network printer to an lpt port, the command format is net use *lpt_port* *computer**printer*. So to connect the laserjet on the server frodo to lpt2, you would type **net use lpt2: \\frodo\laserjet**.

Setting up roaming profiles

Another advantage of a domain network is that you can set up roaming profiles. A user can then customize her desktop, log off the computer, log on at a different computer, and get her customized desktop back because it's stored on the domain server. This works great for situations in which users like to customize their desktops but you can't guarantee that they will get the same computer every time they log on to the network.

The individual user settings for a Windows 95/98 client are stored in a registry file named USER.DAT. When you use roaming profiles, the USER.DAT file gets downloaded from the server instead of having to remain on the local hard drive. Thus, as long as you can log on to the domain controller, you can download your USER.DAT file, and therefore your user profile can roam with you.

Setting up roaming user profiles is a two-step process. First, configure the Windows 95/98 client. Then, configure the Samba domain controller.

Configuring the Windows 95/98 client to use roaming profiles

By default, Windows 95/98 clients do not allow individual profiles. But you can easily change that by completing the following steps:

1. **Open the Passwords control panel.**

2. **Click the User Profiles tab.**

3. **To enable individual preferences, select the radio button with the lengthy name that starts with Users Can Customize Their Preferences . . .**

4. **Check the box labeled Include Start Menu and Program Groups . . . if you want the Start menu and program groups customized for each user.**

5. **Click OK and then restart your computer.**

Now, if your Windows 95/98 client is correctly configured to log on to a domain (do you get three fields at the logon screen?), it checks the domain server and the local hard drive for the most recent USER.DAT file to use. When you log off, the Windows client then stores USER.DAT on the domain server. All you have to do now is set up a share for the USER.DAT file on the Samba domain controller.

Configuring the Samba server for roaming profiles

After you configure your Windows client for logging on to a domain controller and you have it set up to use individual user profiles, you need to consider how to store the user profiles. The default behavior is to store each USER.DAT file in the profile subdirectory of each user's home directory. To store the users' profiles in a different directory, use the logon path Samba parameter. The logon path is an option in the global section of the Samba configuration file. In SWAT, you find the logon path option in the Advanced View of the Globals page.

The default value of the logon path parameter is

```
logon path = \\%N\%U\profile
```

This line expands to the following setting:

```
logon path = \\home\user_name
```

Having Samba Join a Windows NT Domain

If your network is already a domain-controlled network and you have Windows NT servers running as domain controllers, you can easily integrate your Samba server into the NT domain.

When you have your Samba server integrated into an existing NT domain, Samba no longer does any password authentication. Instead, the Windows NT domain controllers do the password authentication.

It's not hard to make a Samba server work with an NT domain controller, but you need access to the Windows NT server that is the primary domain controller to let the primary domain controller know about your Samba server. After you add your Samba server to the primary domain controller, make some changes to the Samba configuration file and then have your Samba server join the domain, as we explain in the following sections.

Letting the primary domain controller know about the Samba server

First, you need to inform the Windows NT primary domain controller (PDC) about the Samba server. Using the Server Manager for Domains function on the PDC, add the NetBIOS name of the Samba server to the NT domain.

Setting up the Samba server

After you add the Samba server to the NT domain at the primary domain controller, you need to make some changes to the Samba configuration file and then have the Samba server join the domain.

Changing the Samba server's configuration file

Now that your Samba server has joined the NT domain, you need to make a few changes to the Samba configuration file. Specifically, you need to edit or add four parameters in the global section of the Samba configuration file:

- ✔ security: Set the security parameter to domain — that is, security = domain.

- ✔ workgroup: Set the workgroup parameter to the domain name. For the domain SHIRE, you would use workgroup = SHIRE.

- ✔ password server: You must list the PDC and any backup domain controllers (BDCs) in the password server parameter. For example, if the PDC is named BAGEND and the BDC is named TOOKHALL, the password server line would be password server = BAGEND TOOKHALL.

- ✔ encrypt passwords: The Samba server must be using encrypted passwords. Set this with encrypt passwords = yes.

Samba must be able to resolve the names of the domain controllers. A good way to ensure that Samba can resolve the names of the domain controllers is to add them to the Samba server's /etc/hosts file.

Restart Samba, and you should be on your way. Test that your Samba server has joined the domain with smbclient.

Having the Samba server join the domain

After you add the Samba server to the NT domain at the primary domain controller, you need to have the Samba server join the domain. To join an NT domain from your Samba server, type the following command:

```
# smbpasswd -j domain_name -r PDC_name
```

For example, if SHIRE is the NT domain name, and BAGEND is the NetBIOS name of the primary domain controller for the SHIRE domain, you complete this step by typing the following command

```
# smbpasswd -j SHIRE -r BAGEND
```

If this command executes successfully, you get a confirmation message similar to this example:

```
smbpasswd: Joined domain SHIRE
```

After your Samba server successfully joins this domain, the password is stored in a file named *domainname.Sambaservername*.mac. For example, for the Samba server named BILBO, the filename would be SHIRE.BILBO.mac. The password file for an NT domain is stored in the same directory as the smbpasswd file, which is typically /usr/local/samba/private.

Using Samba as a Windows NT Primary Domain Controller

If you want to make Samba work with Windows NT domains, you need to get the development version of Samba, which is equivalent to version 2.1 at the time of this writing. Because this development version changes so often (several changes daily), you need to use a special software program called CVS to download the latest software and then you need to compile it.

The Samba team recommends against using Samba as an NT primary domain controller because the software is still in the beta stage of development. However, many people use it as such, so if you're in the position where you need a primary domain controller for your NT clients, you can at least consider it. You do, however, need to be comfortable with using some esoteric Linux commands and compiling Samba.

Getting the version of Samba that acts as an NT primary domain controller

Because the version of Samba that supports being an NT primary domain controller is beta software that is being developed daily, you can't download the binaries. Instead, you need to get the latest source code and compile it. Fortunately, the CVS software setup utility fits the bill — it's designed to download newly written source code and keep your source code synchronized with the development software.

The source code for CVS is available on the Web at the following site: http://CVS.samba.org/cgi-bin/CVSweb.

Alternately, you can get the Samba CVS code by using the CVS client at the command line. Before you can download the Samba CVS code, you need a CVS client. If your server doesn't have one, download one from http://www.cyclic.com.

When you finally get a working CVS client, you can use the following command to retrieve the Samba CVS code:

```
# cvs -d :pserver:CVS@samba.org:/CVSroot login
```

When you're prompted for a password, type **cvs**.

After you download the Samba source code with CVS, you need to expand it into a target directory. The following command expands the source code into a directory containing the Samba source code:

```
# cvs -d :pserver:CVS@samba.org:/CVSroot co Samba
```

Next, merge the newest additions to the existing code with the following command:

```
# cvs update -d -p
```

After you merge the code, you can then compile Samba. See Chapter 2 for details about compiling Samba from the source code.

Setting up the Samba server as a Windows NT domain controller

After you obtain a copy of the beta version of Samba that enables Samba to act as an NT primary domain controller, how do you make Samba act as an NT primary domain controller?

Using encrypted passwords

You must set up your Samba server to use encrypted passwords, and the smbpasswd file must have an entry for every user who will connect to the Samba server. This section briefly describes the process, which we cover more thoroughly in Chapter 9.

To make your Samba server use encrypted passwords, you need to add (or modify) two parameters in the global section of the smb.conf file: encrypt passwords and smb passwd file.

Set the encrypt passwords parameter to yes. The smb passwd file parameter must point to the location of the smbpasswd file if the smbpasswd file is not in the default location. The smbpasswd file contains the encrypted passwords in a Windows-networking-formatted fashion.

After you make the changes to the Samba configuration file to enable encrypted passwords, you need to populate the smbpasswd file with encrypted passwords. Fortunately, Samba includes a script to start the smbpasswd file with the contents of the /etc/passwd file. The following line populates the smbpasswd file in /usr/local/etc with the contents of the /etc/passwd file:

```
# cat /etc/passwd | mksmbpasswd.sh > & /usr/local/etc/smbpasswd
```

After you create the smbpasswd file, assign an encrypted password for each user. To do that, you need to be logged on as the superuser. Then, simply type **smbpasswd *username***, and give the password twice.

If you're creating a Samba server from scratch to be used as an NT primary domain controller, you might want to avoid creating and populating the smbpasswd file until after you've added the client access, as we describe in the next section.

If you need a more in-depth treatment of encrypted passwords, refer to Chapter 9.

Adding client access

Next, you must add an account to the Samba server that you plan to use as the primary domain controller for each client that will access it. Basically, you add an account in the /etc/passwd file for each client and add the corresponding entry to the smbpasswd file.

The user name for this client account will be the client's NetBIOS name with a $ appended. For the client smaug, the user name you would add on the Samba server would be smaug$. You have to assign a unique user ID (UID), and because the shell and home directories aren't being used, they can be set to /bin/False and /dev/null.

After you add the client's user account to the /etc/passwd file, you need to add the client to the smbpasswd file. The following command adds the client to the smbpasswd file:

```
# smbpasswd -a -m smaug
```

Modifying the smb.conf file

You must configure three global parameters and add a netlogon share to the Samba configuration file for Samba to be an NT primary domain controller. The three parameters to check are `security`, `workgroup`, and `domain logons`:

- Set the `security` parameter to user.
- Set the `workgroup` parameter to the domain name.
- Set the `domain logons` parameter to yes, to tell the clients that Samba is the primary domain controller.

Next, add the netlogon share. All the Windows clients need to be able to attach to the netlogon share when they first log on. Here is a netlogon share example:

```
[netlogon]
comment = Netlogon share for Windows PDC
path = /usr/local/samba/netlogon
guest ok = no
read only = yes
browseable = yes
locking = no
force create mode = 0644
force directory mode = 0755
write list = rot, @wheel
```

This example includes a few Samba parameters that we do not discuss in previous chapters: `locking`, `force create`, and `force directory mode`. `Locking` causes all client file lock and unlock requests to succeed, regardless of whether those requests actually do succeed. This is a dangerous parameter to use in most situations. The `force create mode` and `force directory mode` parameters set the permissions for any files and directories created by Samba. These three parameters are available in SWAT under the Advanced View for the share.

After you make these changes, restart Samba. When Samba starts up again, it should create a file named *domainname*.SID, usually in /usr/local/samba/ private, with permissions of rw-r--r--. If this file gets changed or corrupted, domain members will not be able to log on, and you will have to add them to the domain again.

Customizing your Samba primary domain controller

After your Samba server is working as a primary domain controller, you can do a few things to make it more useful:

> ✔ Set up a file that maps NT domain user names with Linux user names.
>
> ✔ Set up a batch file to map network drives, so all users have the same drive mappings.
>
> ✔ Enable roaming profiles.

Mapping NT user names to Linux user names

You can set up a file that Samba can use to map an NT domain user name with a Linux name and then reference that file with the domain user map option. The format of this file is one record per line, using the following format:

```
unixusername = [\\domainname\]NTusername
```

The following example maps the UNIX user root to the NT user administrator:

```
root = administrator
```

The following example shows the domain user map parameter referencing the file NTusers in the /usr/local/samba/lib directory.

```
domain user map = /usr/local/samba/lib/NTusers
```

Mapping network drives

With the Samba parameter logon script, you can have a batch file run on the Windows client as soon as a user successfully connects. You can use the batch file to map network drives using the net command. For more information and examples of mapping network drives with a batch file, see the section "Using Samba as a Domain Controller for Windows 95/98 Clients," earlier in this chapter.

Roaming profiles

You can set up roaming profiles on the server as you would set them up for a Windows 95/98 client. See the section "Setting up roaming profiles" earlier in this chapter.

Setting up the Windows NT client

It's easy to set up your Windows NT client to work with an NT domain. Open the Network control panel and click the Identification tab. Click Change and add the domain name. Click OK to join the domain, and you should get a confirmation message.

Windows 2000 Domains

Due to changes Microsoft has made in the network protocol, Windows 2000 clients cannot log on to a Samba primary domain controller. However, the code to enable it should be in the beta version of Samba (2.1).

Part IV
Troubleshooting Samba

The 5th Wave   By Rich Tennant

©RICHTENNANT

"What is it Lassie? Is it Gramps? Is it his hard disk? Is he stuck somewhere, girl? Is he trying to write CGI programs to a Unix server running VRML? What, girl, what?!"

In this part . . .

What, you're having problems? No problem. This part has a plethora of troubleshooting advice. Snafus come in all shapes and sizes and from any number of different sources, so we break down the approach as follows.

The primary players are Linux, Windows, and Samba. Chapter 13 lays out all the Linux and Windows utilities, logs, and techniques for solving pesky little errors and no-ops. If you think Samba might be the culprit, Chapter 14 is all for you.

Also, see Part VI, "The Part of Tens," which includes lots of helpful troubleshooting tips, reminders, and summaries.

Chapter 13

Troubleshooting Samba with Linux and Windows

• •

• •

*T*he first step in troubleshooting Samba is to start at the operating system level, meaning Linux or Windows. In this chapter, we show you how to use various Linux- and Windows-based tools that can help you to trouble-shoot Samba. For example, with the `ping` command, available in both Linux and Windows, you can quickly check to see if two computers can connect over the network. Other commands show you what connections you have to the network. We also show you where to look to verify that the network infor-mation is correct.

Troubleshooting with Linux Utilities

Linux comes with many utilities for troubleshooting a network connection. Two of the most basic are `ifconfig` and `ping`. You use `ifconfig` to config-ure a network connection. You can also use it to show the status of the net-work connections. `Ping` is a very common and useful command for testing network connectivity between two computers.

Checking your network connections with ifconfig

The Linux utility for configuring networking is called ifconfig. Although you usually don't need ifconfig to configure networking because much gets done automatically, you can use ifconfig to get a picture of your Samba server's network interfaces.

To use ifconfig in Linux, just type **ifconfig**. Linux stores ifconfig in the /sbin directory, so if you get a command not found error, try typing **/sbin/ifconfig**.

The following example shows what ifconfig might display on your Samba server:

```
[root@olorin george]# /sbin/ifconfig
eth0  Link encap:Ethernet  HWaddr 00:80:C8:FD:B4:FB
      inet addr:192.168.11.3 Bcast:192.168.11.255 \  Mask:255.255.255.0
      UP BROADCAST RUNNING MULTICAST  MTU:1500  Metric:1
      RX packets:180 errors:0 dropped:0 overruns:0 \ frame:0
      TX packets:194 errors:0 dropped:0 overruns:0 \ carrier:0
      collisions:0 txqueuelen:100
      Interrupt:10 Base address:0xe800

lo    Link encap:Local Loopback
      inet addr:127.0.0.1  Mask:255.0.0.0
      UP LOOPBACK RUNNING  MTU:3924  Metric:1
      RX packets:0 errors:0 dropped:0 overruns:0 \ frame:0
      TX packets:0 errors:0 dropped:0 overruns:0 \ carrier:0
      collisions:0 txqueuelen:0
```

What does this tell you? First, we had to call ifconfig directly from its location, with /sbin/ifconfig, because the path for locating files wasn't set correctly.

Next, the server has two network interfaces: the loopback port (lo) and the network interface card (eth0). Every Linux server has the lo port. And for a server, you need at least one network port, although it might not be named eth0. If your network card doesn't appear, reboot and try /sbin/ifconfig again. If that doesn't do it, consider using a different card or reinstalling your server software.

The second line of each section displays the Internet addresses the network card and the loopback port are using. The network card is using 192.168.11.3, and the loopback port is using 127.0.0.1. The loopback port's address never changes, but check to make sure that the network card's address is what you expect it to be.

Use ifconfig to see that all the network interfaces you expect are available. You can also check that the correct network addresses are being used. You can use ifconfig for other more advanced uses, such as configuring the network interfaces while the Linux server is running, or to gain greater knowledge of what's happening on the network for debugging purposes (but that's beyond the scope of this book).

The syntax for ifconfig might differ somewhat for other UNIX systems. For example, in Solaris, you type **ifconfig –a** to see all the network interfaces. You might need to check the ifconfig man pages for your particular version of UNIX.

Contacting a remote computer with ping

Ping is a very common and useful command for testing network connectivity — so useful and common that you can find it on almost any networked computer. Typically, you use ping to test network connectivity to a computer.

To test connectivity at the most basic level, you need to know the IP address of the computer you want to verify. For example, if you wanted to find out if your Samba server is connected to the computer with the IP address of 192.168.11.5, you would type this command:

```
# ping 192.168.11.5
```

If the network connection is successful (that is, your server can see the computer with the IP address of 192.168.11.5), you should get back something like this:

```
PING 192.168.11.5 (192.168.11.5) from 192.168.11.3 : 56(84) bytes of data.
64 bytes from 192.168.11.5: icmp_seq=0 ttl=255 time=2.5 ms
64 bytes from 192.168.11.5: icmp_seq=1 ttl=255 time=1.4 ms
```

With this output, the two computers can see each other, so if you're having trouble with a Samba connection, it isn't at the basic TCP/IP level. If your screen is filling up with 64 bytes from . . . lines, and you're wondering how to stop them, just press Ctrl+C.

If the two computers can't see each other over the network, you would get output similar to this example:

```
PING 192.168.11.5 (192.168.11.5) from 192.168.11.3 : 56(84) bytes of data.
From olorin (192.168.11.3): Destination Host Unreachable
```

If you're having trouble with a client accessing the Samba server, and ping gives you output like this example, you know that no network connectivity exists between the two computers, and Samba won't work. To determine which of the two computers is having trouble, try to ping a different computer from each one. By using ping to divide and conquer in this way, you can narrow down the location of your network connectivity problem.

Usually, you can also `ping` a computer using its network name. For example, instead of typing **ping 192.168.11.5**, you can type **ping terrapin**. Assuming terrapin has the IP address of 192.168.11.5, these two commands are identical. If you have more than three or four computers on the network, you'll probably come to prefer names over IP addresses.

Sometimes, using `ping` with the IP address works, but using `ping` with the name doesn't. Assuming you have the right name and IP address, the problem rests with either the Linux machine's /etc/hosts table or the naming service (NIS, NIS+, DNS) you use for IP-address-to-hostname lookup. Double-check your /etc/hosts table to make sure it's accurate, or double-check your naming service setup.

Checking who's connected with netstat

Another useful Linux command for diagnosing your network problems is `netstat`. You use `netstat` for looking at active network connections. With this information, you can see what computers are connected to your server, and how.

The following example shows the result of typing **netstat** on the Samba server:

```
[root@olorin george]# netstat
Active Internet connections (w/o servers)
Proto Recv-Q Send-Q Local Address          Foreign \ Address          State
tcp        0      0 olorin:netbios-ssn     liberty:1603 \             ESTABLISHED
tcp        0    126 olorin:Telnet          liberty:1039 \             ESTABLISHED
```

On the fourth line, you can see a netbios-ssn connection to olorin (the Samba server) from liberty (the Windows 98 workstation). Because Samba uses NetBIOS connections, the netbios-ssn connection indicates that someone using the computer named liberty has a Samba connection to this Samba server. If users claim that they're connecting to a Samba server but they're not seeing what they should, you could use `netstat` to verify that they have a NetBIOS connection from their computer to the Samba server.

The fifth line shows that you have a telnet session from liberty to olorin. As this example demonstrates, you can use `netstat` to see how others are connecting to your Samba server.

In addition to verifying connections, you can use `netstat` to count the users who connect. With this information, you can figure out how much RAM your server needs. The following line uses `netstat` and `grep` (with the `-c` option) to count the number of Samba connections to your server:

```
[root@olorin george]# netstat | grep -c netbios
1
```

This command uses `netstat` to list all the connections to the server named olorin. Then, it uses `grep` to get all the lines with netbios in them, and the `-c` option counts the lines that `grep` finds. It looks like olorin has it pretty easy with only one Samba connection to it right now. Try that command in the middle of the day on your Samba server to get an idea of the load it's handling.

Resetting a user's password with passwd

Users forget their passwords. Technically, you could decipher a password from the encrypted one in the system (and a fast workstation might take only about a day to figure it out), but it's much easier just to issue a new one. At the root prompt, type **passwd *username*** and then type the new password and type it a second time to confirm. Then, send the user off with a friendly reminder to please remember that new password.

If you are using encrypted passwords on your Samba server, you will need to reset the password with the `smbpasswd` command. If your password chat is not working correctly in Samba, or you are not using the password chat, you will have to change the password in Linux to match using the `passwd` command.

Checking across routers with traceroute

To test your Samba server's connectivity across a router, use `traceroute`. You won't find `traceroute` in every version of UNIX, but Linux and FreeBSD have this command. Like many other superuser commands, `traceroute` lives in the /usr/sbin directory. So if you can't call it by typing **traceroute**, try **/usr/sbin/traceroute**.

The most basic use of `traceroute` is to see how the network connects to a distant host. Type **traceroute *hostname***, where *hostname* is the name of the distant host you want to trace. You should get back the router address that `traceroute` takes. It can help you make sure you are using the correct router.

If you can't connect, the output from `traceroute` can help you determine where in your network the connection is broken, and you can then tell your network administrator.

You can also use `traceroute` when you are trying to connect a Windows client and a Samba server through a router. If you can't connect with `traceroute`, you won't be able to connect with Samba.

Testing your printer with lptest

If you're having printer problems, you can test the functionality of the printer at the most basic level by using the `lptest` command to send output directly to the printer port. The following example prints 10 lines of 30 characters each and sends those lines to the printer at /dev/lp0 (which corresponds to lpt1 in the Windows world):

```
# lptest 10 30 > /dev/lp0
```

Next, test your printer by sending the output through the /etc/printcap file. Look through your /etc/printcap file for the printer you want to test, and pipe the output of the `lptest` command to it. For the printer lp, you would type this command:

```
# lptest 10 30 | lpr
```

Finally, if you're on a Linux server, you can use `printtool` to send test pages to selected printers. You can send ASCII test pages or a PostScript test page.

Checking Linux Rights

If your users complain of troubles accessing files and directories that they think they should be able to access, check the Linux rights. You can set up Samba to give a user rights to a specific directory, but if you do not have the underlying Linux rights set up correctly, the user cannot use that directory.

You can try to access a specific directory by using the `su` command to switch to a specific user. For example, if frodo was complaining that he could not access his directory, you would first switch to the user frodo by typing **su frodo** as the root user. After you switch to frodo, try to access his directory by typing **cd /home/frodo**. If you get a `permission denied` error, you know the rights aren't set up correctly, and you need to change them so Samba can give the correct access to that directory.

You can also use the `ls` command with the `-l` switch (for a long listing) to double-check rights. The following is a "long" listing of the directories of the home directory on the server olorin, formatted to fit the page:

```
[root@olorin /home]# ls -l
total 32
drwx------  4 bilbo     bilbo  4096 Mar 31 21:42 bilbo
drwx------  4 delilahj  504    4096 Apr  1 09:10 delilahj
drwxr-xr-x  2 root      root   4096 Mar 26 23:37 fn
drwx------  4 root      root   4096 Mar 26 22:34 frodo
drwx------ 16 george    george 4096 Mar 27 07:23 george
drwxrwxr-x  2 root      root   4096 Feb 11 23:56 lucky
drwx------  4 neo       wheel  4096 Mar 26 22:33 neo
drwxr-xr-x  2 root      nobody 4096 Sep 25  1999 samba
```

As you can see, the frodo directory is not owned by frodo, but by root. Also, with a rights value of drwx——, only the root user can access that directory. No wonder frodo is having trouble.

To fix this problem, change the group to frodo and the directory ownership to frodo by typing the following commands as the root user:

```
# chgrp frodo frodo
# chown frodo frodo
```

To clarify, here's the syntax of these commands:

```
chgrp desired_group directory
chown desired_owner directory
```

In this syntax, *directory* refers to the directory we are concerned about. The *desired_group* is the group that you want to be associated with the directory after you run the *chgrp* command. Similarly, the *desired_owner* is the user you want to own the file after you run the *chown* command.

A new long listing shows the result:

```
[root@olorin /home]# ls -l
total 32
drwx------ 4 frodo    frodo    4096 Mar 26 22:34 frodo
```

Checking Some Linux Files

In addition to using the utilities that we describe in previous sections of this chapter, you can also check a few important Linux files to see if they are configured correctly. For example, if your /etc/hosts file is not configured correctly, your Linux server might have trouble printing to remote printers. Misconfiguring the /etc/hosts.allow or /etc/hosts.deny files can cause tricky connectivity problems. If a user does not have an entry in the /etc/passwd file, that user cannot connect to a Samba server. Finally, a problem with the /etc/ services and /etc/inetd.conf files can prevent Samba or SWAT from running.

The /etc/hosts file

The /etc/hosts file contains a mapping of computer names to IP addresses. If you're running a naming service that your Linux server can access, like DNS, the /etc/hosts table is not as important, assuming your naming service is working. If you're not using a naming service, you should enter the IP address and name of any computer you might need to access from your Linux server to the /etc/hosts table.

If you are referencing a remote printer by name instead of by IP address in your /etc/printcap file, the remote printer should be in your /etc/hosts file.

You don't need to add your Samba clients to your /etc/hosts table.

The /etc/hosts.allow and /etc/hosts.deny files

The /etc/hosts.allow and the /etc/hosts.deny files can be tricky. Together, they allow only certain IP addresses to connect to your Linux server and prevent others.

If you're using the /etc/hosts.allow file, only computers and networks listed there can connect to your Linux server, except for Samba clients. It's best to be generous here; you might want to include your whole network. For example, if your clients had IP addresses ranging from 192.168.1.2 through 192.168.1.254, you could just include the line 192.168.1. in the /etc/hosts.allow file. On the other hand, if you are going to be the only person connecting to your Samba server via telnet and ftp, perhaps you only want to include your workstation's IP address in the /etc/hosts.allow file.

The /etc/hosts.deny file works the opposite way: Any IP addresses there are denied access.

Samba has its own `hosts allow` and `hosts deny` parameters in the smb.conf file, so the /etc/hosts.allow and /etc/hosts.deny files won't affect Samba, except in the case of Samba being started from inetd or tcpd.

The /etc/passwd file

The /etc/passwd file contains all the users you have on your Linux server. If the users are available in Linux, they are available for Samba. So, for users to access their directory on the Samba server, they need to be listed in the /etc/passwd file.

The /etc/services file

The /etc/services file lists all the services that use the network, the network ports they need to use, and the kind of IP connection they need. If a service is commented out from the /etc/services file, it won't work.

For example, Samba uses ports 137–139, with both TCP and UDP connections, so you need to have six lines for NetBIOS uncommented in the /etc/ services file. SWAT uses only port 901, with a TCP connection.

If you're having trouble with some other tool, look here to see if it is blocked.

The /etc/inetd.conf file

The /etc/inetd.conf file is the configuration file for the inetd metadaemon, the very useful software that acts like a butler, waiting for Internet requests to come in. When they do, inetd routes the requests to the correct software. The inetd metadaemon controls software that runs only by request. Software that runs all the time runs by itself.

If your Samba server runs only when people need it, inetd starts it. The /etc/inetd.conf file will have two corresponding lines for ports 137 and 139. If your full-time Samba server starts running when your Linux server boots, the lines are omitted. See Chapter 14 for more details.

You can also run SWAT from the /etc/inetd.conf file. If you can't connect to it, check for a line that mentions SWAT.

Reviewing Linux Logs

The directory that contains the logging files for a Linux server is usually /var/log. However, you can change that by editing the logging configuration file, /etc/syslog.conf. We tell you more about the Samba logging files in Chapter 14, but you can also learn a lot by looking at the Linux logging files.

If you need help with Samba connectivity, check the Linux log file called messages, or more properly, /var/log/messages. The following listing illustrates how to display the messages file with the `cat` command and using `grep` to filter out the lines that mention Samba:

```
[root@olorin log]# cat messages | grep samba
Feb 29 15:58:45 localhost PAM_pwdb[660]:      \ authentication failure; (uid=0)
            -> george for \ samba service
Feb 29 15:58:46 localhost PAM_pwdb[660]:      \ authentication failure; (uid=0)
            -> george for \ samba service
Feb 29 15:58:48 localhost PAM_pwdb[661]:      \ authentication failure; (uid=0) -
            > george for \ samba service
Feb 29 22:29:17 localhost PAM_pwdb[940]:      \ authentication failure; (uid=0) -
            > george for \ samba service
```

If your user george is complaining of connection problems, these logging messages give you a clue to look into george's password.

Troubleshooting with Windows Utilities

Windows comes with many useful programs for diagnosing and debugging network connectivity problems. They range from our old friend, `ping`, to those unique to Windows, like `winipcfg`. In some cases, the Windows 95/98 versions differ from the Windows NT/2000 ones, so we point out those differences as we come across them. Most of these programs run from the MS-DOS prompt, so assume that you need to be at that prompt to use these tools unless we indicate otherwise. In Windows 2000, the MS-DOS prompt has been renamed as the command prompt. To get the command prompt in Windows 2000, click Start➪Programs➪Accessories➪Command Prompt.

Saving your shoes with telnet

One of the more widely used Windows applications is telnet. With telnet, you can run all the utilities we describe in this section on your Linux server from a telnet session on your Windows client.

Telnet is in the Windows directory for Windows 95/98, in the Winnt/System32 directory in Windows NT, and in the Windows/System32 directory for Windows 2000. You can run it from the command line, but you might find it easier to access telnet from a shortcut (or add it to your Start menu).

After you start telnet, you need to connect to your Linux server. Choose Connect➪Remote System and then type the hostname or IP address in the hostname field. You should then get the logon screen for your Linux server.

Telnet sends passwords out in plaintext. If you are concerned about a password sniffer on your network, you should consider using SSH or OpenSSH. We talk more about SSH and OpenSSh in Chapter 16.

You should log on as your normal user instead of the superuser on the Linux server and only use su to get superuser privileges when needed. Two kinds of users log on as root all the time: those who will eventually delete their hard drive by accident, and those who have already deleted their hard drive by accident. (You have been warned.)

Ping — it's here, but it might challenge you

Like various other systems, Windows has the common network command known as `ping`. To use `ping` in Windows 95/98, NT, and 2000, you need to be at a command prompt (also known as an MS-DOS prompt). Just like the Linux command, type **ping *destination*,** where the destination is the IP address or computer name of the remote computer to which you want to check network connectivity.

The following example shows a successful ping of the Samba server olorin:

```
C:\WINDOWS>ping olorin

Pinging olorin [192.168.11.3] with 32 bytes of data:

Reply from 192.168.11.3: bytes=32 time=1ms TTL=255
Reply from 192.168.11.3: bytes=32 time<10ms TTL=255
```

You should note a couple of interesting points about using ping. First, your Windows 98 system might attempt to dial your ISP. Cancel the dialer before the ping goes to your local network.

Next, the hostname(olorin)-to-IP-address lookup was successful because it returned olorin's IP address (192.168.11.3). Then, you see olorin returning the ping, and fairly quickly, too.

Windows 98 returns only four iterations of replies, but Linux and some other UNIX versions keep returning the ping response until you press Ctrl+C. (You can use Ctrl+C to stop the repetitive response in Windows, too.)

Here is an example of an unsuccessful ping attempt by using the IP address:

```
C:\WINDOWS>ping 192.168.11.6

Pinging 192.168.11.6 with 32 bytes of data:

Request timed out.
```

If you see a Request timed out message, you know that no network connectivity exists between the two computers. Now is the time to make like Julius Caesar and divide and conquer. That is, divide your network into separate parts to conquer the connectivity problem. If you are on a Windows 95/98 client, try rebooting before going too far down the divide-and-conquer route; sometimes, Windows 95/98 will drop the network connection.

Like the Linux ping, you may find that ping works with the IP address but fails with the name. If so, you probably have a problem with the Windows client's LMHOSTS table or the naming service your Windows client is using. We strongly discourage using LMHOSTS tables. We discuss Windows naming services in Chapter 11.

Checking the IP address with ipconfig

Ipconfig is another useful utility that's available only at the command prompt. At its simplest, ipconfig can show your Windows client's IP addresses and subnet masks. If you use ipconfig with the /all flag, you get more detailed output that includes the Windows computer name and the type of network interface cards installed.

If you have Windows 95, you cannot use ipconfig, but it is included with Windows 98, NT, and 2000.

You can also use ipconfig to test DHCP connections by releasing and renewing the DHCP connection. In this way, your client can test a few different IP addresses if the client's addresses are being allocated via DHCP. To release the DHCP-assigned IP address, type **ipconfig /release_all** for Windows 98, or **ipconfig /release** for Windows NT and 2000. To renew the DHCP IP address lease, type **ipconfig /renew_all** for Windows 98, or **ipconfig /renew** for Windows NT and 2000.

Checking the routers with tracert

Use the tracert command to diagnose routing problems. For example, if you access your Samba server through a router and you're currently having trouble accessing it, you can use tracert to help diagnose the problem. In this respect, it's similar to traceroute in the Linux world.

To use tracert, just type **tracert *destination_address***. A timeout indicates a failure to contact the destination address.

You can use tracert to see a computer across the network — for example, a Samba server that is in a different subnet. You can test the connectivity with the IP address or the remote hostname.

If you get an error message such as Destination host unreachable, you have a problem with routing or network connectivity.

Checking NetBIOS resources with nbtstat

To display the NetBIOS statistics for your client, use the nbtstat command at a DOS prompt. Just typing **nbtstat** by itself displays its options. Table 13-1 lists some useful nbtstat options.

Table 13-1	nbtstat Options
Option	*What It Shows*
-r	NetBIOS computer names resolved by broadcast and WINS. Useful for checking how the computer learned about other NetBIOS computers.
-a *computername*	The NetBIOS name table for the specified computer name. Useful for seeing what NetBIOS resources the computer knows about.
-A *IP_address*	The NetBIOS name table corresponding to the computer at *IP_address*, Useful for seeing what NetBIOS resources the computer knows about.
-c	The local computer's NetBIOS name cache.

Using netstat to check network statistics

Use the netstat command to check the TCP/IP network statistics. To view the options for netstat, type **netstat /?**. Table 13-2 describes several useful netstat options.

Table 13-2	netstat Options
Option	*What It Shows*
-a	All the connections and ports
-e	Just the Ethernet connections and statistics
-p tcp	TCP connections
-p udp	UDP connections
-r	The contents of the routing table
-s	The statistics per protocol

If you end up with screens of information, you'll probably want to use the more command, or save this information to a file to review it. To use the more command, type **netstat –a | more**, for example. To save the results to a file named netstat.txt, type **netstat –a > netstat.txt**.

Using the Network Control Panel in Windows 95/98

The Network control panel doesn't do much to help diagnose network problems, but you can use it to check for configuration information such as IP addresses and workgroup names. You need to have a passing familiarity with the Network control panel for any clients so you can recognize when they aren't set up correctly.

You won't find any real difference between the Network control panels in Windows 95 and 98. To open the Network control panel, right-click the Network Neighborhood icon and then choose Properties from the pop-up menu.

In the Network control panel for Windows 95/98, you only need to worry about the properties on the Configuration and Identification tabs. The Access Control tab is only for sharing a resource from the Windows 95/98 machine, which is beyond the scope of this book.

The Configuration tab

When you open the Network control panel, you see the Configuration tab. The large pane on the Configuration tab shows the network client software you have installed, any network cards you have installed, and the network protocols that are running on each card or device.

For a Windows 95/98 client to successfully use a Samba client, you need to have the network adapter installed and using TCP/IP. You also need to have the Client for Microsoft Networks software installed and enabled. Finally, these networking components must be successfully configured to work with your particular network.

Each of these networking components has a Properties dialog box in which you can configure the component to work with your Windows/Samba network. To access these Properties dialog boxes, select the desired component (Client for Microsoft Networks or TCP/IP) on the Configuration tab in the Network control panel and then click Properties.

Checking Client for Microsoft Networks properties

In the Client for Microsoft Networks Properties dialog box, make sure that the Windows NT Domain setting is correct. If this client is going to be part of a Windows NT domain, make sure that the Log on to Windows NT Domain box is checked. Also, ensure that you have the correct domain name entered in the Windows NT Domain box. If you're not in a Windows NT domain, be sure that the box is not checked.

Checking TCP/IP properties

The TCP/IP Properties dialog box has lots of settings, and if you don't get them right, they can cause no end of trouble for your Windows 95/98 client.

To view the TCP/IP properties for your network card, select the component named TCP/IP - *component name* in the list on the Configuration tab in the Network control panel and then click Properties. The TCP/IP Properties dialog box has seven tabs: Bindings, Advanced, NetBIOS, DNS Configuration, Gateway, WINS Configuration, and IP Address. You don't need to configure anything on the Advanced or NetBIOS tabs, so we don't mention them any further.

The IP Address tab

The IP Address tab opens by default when you open the TCP/IP Properties dialog box. Here, you determine whether your client is using DHCP by selecting either the Obtain an IP Address Automatically radio button or the Specify an IP Address radio button. The latter assigns a static IP address to the card. You must enter a unique IP address, and the subnet mask must be correct.

The Bindings tab

The Bindings tab in the XE "Bindings tab, TCP/IP Properties dialog box" TCP/IP Properties dialog box shows the network software that will use the TCP/IP protocol. Client for Microsoft Networks must be available and checked.

The DNS Configuration tab

On the DNS configuration tab XE "DNS Configuration tab, TCP/IP Properties dialog box" in the TCP/IP Properties dialog box, you enable or disable DNS for this client. If DNS is enabled, verify that you have the correct settings for the host and the domain, as well as the addresses for the DNS servers.

The Gateway tab

You use the Gateway tab XE "Gateway tab, TCP/IP Properties dialog box" in the TCP/IP Properties dialog box to enter the IP address of the gateway machine, if any. By *gateway,* we mean the computer that links this client's network to other networks. The gateway machine could in fact be your router.

If you can connect to local Samba servers but have trouble with more remote ones, check your Gateway options.

The WINS Configuration tab

On the WINS Configuration tab XE "WINS Configuration tab, TCP/IP Properties dialog box" in the TCP/IP Properties dialog box, you define how your Windows clients handle a WINS server for mapping local IP addresses to computer names.

If you're not using a WINS server, be sure to disable it here. If you are using WINS servers, ensure that Enable WINS Resolution is selected and you've entered the correct IP addresses for all WINS servers. You can also have your WINS handled by DHCP by selecting Use DHCP for WINS Resolution.

The Identification tab

After checking all your TCP/IP properties, click OK to return to the Network control panel. Then, select the Identification tab. Here, you enter the Windows client computer name and workgroup. It's much less confusing if each computer name is unique, and the computer name must be a valid NetBIOS name. The Workgroup should be set to what you expect it to be (and correctly spelled).

If you get an error message such as `Unable to browse the network` when trying to view shares, you might have a network adapter conflict. Use the System control panel to create a separate hardware profile in which you can disable the possibly conflicting adapter. For example, if you have a dial-up adapter that already has TCP/IP properties applied to it, that could override your TCP/IP settings for your network card and prevent you from connecting to the server. You can also try disabling the adapter directly as follows:

1. **Open the System control panel.**

2. **Click the Device Manager tab.**

3. **Click the plus box to expand the Network Adapters device list.**

4. **Select the suspected adapter and click Properties.**

5. **Check the box labeled Disable in This Hardware Profile and click OK.**

6. **Click OK to close the System Properties dialog box.**

Working with the Network Control Panel in Windows NT

To access the Network control panel in Windows NT, right-click Network Neighborhood and choose Properties from the pop-up menu.

The Identification tab

The first tab in the Network control panel is the Identification tab. You set the Windows client name in the Computer Name field. Set the desired domain or workgroup in the Domain Name field. If you need to change one of these values, click Change and then enter the desired computer name, workgroup, or domain name. Make sure that the choice between workgroup or domain is correct for your network.

The Services tab

The Network control panel's Services tab lists all the installed Network services. For this client to access a Samba server, you must have the following services installed:

- ✔ Computer Browser
- ✔ NetBIOS Interface
- ✔ RPC Configuration
- ✔ Server
- ✔ Workstation

If any of these services are missing, add them with the Add button.

By clicking the Network Access Order button, you can specify the order in which this client looks for objects on the network. For Network Providers, you should see Microsoft Windows Network. Under Print Providers, you should see LanMan Print Services.

The Protocols tab

The Network control panel's Protocols tab lists the network protocols that are loaded on this Windows NT client. TCP/IP must be loaded for this client to access a Samba server.

If you highlight the TCP/IP Protocol and click Properties, you can view the TCP/IP Properties for this workstation. The TCP/IP Properties dialog box has four tabs: IP Address, DNS, WINS Address, and Routing. You would only use the Routing tab to set up a Windows router, which is beyond the scope of this book, so we don't discuss that tab.

The IP Address tab

On the IP Address tab in the TCP/IP Properties dialog box, you specify this client's IP address, or where the client gets its IP address. If this client gets its IP address from a DHCP server, make sure that the Obtain an Address from a DHCP Server box is checked.

If you're not using DHCP to serve IP addresses to your clients, you need to give each client its own unique IP address. You also need to specify the correct subnet mask and the proper default gateway.

The DNS tab

You use the DNS tab in the TCP/IP Properties dialog box to specify how this Windows client interacts with the DNS servers. You should suspect a DNS problem if you can contact another computer by its IP address but not by its name.

You need to check four sections on the DNS tab. The Host Name field is for the name of this client computer. It should match the name on the Identification tab in the Network control panel. The Domain box is for the name of your computer domain. In the DNS Service Search Order box, you enter the IP addresses of your DNS server, and specify the order in which they are searched. The Domain Suffix Search Order is only needed for sites with more than one DNS domain.

The WINS Address tab

On the WINS Address tab in the TCP/IP Properties dialog box, you define how this Windows NT client will work with WINS servers. If you are using DHCP to assign IP addresses for this client, and the DHCP server is also assigning the WINS server, you need only enter the DHCP address on the IP Address tab.

If you're not using DHCP for this client, you can make this client use a WINS server by adding the IP addresses of the WINS servers in the appropriate fields.

This tab also has two check boxes that you probably don't want to check. The first is Enable DNS for Windows Resolution. Although having failed WINS requests go to a DNS server might seem like a good idea, it usually doesn't help resolve the address, and it just wastes network bandwidth.

The second check box you probably don't want to enable is Enable LMHOSTS Lookup. If you were to enable this option, you would need a local file called LMHOSTS to map IP addresses and hostnames. If you have more than a few clients, this rapidly creates a lot more work for you because you have lots of files to maintain.

The Adapters tab

The Adapters tab in the Network control panel displays your network card and its properties. You can't do much here except make sure your network card appears.

The Bindings tab

The Network control panel's Bindings tab shows the connections between your network card and your network services. For Samba to work, you should see the Server, Workstation, and NetBIOS Interfaces services bound to the WINS Client TCP/IP.

Finding Network Information in Windows 2000

Windows 2000 has changed quite a bit from NT. If you're an experienced NT administrator, you'll have to get used to some new ways of finding network information in Windows 2000.

Checking the computer name and workgroup

You identify a Windows 2000 client's name and workgroup in the System control panel. (In Windows NT, you find this information in the Network control panel.) To open the Network Identification dialog box in Windows 2000, follow these steps:

1. **Click Start⇨Settings⇨Control Panel.**
2. **Double-click the System control panel.**
3. **Select the Network Identification tab.**
4. **Click Properties to edit the network identification.**

In the top section of the Network Identification dialog box, you enter the computer name. It must be a valid NetBIOS name and should be unique.

By clicking More, you open the DNS Suffix and NetBIOS Computer Name dialog box, in which you can customize this client for DNS networks (which is beyond the scope of this book).

In the bottom section of the Network Identification dialog box, you can choose between having this client join a workgroup or domain, and you specify the domain or workgroup you want the client to join.

Exploring Windows 2000's Network control panel components

In Windows 2000, you can access the Network control panel directly from the Settings menu. You have one control panel for each connection (for example, one control panel for the dial-up connection and one for the network connection).

To open the Properties dialog box for the Windows 2000 network connections, click Start⇨Settings⇨Network and Dial-up Connections. Then, right-click Local Area Connection and choose Properties. As shown in Figure 13-1, Windows displays the Local Area Connection Properties dialog box.

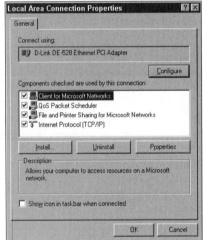

Figure 13-1:
The Local
Area
Connection
Properties
dialog box.

The Local Area Connection Properties dialog box has one tab: the General tab. The top part of the General tab should show you the network adapter you are using. The Configure button takes you to the Configure Network Adapter dialog box.

In the middle of the General tab, you see the network components that the local area connection is using. To access a Samba server, you need to have Client for Microsoft Networks and the Internet Protocol (TCP/IP) installed and enabled. The TCP/IP Properties dialog box has lots of settings that you could configure incorrectly; see the following sections.

Troubleshooting the Network Adapter properties

Access the Network Adapter properties by clicking the Configure button on the General tab in the Local Area Connection Properties dialog box. The Network Adapter Properties dialog box has four tabs: General, Advanced, Driver, and Resources.

On the General tab, the Device Status gives you the status of this network interface card. If it's fine, don't worry. Otherwise, the Troubleshooter button can help you fix it.

The Advanced tab lets you change any configurable properties for this adapter. It's probably best to leave this alone unless you really know what you are doing.

On the Driver tab, you see the driver currently being used by this network card. This is where you go if you need to update the driver.

You can see what system resources your network card is using on the Resources tab. Any resource conflicts should appear at the bottom of the Resources tab in the Conflicting Device list.

Checking the Internet Protocol (TCP/IP) properties

To check the Windows 2000 client's TCP/IP properties, select the Internet Protocol in the Components window in the Local Area Connection Properties dialog box and then click Properties. The General tab displays first, enabling you to choose between DHCP and static IP addressing, with other parameters available via the Advanced button.

Examining the Advanced TCP/IP settings

To access the Advanced TCP/IP settings, click the Advanced button on the General tab in the TCP/IP properties. The Advanced TCP/IP Settings dialog box has four tabs: IP Settings, DNS, WINS, and Options.

On the IP Address tab in the Advanced TCP/IP Settings dialog box, you can configure the IP address, subnet mask, and gateways for this client. Because you can also do that on the General tab, you should only need to confirm any information on this tab.

Check the DNS configuration for this client on the DNS tab. It's probably easiest to just compare these values against a client that has a working DNS configuration.

On the WINS tab, you check this client's WINS settings. A Windows network uses WINS to maintain a listing of computer names and IP addresses. The top section of the WINS tab is where you have your list of WINS servers. Here, you can add, edit, or remove WINS servers. Your network administrator should have this information, or you can just copy it from a working client.

You have two other options in the WINS tab: using an LMHOSTS table and enabling NetBIOS over TCP/IP. You probably don't want to use an LMHOSTS table. It just makes for extra work because you can have a different LMHOSTS table for each client. Adding one server to your network means you have to edit the LMHOSTS table on each client. The other option is to enable NetBIOS over TCP/IP. Because this is the heart of what Samba does, make sure it is enabled.

You use the Options tab to configure TCP/IP filtering and network security. These options go beyond the scope of this book.

Chapter 14

Using Samba to Troubleshoot

*Y*ou can troubleshoot your Samba server by using Linux and Samba commands or by examining the Samba log files. At the most basic level, use Linux commands to see if Samba is actually running. Then, check the configuration files to see if Samba starts when and how you want it to.

Testing Samba at the Linux Level

You can check a few Linux commands and files if you're having trouble with Samba. You can check to see if Samba is running by using the ps command, or you can verify how Samba is supposed to start by looking at the (right) configuration files.

Is Samba running? Checking with the ps command

One of the first troubleshooting steps you can take is to make sure that Samba is running. If Samba isn't running, you certainly won't be able to connect to your Samba server.

Samba consists of two daemons: smbd and nmbd. You can have many copies of these daemons running (one copy of smbd for each connection, and possibly a few copies of nmbd). The ps command displays all the daemons and programs that are running on a Linux system, as well as some information about each daemon and program. The following example shows how you can use ps and grep to find any instances of Samba running. You do not have to log on as root to run this command:

```
[george@olorin george]$ ps -e | grep smbd
  PID       TTY      TIME        CMD
9562        ?     00:00:00       smbd
```

For other operating systems, you might need to use different options with ps. For Solaris, you only need the -e flag with ps, as in the previous example. For FreeBSD, you need to type **ps -a | grep smbd** at the superuser prompt.

What else can you learn from the ps command besides determining whether Samba is running? From the basic ps command (ps -e on Linux), you can identify the process number for smbd and nmbd, which is the number in the first column, under the PID heading. The process number is useful if you need to kill a misbehaving process. The second column is the TTY, or telnet or terminal connection, on which the process is running. Samba doesn't really run on a specific TTY, so you will see ?. The TIME column states the amount of CPU time that process has used.

If you want more information on what your processes are doing, you can use the l flag with ps for a long listing. The following example is a small section of a sample long process listing on the Linux server:

```
[root@olorin george]# ps -el | more
F   S UID PID PPID C PRI NI ADDR SZ WCHAN TTY TIME CMD
140 S   0 526   1 0  60  0    - 603 do_sel ? 00:00:00&   smbd
140 S   0 537   1 0  60  0    - 497 do_sel ? 00:00:00&   nmbd
```

New information in the long listing includes the S (status) column, which tells you about the state of the process. You should be very concerned if you see processes with a state of Z — these are zombied processes, so-called because they should have been killed when the program stopped, but now they are just taking up system resources. (However, they won't affect your system until you have lots of them.)

How does Samba start?

When troubleshooting, you also need to know how Samba is supposed to start. If you have Samba configured to start at boot time but it doesn't start when your server does, your Linux server isn't much use as a Samba server. Alternatively, if you set up your server so Samba only starts if someone tries to connect to it, you should make sure that this works.

Checking if Samba starts at boot time

If Samba is supposed to start when your server starts, you should find a listing for Samba in the proper server initialize file. Where you look depends on the kind of server you're running — a System V-type server or a BSD-type server.

Linux is a System V-type of UNIX, at least as far as starting and stopping the system goes. (If we were talking about printers, we could refer to it more as a BSD-type of system.) Solaris is another well-known System V UNIX OS. System V servers use *numbered* run-level control files to determine what daemons start up at boot time.

FreeBSD, NetBSD, OpenBSD, and SunOS4.1.3 are examples of BSD UNIX systems. BSD UNIX systems use *named* run-control files, such as rc.local, to determine what daemons should start at boot time.

How should Samba start with Linux and other System V servers?

System V servers have different run levels. Depending on the run level, the server might have only the bare minimum of programs running (usually, run level 1), the networking services (typically, run level 2), or a full multiuser system (typically, run level 3).

The default run level is usually 3, for a fully networked multiuser system. However, Caldera OpenLinux uses a default run level of 5, which is like 3 plus X Window. You set the default run level in the /etc/inittab file. The following section from the /etc/inittab file on a Samba server shows a default run level of 3:

```
# Default runlevel. The runlevels used by RHS are:
#   0 - halt (Do NOT set initdefault to this)
#   1 - Single user mode
#   2 - Multiuser, without NFS
#   3 - Full multiuser mode
#   4 - unused
#   5 - X11
#   6 - reboot (Do NOT set initdefault to this)
#
id:3:initdefault:
```

Associated with these run levels are run control directories, which are named rc0.d, rc1.d, rc2.d, and so on, all the way up to rc6.d. In Linux, you find these directories in the /etc/rc.d/ directory. These directories contain scripts that can start or stop various Linux daemons, depending on the initial character of the script name. If the script's name starts with a K, the script kills a daemon, and if the name starts with an S, the script starts a daemon.

When you invoke a run level, or the system goes to its default run level, the scripts in the associated run level run in a specific order. First, the K scripts run in increasing sequential order to kill any needed daemons. For Red Hat Linux level 3, K20rstatd runs before K55route. After the K scripts run, the scripts starting with S run, again in increasing order.

Running Samba in run level 3 makes the most sense. So if you plan to start Samba at boot time, set run level 3 as the default run level, and you should have a script to start Samba in the run level 3 directory (rc3.d).

Now, here is one of those curveballs that makes Linux so loveable. A master run control directory named init.d is located in /etc/rc.d. The init.d directory contains all the master scripts to start and stop all the system's processes. For example, `/etc/rc.d/init.d/smb start` starts Samba and `/etc/rc.d/init.d/smb stop` stops it.

Instead of having two or three copies of each script spread throughout the run control directories, which makes it very hard to change them, the scripts in the run control directories are really just links to the scripts in the init.d directory. To convince yourself, look at the run control directory with the `ls -l` command — for example, **ls -l /etc/rc.d/rc3.d**. Instead of actual scripts, you will see a bunch of links to scripts in /etc/rc.d/init.d.

What this means for Samba is that the /etc/rc.d/rc3.d directory should have a script that starts with K and links to the /etc/rc.d/init.d/smb script. It should also have a script that starts with S and links to the /etc/rc.d/init.d/smb script (yes, the same script).

If the links are missing, you can easily add them. Just follow these examples:

```
olorin# ln -s /etc/rc.d/init.d/smb K35smb
olorin# ln -s /etc/rc.d/init.d/smb S98smb
```

The next time your Linux server starts, Samba should start, too. You can verify that Samba started with the `ps -e` command.

How should Samba start with BSD servers?

BSD UNIX servers use named run control files, such as rc.local, rc.conf, and rec.network, to determine what daemons get started and when the daemons get started. Samba typically starts from the rc.local file, but the exact syntax varies depending on where the Samba binaries live. For a FreeBSD system that keeps the Samba binaries in the /usr/local/sbin directory, you would add the following two lines to the rc.local file:

```
echo " smbd" && /usr/local/sbin/smbd -D
echo " nmbd" && /usr/local/sbin/nmbd -D
```

If the system stores the Samba binaries in a different directory from /usr/local/sbin, just use the different path in the lines you add to the rc.local file.

Checking if Samba starts automatically when requested

In another kind of server configuration, Samba only starts when the server gets a request over the network for a Samba service. This makes sense for a server that only occasionally serves Windows files, such as a workstation that people access only a few times a day.

To set up Samba-on-request, you need to check the inetd daemon, which monitors requests coming in from the network and then starts the required program. You need to check two files to make sure inetd recognizes Samba requests and successfully starts Samba.

First, check the /etc/services file, which inetd uses to identify the ports on which it should listen for Samba requests. Verify that the /etc/services file has two lines that tell inetd to listen for Samba requests on ports 137 and 139:

```
netbios-ns 137/udp
netbios-ssn 139/tcp
```

The second file that inetd needs to start Samba is the inetd configuration file, /etc/inetd.conf. This file tells inetd what to do when it gets a request from a port listed in the /etc/services file. The following two lines must be present and uncommented in the /etc/inetd.conf file for inetd to start Samba:

```
netbios-ssn stream tcp nowait root & /usr/local/sbin/smbd smbd
netbios-ns dgram udp wait root /usr/local/sbin/nmbd & nmbd
```

These two lines might vary depending on the location of the Samba binaries. Also, some versions of UNIX use `netbios_ssn` instead of `netbios-ssn`. You do need to make sure that netbios-ssn is spelled the same in both the /etc/ services and the /etc/inetd.conf file.

If you make any changes to the /etc/inetd.conf file, restart the inetd daemon to make the changes take effect. The easiest way to restart inetd is to find its process number and send a `kill -HUP` signal to the inetd file. So if the process number for inetd is 5877, you would type the following command:

```
# kill -HUP 5877
```

Testing Samba with its own Diagnostic Utilities

Samba comes with several handy testing utilities:

- `testparm`: Checks the syntax of your Samba configuration file, smb.conf
- `smbclient`: Enables Linux or UNIX systems access to smb shares
- `smbstatus`: Shows what connections are active
- `nmblookup`: Verifies that your Samba server is connected to clients
- `testprns`: Tests Samba printers

Testparm

The Samba `testparm` command tests the smb.conf file for syntax errors (but not for the correctness of the shares you've created). If `testparm` gives the OK for your smb.conf file, it means that the syntax is correct and the variables are spelled right, but it doesn't test the functioning of your shares. For example, you could create a Samba configuration file that is perfectly written, but it doesn't give anyone at your company access to shares. Even keeping this in mind, `testparm` still is a useful tool in your Samba tool chest.

In addition to using `testparm` to check the correctness of your smb.conf file, you can use it to check that you're accessing the correct smb.conf file, to search for Samba variables, and to check for access to the Samba server from a remote host.

Are you accessing the correct smb.conf file?

You can have multiple Samba configuration files on your system. In fact, some installations of Samba come with several sample smb.conf files. How then, do you know which is the correct one? The first output from `testparm` provides the location of the smb.conf file that Samba is reading, so that's how you know. If you're not sure where the smb.conf file is, you can again use `testparm` to find it.

The following listing shows the first few lines of the `testparm` output, indicating the smb.conf file is located in /etc/:

```
[root@olorin george]# testparm
Load smb config files from /etc/smb.conf
Processing section "[homes]"
```

Searching for Samba parameters with testparm

Because `testparm` outputs all the values of the Samba variables, you can use it to find the value of a specific variable — for example, the location of the encrypted password file. Because `testparm` scrolls the output so fast, save it into a file for easier searching.

The following example shows the root user redirecting the output of `testparm` to a file named testparm.txt. You have to press Enter twice:

```
[root@olorin george]# testparm > testparm.txt
```

After you create a file from the `testparm` output, you can use `grep` to search for variables. For the examples that we describe in the following sections, we assume that you have created and named the file testparm.txt.

Searching for password information with testparm

If you need to locate the password file or find out what the settings are, you can save the output of testparm into a text file and then grep on the word "passwd" to display all the Samba variables with "passwd" in them:

```
[root@olorin george]# grep passwd testparm.txt
        min passwd length = 5
        smb passwd file = /etc/smbpasswd
        passwd program = /bin/passwd
        passwd chat = *old*password* %o\n & *new*password* %n\n *new*password* &
                %n\n *changed*
        passwd chat debug = No
```

The output shows that the Samba server olorin has a minimum password length of 5 characters and it has an smbpasswd file, so it is probably using encrypted passwords.

Searching for log files with testparm

You might find it useful to search for the logging files and level with the output from testparm. The following example shows search results for "log" in the testparm output:

```
[root@olorin george]# grep log testparm.txt
        log level = 2
        syslog = 1
        syslog only = No
        log file = /var/log/samba/log.%m
        max log size = 50
        timestamp logs = Yes
        logon script =
        logon path = \\%N\%U\profile
        logon drive =
        logon home = \\%N\%U
        domain logons = No
```

This output states that the logging level is 2, which is a useful level for debugging setup problems.

You can avoid using a file, and just send the output of testparm to grep. For example, to look for the word "passwd" in the output of testparm using grep, type **testparm | grep passwd**.

Checking access from a remote computer with testparm

You can also use testparm to test access to the Samba server from a remote client based on the hosts allow and hosts deny Samba parameters. You need to use the remote client's hostname and IP address with testparm to make it work.

The following listing shows the output from using testparm to test the connection from the Windows 98 client named liberty that has an IP address of 192.168.11.2:

```
[root@olorin george]# testparm liberty 192.168.121.2
Load smb config files from /etc/smb.conf
Processing section "[homes]"
Processing section "[printers]"
Processing section "[lucky]"
Processing section "[Win98]"
Processing section "[cdrom]"
Loaded services file OK.
Allow connection from liberty (192.168.121.2) to homes
Allow connection from liberty (192.168.121.2) to &  printers
Allow connection from liberty (192.168.121.2) to lucky
Allow connection from liberty (192.168.121.2) to Win98
Allow connection from liberty (192.168.121.2) to cdrom
```

The listing shows that liberty has access to every share. If a user on liberty is having trouble, focus on the user name or password because the machine connection looks good.

Smbstatus

For a quick look at what connections Samba is serving, use the smbstatus Samba program. By applying different options to smbstatus, you can see what a specific user is doing, which files are locked, what shares are being used, or what processes Samba is running.

Just typing **smbstatus** by itself gives a summary of the connections that your Samba server is running:

```
$ smbstatus

Samba version 2.0.3
Service uid     gid   pid   machine
----------------------------------------------------
george  george  wheel 62812 liberty & (192.168.11.2) Sat Apr  8 18:08:59 2000

Locked files:
Pid    DenyMode   R/W      Oplock          Name
----------------------------------------------------------
62812  DENY_NONE  RDONLY   EXCLUSIVE+BATCH & /usr/home/george/last.txt   Sat
             Apr  8 18:09:5 2000
62812  DENY_NONE  RDONLY   EXCLUSIVE+BATCH & /usr/home/george/Shortcut to
             SMBEDIT.lnk   Sat Apr  8 18:09:24 2000

Share mode memory usage (bytes):
    1048256(99%) free + 232(0%) used + 88(0%) overhead& = 1048576(100%) total
```

The output identifies the version of Samba as 2.0.3. The next section shows the shares that are being used — in this case, just the share named george. You can see that the user named george is being served by the Samba process with the ID of 62812 and he is connected from the client named liberty, which has an IP address of 192.168.11.2.

Below the section for the share, the section for Locked files lists all (two) files that are in use: /usr/home/george/last.txt and /usr/home/george/Shortcut to SMBEDIT.lnk. Finally, you see a summary of the Samba server's memory use.

To get just a particular set of information from smbstatus, use flags. For example, to list only the shares being used, type **smbstatus -S**. If you were curious as to what shares a specific user was accessing, you would type **-u** and the user name. For example, to see what shares and files the user jstraw is accessing, type **smbstatus -u jstraw**.

To find out what files are locked, use the -L flag — that is, type **smbstatus -L**. Finally, to see what processes Samba is using, use the -p flag.

Smbclient

The smbclient program was developed to give Linux or UNIX machines access to Windows or SMB shares. Because a Samba share is an SMB share, you can use smbclient to access a Samba share. In troubleshooting terms, you can connect to a Samba share from the Linux workstation that's running Samba to check out the shares. You don't need to go to a Windows client to check it; you can do it at the command line with smbclient.

Seeing the available shares with smbclient

To see what shares are available on the Samba server, you can telnet in and run smbclient as follows:

```
$ smbclient -L terrapin -N
Added interface ip=192.168.11.5 bcast=192.168.11.255 & nmask=255.255.255.0
Domain=[WORKGROUP] OS=[UNIX] Server=[Samba 2.0.3]

        Sharename      Type      Comment
        ---------      ----      -------
        samba          Disk      Samba directory
        testparm       Disk      run testparm
        test           Disk
        IPC$           IPC       IPC Service (Samba Server)
        lp             Printer   \Canon BubbleJet & BJC-4300

        Server                   Comment
        ---------                -------
        OLORIN                   Samba 2.0.5a
        TERRAPIN                 Samba Server

        Workgroup                Master
        ---------                -------
        WORKGROUP                TERRAPIN
```

You can find out a lot about the Samba server from this output. First, note that this Samba server is using IP address 192.168.11.5, which is good — if Samba was using the loopback port 127.0.0.1, it wouldn't be communicating on the network, and therefore wouldn't make a very good server.

Next, you see the workgroup or domain name, which is WORKGROUP, and the Samba version.

Below the share listing, you see the server and workgroup information. The Server/Comment section lists the other Samba servers in the workgroup.

Checking the shares for a specific user

You can use smbclient to see what shares are available for a specific user. To do so, add the -L flag and the name of the Samba server, plus the -U flag and the name of a user. You also have to supply the user's correct password. The following example shows how you use these smbclient flags with the Samba server named terrapin and the user named george:

```
$ smbclient -L terrapin -U george
```

Checking a specific share with smbclient

To check a specific share, you can use smbclient to try to connect to it. Provide the share name by its uniform resource location, and add the name of the user with the -U flag. The following example shows an smbclient connecting to the share named alli on the server terrapin as the user alli:

```
terrapin# smbclient //terrapin/alli -U alli
Added interface ip=192.168.11.5 bcast=192.168.11.255 & nmask=255.255.255.0
Password:
Domain=[WORKGROUP] OS=[UNIX] Server=[Samba 2.0.3]
smb: \> ls
  .cshrc              H      464   Sun Aug 15 12:00:13 1999
  .login              H      559   Sun Aug 15 12:00:14 1999
  .login_conf         H      139   Sun Aug 15 12:00:15 1999
  .mailrc             H      311   Sun Aug 15 12:00:15 1999
  .profile            H      700   Sun Aug 15 12:00:16 1999
  .shrc               H      832   Sun Aug 15 12:00:17 1999
  .mail_aliases       H      351   Sun Aug 15 12:00:17 1999
  .rhosts             H      257   Sun Aug 15 12:00:18 1999

    47102 blocks of size 8192. 7104 blocks available
```

At the smb: \> prompt, you can type **ls** to see what files are available. That can help you determine what files the user can actually see (as opposed to what files the user expects to see).

Checking your printer with smbclient

You can also use smbclient is to test a Samba printer. You can connect to the printer share and send it a file to see if the file prints. Use smbclient to connect to a printer like you are connecting to a specific share — with the printer name as a uniform resource location and the -U flag and user name — and add -P for a printer share. For the Samba server with a printer share named lp, the following example prints the /etc/hosts file with the put command:

```
terrapin# smbclient //terrapin/lp -U george -P
Added interface ip=192.168.11.5 bcast=192.168.11.255 & nmask=255.255.255.0
Password:
Domain=[WORKGROUP] OS=[UNIX] Server=[Samba 2.0.3]
smb: \> put /etc/hosts
putting file /etc/hosts as \/etc/hosts (1.1801 kb/s) & (average 1.1801 kb/s)
```

Checking your Network Neighborhood with smbclient

You can see what computers are available in your Network Neighborhood by using smbclient. The following command uses -L with an asterisk to list all the computers in the Network Neighborhood. The -U with the user name george is to make sure you know the right password to use when prompted:

```
$ smbclient -L "*" -U george
Added interface ip=192.168.11.5 bcast=192.168.11.255 nmask=255.255.255.0
Got a positive name query response from 192.168.11.5 ( 192.168.11.5 )
Password:
Domain=[WORKGROUP] OS=[Unix] Server=[Samba 2.0.3]

        Sharename      Type      Comment
        ---------      ----      -------
        samba          Disk      Samba directory
        testparm       Disk      run testparm
        test           Disk
        IPC$           IPC       IPC Service (Samba Server)
        lp             Printer   \Canon BubbleJet BJC-4300
        george         Disk      Home Directories

        Server         Comment
        ---------      -------
        CREAKY
        OLORIN
        TERRAPIN                 Samba Server

        Workgroup      Master
        ---------      -------
        WORKGROUP      TERRAPIN
```

Nmblookup

The nmblookup program was developed with Samba to let a Linux server query your network. Nmblookup sends out messages and displays what computers respond to the messages.

Nmblookup is a part of Samba that interacts with the network. With nmblookup, you can verify that a Windows client is correctly set up for Samba, and you can look at all the computers on your Windows network. You can also use nmblookup to verify that your Samba server is using the correct IP addresses. Finally, you can use nmblookup to find the master browser for a workgroup.

Checking a remote Windows client with nmblookup

If you have only one Samba server and a specific client can't connect to it, narrowing down the problem may be difficult. You can use nmblookup to verify that a Windows client is correctly set up for SMB networking. Use nmblookup with the -B flag (for broadcast) and the Windows client's NetBIOS name. The following example shows a search for the client named liberty, with a successful return of liberty's IP address:

```
terrapin# nmblookup -B liberty
Sending queries to 192.168.11.2
```

You can also use nmblookup with the -B flag to check for a remote SMB server, be it a Windows server or a Samba server. To look for a remote Samba server, just use the Samba server's NetBIOS name. If you don't get the remote Samba server's IP address returned, nmbd (and thus Samba) is not set up correctly on the remote Samba server.

Checking the network with nmblookup

To see all the computers on your local subnet, use nmblookup with the -d flag. The following command shows how you search for all the computers on your local subnet with nmblookup:

```
terrapin# nmblookup -d 2 "*"
Added interface ip=192.168.11.5 bcast=192.168.11.255 nmask=255.255.255.0
Sending queries to 192.168.11.255
Got a positive name query response from 192.168.11.3 & ( 192.168.11.3 )
Got a positive name query response from 192.168.11.2 & ( 192.168.11.2 )
Got a positive name query response from 192.168.11.5 & ( 192.168.11.5 )
192.168.11.3 *<00>
192.168.11.2 *<00>
192.168.11.5 *<00>
```

This application of nmblookup returns the IP address that the Samba server is using (192.168.11.5), the broadcast address (192.168.11.255), and the netmask address (255.255.255.0). You can also see that two other computers are running Samba or Windows networking in this workgroup: the computers at 192.168.11.2 and 192.168.11.3.

Finding the master browser with nmblookup

You can use nmblookup to find the master browser of a workgroup. If you want to have your Samba server accessible from remote subnets, you make the setup process much easier if you know the master browser in the remote subnet.

To find the master browser for a workgroup, use the -M flag and the name of the workgroup. The following example finds the master browser for the workgroup named AGENTS:

```
terrapin# nmblookup -M AGENTS
Sending queries to 192.168.11.255
192.168.11.5 AGENTS<1d>
```

For the workgroup named AGENTS, the master browser has an IP address of 192.168.11.5. You can then use nmblookup with the -S and -A flags and the IP address to find the name of the master browser:

```
terrapin# nmblookup -S -A 192.168.11.5
Sending queries to 192.168.11.255
Looking up status of 192.168.11.5
received 7 names
        TERRAPIN       <00> -            B <ACTIVE>
        TERRAPIN       <03> -            B <ACTIVE>
        TERRAPIN       <20> -            B <ACTIVE>
        .._MSBROWSE__. <01> - <GROUP>    B <ACTIVE>
        AGENTS         <00> - <GROUP>    B <ACTIVE>
        AGENTS         <1d> -            B <ACTIVE>
        AGENTS         <1e> - <GROUP>    B <ACTIVE>
num_good_sends=0 num_good_receives=0
```

This looks like a lot of confusing information, which isn't surprising because NetBIOS is a confusing protocol. The first column is the name of the NetBIOS resource that nmblookup found.

The second column is the resource byte for each resource, which tells NetBIOS clients such as Samba the type for the resource listed in the first column. A resource byte of <00> refers to a computer or workgroup name. Because the first occurrence of <00> does not include the word <GROUP>, this output tells you that the computer with the IP address of 192.168.11.5 is named TERRAPIN. The second occurrence of the <00> resource byte has the word GROUP on that line, which tells you that this computer belongs to the workgroup named AGENTS.

A resource byte of <1d> means this computer is the master browser for the workgroup listed on the <1d> line. A resource byte of <1b> indicates the computer is the primary domain controller for the domain mentioned on the <1b> line.

Testprns

Testprns is a simple program for testing whether a printer name is valid for Samba. Testprns searches the /etc/printcap file for the named printer. To test the validity of a printer name, just type **testprns *printername***.

Reviewing Samba Logs

You can troubleshoot Samba by looking through the Samba logs. The Samba logs contain messages from the Samba daemons. The amount of information included depends on the value of the log level parameter. Also, the location of the information depends on the log files parameter. You can restrict the size of the log files. The log file that gets the messages depends on the syslog parameters.

Samba parameters used for logging

Several Samba parameters determine the location of the logging files and the amount of information that is logged on your Samba server. We cover the most important ones here.

How much information do you want?

The log level parameter (also known as the debug level) determines how much information Samba saves in the log. If the log level parameter isn't set high enough, you might not get enough information in your log file to help you solve problems. If you set it too high, you might get huge log files and too much information.

The default log level value is 0, which logs only very critical messages. Most administrators find a log level of 2 to be a useful value for day-to-day server operations. It provides enough information to solve most problems, and the log files stay at a convenient size.

For tougher configuration and connectivity problems, you might want to increase your log level to between 3 and 5. Log levels of 6 and greater give so much information that they're really only useful if you're a Samba developer.

In SWAT, you set the log level parameter on the Globals page in the Logging Options section. In the smb.conf file, log level is a global parameter.

Just where is that log file?

The log file parameter enables you to specify the location for the Samba log files. The usual form is a path, such as /var/log/samba, with an expanding name — for example, Log.%m. The %m is a Samba variable that relates to the NetBIOS name. With %m included in the log file's Samba parameter, you get a log file for the smbd daemon (log.smb), another for the nmbd daemon (log.nmbd), and a log file for each client (log.*clientname*).

In SWAT, you set the `log file` parameter on the Globals page in the Logging Options section. In the Samba configuration file, smb.conf, `log file` is a global parameter.

How big is that log file?

If you are using a high log level, you can limit the maximum log file size with the `max log size` parameter, which sets the maximum size of the log files in kilobytes. The default value of `max log size` is 50. If the log size exceeds the maximum setting, Samba renames the log file with a .old extension (overwriting any existing files with the .old extension) and starts a new log file.

In SWAT, you set the `max log size` on the Globals page in the Logging Options section. In the smb.conf file, set `max log size` in the global section.

Which messages go where: `syslog` and `syslog only`

The `syslog` and `syslog only` parameters determine which Samba messages get logged in the Samba log files and which Samba messages get logged to the operating system log files.

The `syslog` parameter determines which level of Samba messages gets sent to the operating system log files. Samba messages that are less than the level of the syslog go to the operating system logs. So, for a syslog value of 1, any Samba messages generated at a log level of 0 go to the operating system logs.

Use the `syslog only` parameter to send Samba messages only to the operating system logs and not to Samba log files. If you're not getting any messages in the Samba log files, check to see if the `syslog only` parameter is set to yes.

In SWAT, set the `syslog` and `syslog only` parameters in the Advanced View of the Globals section under the Logging Options. In the smb.conf file, `syslog` and `syslog only` are global parameters.

Using log files

So, what kind of information can you get from the log files?

Seeing what's going on in the network with the log.nmb file

The log for nmbd messages, log.nmb, logs the messages the nmbd daemon sends when it interacts with the Network Neighborhood. Depending on the log level, you can see requests from clients and information on who the master browser is.

The following lines from log.nmb show a browser election starting between the Samba server at 192.168.11.5 and another server at 192.168.11.4. To generate this output, type **grep master log.nmb | more**.

```
[2000/01/13 21:21:52, 0] &
            nmbd/nmbd_incomingdgrams.c:process_local_master_&announce(309)
            process_local_master_announce:  & Server WORKGROUP at IP
            192.168.11.4 is & announcing itself as a local master browser for &
            workgroup WORKGROUP and we think we are master. & Forcing election.
[2000/01/13 21:21:52, 0] & nmbd/nmbd_become_lmb.c:unbecome_local_master_ & suc-
            cess(156)Samba name server TERRAPIN has & stopped being a local
            master browser for  workgroup WORKGROUP on subnet 192.168.11.5
[2000/01/13 21:22:05, 0] & nmbd/nmbd_become_lmb.c:become_local_master_& stage
            2(406)Samba name server TERRAPIN is now &  a local master browser
            for workgroup WORKGROUP & on subnet 192.168.11.5
```

If you see output like this, investigate the computer with the IP address of 192.168.11.4. Or perhaps verify that your Samba server always wins browser elections.

Checking Samba's health by viewing the log.smb file

You can get an idea of how Samba is running by viewing the log.smb file. The following example shows that Samba thinks the word *coment* is an unknown parameter, but it is probably just *comment* misspelled:

```
[1999/08/15 08:45:21, 0] & param/loadparm.c:map_parameter(1587) Unknown & para-
            meter encountered: "coment"
```

Search through the smb.conf file for *coment* and correct it.

Seeing what a client is doing with client name logs

The default log file setup causes logging files to be created for each client computer. This is a good thing. If Phil, who uses the computer alembic, complains of an inability to get to his files, start by looking through the file named log.alembic.

The following line from the log.olorin file shows the user george connecting to the share named george:

```
[2000/03/22 00:01:41, 1] & smbd/service.c:make_connection(488)olorin &
            (192.168.11.3) connect to service george as & user george
            (uid=1001, gid=0) (pid 34929)
```

The next example shows a line from the log.olorin file in which the user george has apparently mistyped or forgotten his password. You can reset the password using smbpasswd if george comes to you complaining that he can't access his files.

```
[2000/04/09 22:24:05, 1] & smbd/password.c:pass_check_smb(528)smb_password_&
            check failed. Invalid password given for user & 'george'
```

Setting the debug level permanently

After your Samba server is up and running with no problems, you probably want to set the log level to a reasonable level and keep it there. Set the log level parameter to a reasonable value (0 to 2 for a normal server; 0 is usually sufficient) and restart the server.

In SWAT, you set the log level parameter on the Globals page in the Logging Options section. In the smb.conf file, log level is a global parameter.

Temporarily changing the debug level

Sometimes, you want to increase or decrease a Samba process temporarily, or at least until the Samba server gets rebooted. To do this, find the process ID of the Samba daemon for which you want to change the log level and then send it the appropriate signal.

If you're not sure of the correct process ID for the Samba daemon (because each Samba connection has its own process ID), you can use smbstatus to get a list of connections and process IDs.

To increase the logging level of a running Samba process by one, find the process ID and send it the USR1 signal. The following example shows how you increase the logging level of the Samba process that has a process ID of 64255:

```
# kill -USR1 64255
```

Similarly, if you want to decrease the logging level of a running Samba process, find the process ID number and send it the USR2 signal. For a Samba process with an ID of 64260, the following example decreases the logging level by one:

```
# kill -USR2 64260
```

Part V

Maintaining Your Samba Server

The 5th Wave   By Rich Tennant

"C'MON, BRICKMAN, YOU KNOW AS WELL AS I DO THAT 'NOSE-SCANNING' IS OUR BEST DEFENSE AGAINST UNAUTHORIZED ACCESS TO PERSONAL FILES."

In this part . . .

Well, now that you've figured everything out, how do you keep it together? This part covers essential practices that keep your network safe and secure.

Just when you think you can take a break from all this work, somebody loses something and comes crying hysterically to you. If you have already done a full backup, you can slap the lost file into crybaby's home directory, pronto. Chapter 15 clues you in on conducting backups, so now you're a hero.

Unfortunately, when it comes to network security, you probably won't be seeing much hero action. Ensuring security is a fundamental and thankless part of your job, so if you overlook something, you get the opposite of hero, and how! Chapter 16 covers all the important details about maintaining a secure Samba server.

Chapter 15

Backing Up the Server

. . . .

In This Chapter

▶ Choosing a backup device

▶ Choosing a backup method

▶ Configuring your backup system

▶ Restoring data

. . . .

One of your more important responsibilities as a Samba administrator is backing up all essential data. The importance of backing up varies depending on your Samba server's application. If you're only using it as a print server, you might want to back up only your configuration data. If your Samba server stores your company's most important files, you want a complete backup process.

First, you need to choose a backup device (medium). Backup devices range from the floppy-disk drive that you find on almost every Linux server to gigabyte tape drives that cost thousands of dollars. The backup device you choose depends on how much data you have to back up, how quickly you need to repair a damaged server, and, of course, your budget.

After you select a backup device, you need to choose your backup method. For many purposes, the software included with your Linux server, such as `tar`, is adequate, particularly if you use a script and run the backup with an automatic task scheduler like `cron`. For larger, more complex servers, you might want to use custom backup software that enables you to retrieve specific files from your backups — for example, in case a user deletes important files. You should also be concerned with the ability of the backup method to deal with corrupted data files. Does a corrupt data file ruin the whole archive or just the one file in the archive?

Finally, you need to enable and manage your backup process. How often will you back up your server? Will you do full backups or partial backups? How will you store your backup media? The answers to these questions depend on how quickly the data on your server changes, how long it takes to do a backup, and how much data fits on your backup media.

Choosing a Device

The first part of designing a backup strategy is to decide on the backup device to use. Backup devices range from a floppy-disk drive that holds a little more than a megabyte of data on one disk to a tape drive that holds several gigabytes of data. The device you pick depends on how much data you need to back up, how much you can interact with the backup device, how quickly you need to restore your Samba server, and how much you can afford to spend.

Floppy-disk drives

Floppy-disk drives have the advantage of being ubiquitous: nearly every Linux server has one. On the other hand, they have the disadvantage of being slow and unreliable, and they have low capacity. Hence, using a floppy as a backup medium makes sense in only a few instances. For example, you might want to transfer a few small files to another machine for which the network connectivity is poor. Or you might want to keep a few commonly used configuration files on a floppy that you keep in a notebook. Or you might have a Samba server that has only a few customized files, such as with a print server.

If you don't have boot and rescue floppies for your server, you should create them. If you don't know how to create boot and rescue floppies, see the section "Creating Linux boot and rescue disks," later in this chapter.

Mounting and unmounting floppy disks in Linux

Like many other file systems in Linux, you need to mount and unmount DOS-formatted floppies to use them. The following line mounts a DOS-formatted floppy to the /mnt/floppy directory:

```
# mount -t msdos /dev/fd0 /mnt/floppy
```

And of course, when you're done with the floppy, you need to unmount it, like the next example shows:

```
# umount /dev/floppy
```

After the floppy is unmounted, you can safely eject it from the drive.

If you are only going to be exchanging floppies with other Linux systems and you're using `tar`, you don't need to mount and unmount the floppies. The `tar` command does not need to have the floppy mounted to write to it.

When to use floppy disks

Floppies are generally a poor choice for backups because they are slow, error prone, and have a small capacity. However, in a few situations, you might find floppies useful. If you need to transfer a small file and the network connectivity is poor (perhaps the network is not configured yet), floppies are a good choice. If you want to back up configuration files for a server, you can use the `find` command to list the changed ones and then back them up to the floppy.

Transferring small files with tar

Floppies do work well for transferring small files to another Linux system. The following example shows how to transfer the smb.conf file onto a floppy disk using the `tar` command:

```
# tar cvf /dev/fd0 /etc/smb.conf
```

And when you get to the next Linux server and you want to copy the file from the floppy, you would type this command:

```
# tar xvf /dev/fd0 /etc/smb.conf
```

Transferring small files with cp

If you are planning to exchange floppies with a Windows machine, you need to mount the DOS-formatted floppy first. After you've mounted the floppy, you can then copy files to it using `cp`. The following example copies the smb.conf file to a floppy:

```
# cp /etc/smb.conf /mnt/floppy
```

Transferring files with mtools

A final way to work with DOS-formatted floppies is to use the `mtools` suite of programs. The `mtools` suite of programs are freeware programs that enable you to manipulate DOS-formatted floppies. They are included with Linux and FreeBSD and are available for Solaris.

The `mtools` commands correspond to the respective DOS commands, but they are preceded with an m. Instead of `copy`, you would type `mcopy`. Instead of `cd`, you would type `mcd`. Instead of `dir`, you would type `mdir`.

Finding and backing up recently changed files

You might need to find which files have been changed recently. Perhaps you installed a print server on May 8 and then configured it on May 9. The files that make your print server work that differ from the files installed on May 8 would all be dated May 9. Now, it's May 10 and you want to back up all those files. You can use the following `find` commands to list all those files, and then back them up using `tar`:

```
# find /etc -mtime -2 -print >> /root/changed.txt
# tar cvf /dev/fd0 -T /root/changed.txt
```

The first long command searches for all files that have been modified within the last 2 days (the -mtime -2 switch). It begins searching at the /etc directory and then stores the filenames in the directory /root/changed.txt. The next command applies tar with the -T option to read a list of files from the /root/changed.txt directory and then tars them to the floppy drive.

You might want to test this first by sending the output to a temp directory because the tar file might be too big to fit on a floppy disk.

Backing up configuration files

The configuration files for your Linux server often don't take up much space, so you might be able to fit them all on one floppy. These files include the /etc/hosts file that lists the computers your server knows about; the /etc/passwd, /etc/shadow, and /etc/group files that contain your user information; and the Samba configuration files such as the smb.conf file and the smbpasswd file.

All in all, these are good files to duplicate for emergencies and troubleshooting. Ideally, you should back up the entire /etc directory and the Samba configuration files. But because the entire /etc directory usually doesn't fit on a floppy, you might need to pick and choose which files to back up. The following script is a good place to start. It uses tar to copy files to the floppy drive. Modify this example to include other files:

```
#! /bin/sh
tar cvf /dev/fd0 /etc/hosts
tar rvf /dev/fd0 /etc/passwd
tar rvf /dev/fd0 /etc/shadow
tar rvf /dev/fd0 /etc/smb.conf
tar rvf /dev/fdo /usr/local/etc/private/smbpasswd
```

If you need help on writing scripts, Appendix E provides a brief introduction to script writing.

Creating Linux boot and rescue disks

If you don't have boot and rescue floppy disks for your Samba server, you should create them. The following examples use the dd command to copy the boot and rescue images to floppy disks. They should work for most versions of Linux. If not, check your Linux documentation.

The following command creates a boot disk:

```
# dd if=/mnt/cdrom/images/boot.img of=/dev/fd0
```

You need to be in the directory that contains the boot image, which is usually on the Linux CD. For Red Hat, the boot image is located in the images directory.

The command to create a rescue disk is nearly identical. Use the file named rescue.img instead of the file named boot.img. We explain the dd command in greater detail later in the chapter (see the section "Using software you already have on your Linux workstation").

Zip drives

Zip drives are very common, and they hold a fair amount of data, from 100 to 250MB. They might not hold enough to back up a server or even a directory of user's shares, but a Zip cartridge should be able to hold an individual user's files (depending on the size of the files — no mp3 archives, please).

We discuss mounting and unmounting Zip drives in depth in Chapter 8, so we just do a quick overview here. Zip drives come in ATAPI, SCSI, and parallel-port configurations. ATAPI Zip drives are installed internally and share the hard-drive cables. Parallel-port Zip drives are external, and SCSI can be either internal or external.

To mount a DOS-formatted Zip disk into an ATAPI drive that is the second IDE hard drive on your server, you would type this command:

```
# mount -t msdos /dev/hdb4 /mnt/zip
```

Parallel and SCSI Zip drives both appear as SCSI drives. For parallel-port drives, you need to make sure the parallel-port drivers are loaded. The following command is an example of mounting a Windows 95-formatted disk into a parallel port or SCSI Zip drive:

```
# mount - t vfat /dev/sd4 /mnt/zip
```

When done, you need to unmount the Zip disk before it can be safely ejected. You do so by typing **umount /mnt/zip**.

CDR/CDRW

Recordable CDs (CDRs) and rewritable CDs (CDRWs), also called CD "burners," are also becoming very common. CDs hold a decent amount of data, and the media are very inexpensive. With a capacity of up to 660MB, you might find several uses for a CDR drive in your backup scheme.

CDR and CDRW drives are mostly available in SCSI and ATAPI format. SCSI CD burners are generally more expensive than ATAPI drives but have better performance and are easier to integrate with Linux than ATAPI drives. If you have an ATAPI drive, you have to make the kernel treat it as a SCSI drive. Either format should work as a backup drive, so choose whichever is more convenient for you.

CD writing is a two-step process in Linux. First, you make a CD image on your hard drive (which again requires about 650MB of space). Then, you write the CD image to the CD. Hence, you need to have a significant amount of free space on your hard drive for this backup method to work.

For Linux, the CD-Writing-HOWTO text file goes into much greater detail on how to use your CD burner. For example, on Red Hat's Linux CD, the CD-Writing-HOWTO file is located in the /doc/HOWTO directory. Otherwise, look for the CD-writing help at your Linux distribution's Web site, such as http://www.RedHat.com or http://www.calderasystems.com.

CDR software

You need two types of software to burn a CD on the Linux platform. You need one package to generate the CD image and another to write the CD image to the CD. In Red Hat Linux, the software for creating CD images is called mkisofs and the software for writing a CD image to a CD is called cdrecord.

If you have an ATAPI IDE CDR or CDRW

ATAPI IDE CDR drives take a little more work to use with Linux because you have to make the Linux system think they are SCSI drives for the CD software to work. You can make Linux think your ATAPI drive is a SCSI drive with the ide-scsi driver. You have to tell the kernel that the ATAPI CDR drive should use the ide-scsi driver by passing the kernel this information in the lilo.conf or the chos.conf file.

For the ATAPI device /dev/hdc, you would add the following line to the section that describes the Linux system in the lilo.conf file:

```
append="hdc=ide-scsi"
```

Now when the system boots, the ATAPI IDE CD burner appears as a SCSI CD burner to the CD recording software.

SCSI CDR drives work easily in Linux after you have them installed correctly. You don't need to do anything special to make them work with the CD writing software.

The next sections describe how to create and copy the CD image in Red Hat Linux.

Creating the file system using mkisofs

Writing a CD in Linux is best done as a two-step process. For Red Hat Linux, first create the CD image using mkisofs and then write the CD image to the CD using cdrecord. The following example shows mkisofs creating a CD image named cd_image with the contents of the /mnt/nbackup directory. The /mnt/backup directory has already been filled with as much as 650MB of files to be archived.

```
# mkisofs -r -c cd_image /mnt/backup/
```

Copying the file system to the CDR using cdrecord

After you make a CD image using mkisofs, you are ready to burn it to the CD using cdrecord. First, though, you need to identify the SCSI device to which your CD burner has been mapped. To do so, use the following command:

```
# cdrecord -scanbus
```

From the output of cdrecord, you can identify the SCSI bus for the CD burner (SCSI_BUS), the SCSI ID of the CD burner (SCSI_ID), and the #### of the CD burner (SCSI_LUN), You need these three items to use cdrecord.

For example, the CD burner has SCSI_BUS=0, SCSI_ID=6, and SCSI_LUN=0. The CD burner is a 2X burner. The following command burns the CD image cd_image onto the blank CD.

```
# cdrecord -v speed=2 dev=0,6, -data cd_image
```

Using rewritable CDRs in Linux

If you have a CDRW drive, you can use CDRW (rewritable CD) blanks in your CD burner. The cost per disk is higher than the cost per disk for write-once CDs (CDRs), but you can reuse them many times.

Internal hard-disk drives

A second hard-disk drive can serve as a very fast, convenient, and inexpensive backup device for your Samba server. On the other hand, because it is installed inside your computer, you cannot store this backup device offsite. If you have an extra computer to act as a backup server, you can swap hard drives and get your data back in a matter of minutes.

Using internal hard drives also has a disadvantage because you have only one set of backup files. Contrast this with removable media, which you can manage in such a way as to allow you to rebuild your system to any specified date. For example, if you've had a virus infect all your user files in the last two weeks, the backup on the hard drive will also be infected, but the backup tapes from three weeks ago would be clean.

Preparing a second hard drive

The first step in using a second hard drive as a backup device is to prepare. You need to partition it and then format the partitions:

1. **Start by determining the partition geometry of your current hard disk by typing** df -k.

   Each partition is on a separate line of the output. The first column identifies the actual hard drive partition the file system is mounted to, and the second column shows the size of the partition in 1k blocks.

2. **Decide which partitions you want to duplicate on the second hard drive.**

   If you don't have enough disk space, just duplicate the partitions that contain your user data. You can always reinstall your programs from your CDs.

3. **Use** fdisk **on the second hard drive to duplicate the partitions you need.**

   They should be the same size or slightly bigger than your existing partitions. For more details on using fdisk, see *RedHat Linux For Dummies,* by Jon Hall and Paul Sery.

4. **Format the partitions on the hard drive with** mke2fs -c /dev/hdb*n,* **where** *n* **is the partition number for each Linux partition on the second hard drive.**

   This command formats the partitions in the Linux disk format.

5. **Create directories to mount the partitions of the second hard drive —** **for example, /mnt/backup*n,* where** *n* **is the number of the partition.**

6. **Mount each partition of the second hard drive to the newly created mount points.**

   For example, type **mount /dev/hdb1 /mnt/backup1, mount /dev/hdb2 /mnt/backup2,** and so on.

Backing up a section of your hard drive

If you don't have enough space on your second hard drive to back up your entire primary hard drive, you might decide just to back up a section of your hard drive, perhaps the home directory partition.

Assuming that your home partition is named /dev/hda5, the following command lists the files on your home partition and backs them up to the partition /dev/hdc5:

```
# mount /dev/hdc5 /mnt/tmp5
# find /home -print | cpio =pvum /mnt/tmp5
```

Backing up your entire hard drive

If you have two hard drives that are identical in capacity, you can back up your first hard drive entirely to your second hard drive.

For each partition, mount it to a tmp directory and copy the files from the source partition to the target partition. The following commands do so for partition 1:

```
# mount /dev/hda1 /mnt/tmp
# find . -mount | cpio -pvum /mnt/tmp
# umount /dev/hda1
```

You could implement each of these three commands for each partition in a script file, or do it with a loop in a script file if you are feeling particularly adventurous. Appendix E gives a brief overview of script writing.

Tape drives

Tape drives range in storage size from several hundred megabytes to several gigabytes. They also range in interface, from parallel-port interfaces to floppy-drive interfaces to SCSI interfaces.

Floppy and parallel-port tape drives

Floppy tape drives are cheap and common, but their capacity is generally much smaller than server hard drives. They also aren't very reliable and generally aren't preferred for server use. But if it's all you've got, make the most of it; just test it a few times to make sure it works.

Linux has support for floppy tape drives. Other UNIXes have no or very little support. Linux uses the ftape driver to access the floppy tape drive.

Support for parallel-port tape drives is similar to that for floppy tape drives: Some drives are supported in Linux, and there is little support in other versions of UNIX.

Look for the Ftape-HOWTO document on your Linux CD for more detail on which tape drives are supported and how to use them.

Floppies and floppy tape drives

Because floppy drives and floppy tape drives use the same controller, you can't use them at the same time. At first, that might not seem like much of a problem, except the only time you really want to use both the floppy disk and the floppy tape drive is when you are recovering from a system crash. The recommendation is to boot from the floppy, set up a RAM disk, and then unmount the floppy and use the RAM disk for recovery. Or have two floppy controllers: one for the floppy drive and one for the tape drive.

When you make your boot disk, make sure that you include the right tools to retrieve your archives, such as `tar` (or `cpio`, or whatever archiving software you are using) and `mt`.

Formatting tapes

You need to format tapes before you can use them. You can format them in Linux with the `ftformat` program.

Backing up to a floppy tape drive using tar

It's easy to back up your server to the floppy tape drive. Just use the device /dev/ftape. The following example backs up the /home directory to the floppy tape drive:

```
# tar cvf /dev/ftape /home
```

Restoring from a floppy tape drive

To restore an archive from a floppy tape drive, follow this example:

```
# tar xvf /dev/ftape
```

Limitations of floppy tape drives

At the moment, you can't append files to an existing tar file on a floppy tape drive. And as mentioned before, floppy tape drives aren't noted for their reliability, so if you are using them in your backup scheme, test the floppy tape drive a few times first.

SCSI tape drives

SCSI tape drives are the preferred tape drive for larger or crucial servers. Their size can range from less than a gigabyte to tens of gigabytes. The more expensive SCSI tape drives have automatic cartridge changers for very large backup capacities.

After you successfully install your SCSI tape drive, using it is easy. Most backup programs were written with SCSI tape drives in mind.

Backing up an archive onto a SCSI tape drive

Backing up an archive to your SCSI tape drive will probably be a frequent task. The following commands list all the files on your server, starting at your root directory, and pipe them to the `cpio` command to back them up to the SCSI tape drive on device /dev/rst8:

```
# find / -print | cpio -ocvB > /dev/rst8
```

Restoring an archive from a SCSI tape drive

At some point in your administrator career, you will have to restore an archive from your SCSI tape drive. Perhaps you are recovering from a crash, or you need to retrieve a database that came on SCSI tape. The following example shows the use of the `tar` command to retrieve the archive from the SCSI tape drive:

```
# tar xvf /dev/rst8
```

Retrieving a specific file from a SCSI tape drive

Say you want to retrieve a part of an archive from your SCSI tape drive. Maybe you are moving your home directory to a bigger hard drive. You've backed up the original partition, installed the new, bigger hard drive, and are ready to install the /home directory on the new drive. The following command retrieves the /home directory on the SCSI tape drive:

```
# tar xvf /dev/rst8 /home
```

Choosing a Method

After you decide on the backup device, you need to choose a backup method. Linux comes with software for backing up hard drives, but you might want to use special software that works better for different needs.

Using software you already have on your Linux workstation

Your Linux server (as well as most other UNIX servers) already comes with some backup software, specifically `tar`, `cpio`, and `dd`.

tar

The most common Linux backup program you will use is tar, although you will probably use it for many other things in addition to backing up your server. The tar program combines files into one big file. Many software programs are distributed as one big tar file. Tar generally doesn't do any data compression. The tar file, composed of many smaller files, is the same size as the individual file sizes added together.

The `tar` command looks very confusing at first. Typical `tar` command syntax begins with the word `tar`, followed by a three-letter group, followed by several file paths. To make it easier, there are four main types of tar operations:

> ✔ `tar cvf` creates a tar file.
>
> ✔ `tar xvf` extracts files from a tar file.
>
> ✔ `tar rvf` adds files to an existing tar file.
>
> ✔ `tar tvf` lists the files in a tar file.

Because `tar` was originally designed to work with magnetic tapes, numerous commands (usually dealing with block size) only make sense when you are referring to magnetic tape. Don't be thrown by them.

Using cvf to create a tar file

To create a file, start your `tar` command with **tar cvf** and then add the name of the tar device and the name of the file or files to tar. For example, if you wanted to take the /etc/passwd and /etc/group files and back them up as one big file named /etc/userinfo, you would type this command:

```
# tar cvf /etc/userinfo /etc/passwd /etc/group
```

For the next example, if you wanted to copy the entire contents of the /home and the /usr directory to the tape drive named /dev/rmt/0, you would type the following:

```
# tar cvf /dev/rmt0 /home /usr
```

TIP

Scheduling jobs with cron

Backup programs work best when no one else is using your system. If a backup program can run late at night, it shouldn't have to worry about which files are being used by other users or whether the backup process is taking up too much CPU time. You're probably not looking forward to coming into your office at 2:00 a.m. to back up your server, but thanks to a program called cron, you don't have to.

Cron is a program that reads a file called a crontab and then runs programs listed in the crontab file at specified times and dates. Each entry in the crontab has six fields:

✔ The first field details which minutes of the hour the command should be executed. This value can range from 0 to 59.

✔ The second field tells cron which hours of the day the command should execute, with values ranging from 0 to 23.

✔ The third field in a crontab record tells which days of the month the command should be executed. Values from 1 to 31 are valid.

✔ The fourth field specifies in which months of the year the command should be executed. A valid range for the month field is 1 to 12, with January being 1.

✔ The fifth field in a crontab record is for the days of the week the command should run. This can range from 0 to 7, with Sunday being both 0 and 7.

✔ The sixth field in the crontab record holds the command to be executed.

Valid values for the first five fields are a single number, an asterisk for every number, two hyphenated numbers for a range of numbers, or several comma-separated numbers. For example:

```
55 9 * * 1-5 /usr/bin/echo
    "Coffee break" > /dev/
    console
```

This example sends the message "Coffee Break" to the console window on the server at 9:55 a.m. every Monday through Friday. This is cute, but not very interesting. Where cron becomes very useful is when you use it to launch backup scripts, which is almost as powerful as you being there to run the script yourself.

For some backup schemes, you might have one cron job calling a script that executes a full backup on Saturday night and a separate cron job that calls a script executing a partial backup every night at midnight. For additional complexity, you might have a few other cron jobs that clean out log files, run reports, and do other administrative tasks that take too long to do during the day.

View the records in a crontab file by typing **crontab -l**, which displays the crontab records for the user you are logged on as. To view a different user's crontab file, type **crontab -l -u user_name.**

To edit a crontab file, type **crontab -e**. For Linux, the default cron editor is usually vi. For other UNIXes, the default cron editor is often ed. You might want to set your editor value to something a little more friendly. For the bash shell, which is the most common Linux shell, the following

example sets the EDITOR variable to pico and then exports this value to the shell environment. After the value is exported, when you start editing the crontab file, you will edit it with pico instead of vi.

```
# EDITOR=pico
# export EDITOR
```

You can check that the EDITOR variable has been properly sent by checking the shell environment with the env command. To make this environment variable change permanent, you would edit the .profile file in the user's home directory.

To edit another user's cron file, type **crontab -e -u user_name.**

If you ever need to remove the crontab file (perhaps it's trying to back up the server every minute), just type **crontab -r.**

Two files determine which users can and can't use crontab: cron.allow and cron.deny, located in the /etc/cron.d directory. If cron.allow exists, only the users listed in the cron.allow file can use crontab. If no cron.allow file exists, the cron.deny file determines who is denied access. Every other user is allowed to use cron.

If neither the cron.allow nor the cron.deny file exists, two things can happen depending on your version of crontab. In one case, only the superuser can use crontab, and in the other case, all users can use crontab. If it is important that access to cron is restricted, use cron.allow or cron.deny instead of wondering who has crontab access.

Extracting all the files from a tar archive with xvf

A tar file full of user data isn't worth much unless you know how to get the data out. This is where the tar xvf command comes in. To get the files from the tar file stored on the floppy drive, you would type this command:

```
# tar xvf /dev/fd0
```

Extracting a specific file from a tar archive with xvf

Sooner or later, users will come to you asking for help with a deleted file. Maybe they were cleaning up their user directory and accidentally deleted their progress report. If the server was backed up before the file was deleted, you will have a copy of it somewhere in the tar archive (this is a good argument for frequent backups). If you untar the whole user directory, you overwrite what that user worked on today, so you need to untar just one specific file. To show you how to untar just one file, the following command retrieves the file progress.doc in the /home/merlin directory from the tar file on the tape device:

```
# tar xvf /dev/rmt0 /home/merlin/progress.doc
```

Adding to a tar file with rvf

To add a file or two to an existing tar file, use `tar rvf`. For example, to add the file /usr/local/etc/private/smbpasswd to the tar file named /etc/userinfo, you would type this command:

```
# tar rvf /etc/userinfo & /usr/local/etc/private/smbpasswd
```

Seeing what files are in a tar file with tvf

Use the `tar tvf` command to list the files in a tar file. For example, you could check whether the progress report mentioned in the previous example is named progress, progress.doc, or MayProgress. To list the files in the tar file on the /dev/rmt0 tape drive, you would type this command:

```
# tar tvf /dev/rmt0 /home/merlin
```

Other tar options

Table 15-1 lists a few more options you can use after you get familiar with `tar`.

Table 15-1	Additional tar Options
Option	*What It Does*
-b *N*	Specify that the files are in block size *N*, used for tape drives.
-o	Specify that the files being extracted get the user and group rights of the person running the tar operation, instead of what the rights were when the tar file was created.
-M	Specify that the tar file is a multivolume tar file.
-T *file_name*	Read in a list of files to be extracted or created from the file *file_name*.

Option	What It Does
-u	Update a tar file with new files or newer files compared to the files in the tar file.
-W	Verify the tar file after writing it.
-w	Run tar in interactive mode.
-Z	Expand or shrink the file size with compress.
-z	Expand or shrink the file size with gzip.

Tar has many other options, but not all of them are available in every flavor of UNIX. Be sure to check the man pages first if you want to do something special with tar.

dd

We refer to dd earlier in this chapter, when we describe the steps for creating the Linux boot and rescue disks. You primarily use dd for copying data between differently formatted devices — for example, from a hard drive to a floppy disk. You can also use it to copy data between two formats, such as from ASCII to EBCDIC format.

The usual format for dd is dd if=input_file of=output_file options. In the example for creating a boot disk, the input file is boot.img, and the output file was the floppy drive, /dev/fd0.

Like tar, the dd command is designed to work with tape drives, so dd has many options that only make sense when applied to tape operations.

dd options

The dd command has many options. Table 15-2 describes some of the more important ones.

Table 15-2	dd Options
Option	**What It Does**
bs = *n*	Set the input and output block size, in bytes.
ibs = *n*	Set the input block size, in bytes.
obs = *n*	Set the output block size, in bytes.
cbs = *n*	Specify the conversion block size, in bytes.

(continued)

Table 15-2 *(continued)*

Option	What It Does
files = *n*	Copy and concatenate *n* input files, and then quit.
skip = *n*	Skip *n* input before copying the input file.
iseek = *n*	Seek *n* blocks from the beginning of the input file before copying.
oseek = *n*	Seek *n* blocks from the beginning of the output file before copying.
count = *n*	Copy only *n* input blocks.
conv = *value*[, *value*] ...	Convert the input file using the conversion specified by *value*. Some types of conversion options are
block:	Convert variable-length records, terminated by a newline, to fixed-length records.
unblock:	Convert fixed-length records to variable-length records.
lcase:	Convert uppercase to lowercase.
ucase:	Convert lowercase to uppercase.
noerror:	Continue processing even if an error occurs.
sync:	Pad every input block to the size of ibs.

Using dd

The following command uses dd to convert every letter in the input file to lowercase:

```
# dd if=input_file of=output_file conv=lcase
```

cpio

The cpio command is the third very common backup command, along with tar and dd. Use the cpio command to copy files to and from an archive.

cpio options

Table 15-3 lists some useful options for cpio.

Table 15-3	cpio Options
Option	*What It Does*
-o	Create an archive by reading the input names from standard input and copying those files to standard output.
-i	Extract the archive file specified by the standard input.
-p	Read a list of filenames from the standard input.
-B	Change block input/output record size to 5,120 bytes from the default of 512 bytes.
-c	Read or write the header in ASCII.
-H *format*	Read or write the header in tar, bar, crc, odc, or utar formats.
-A	Append to an existing archive.
-C *n*	Block input/output *n* bytes to the record.
-d	Create any needed directories.
-E *file_name*	Use the file *file_name* to read a list of files to be extracted from the archive.
-f	Read in all files, except those that match the pattern given.
-I *file_name*	Use the file *file_name* to get a list of files to be read into the archive.
-k	Try to skip any corrupted file headers and I/O errors encountered.
-l	Link files rather than copying them, if possible.
-L	Follow symbolic links.
-m	Retain the previous file modification time.
-M *text*	Display the text when you need to change the backup media.
-O *file*	Send the output of cpio to a file.
-P	Preserve file ACLs.
-R *id*	Make each extracted file be owned by the user with user ID of *id*. Give each file the group rights of the user ID.
-t	Print a table of contents of the file inputs.
-u	Copy unconditionally, by copying over older files with newer ones.
-v	Verbose output.

Using cpio

The following example uses the find command to copy the directory through cpio and the tape drive:

```
# find . print | cpio -ocBv > /dev/rmt0
```

mt

The mt command is only used with tape drives. It enables you to manipulate the tape drive and is usually used with tar to get to a specific tar file on a tape. For example, if backing up your entire server takes only 1GB, and your tape holds 2.5GB, you can use mt to move to a blank section of a tape after you tar your first backup to it.

Table 15-4 describes several useful options for mt.

Table 15-4	mt Options
Option	*What It Does*
-f *tape_device*	Make mt operate on the tape drive named *tape_device*.
status	Display the status of the tape drive.
rewind	Rewind the tape.
retension	Wind and rewind the tape to fix the tension.
erase	Erase the tape.
fsf *n*	Forward-skip *n* tape files.
bsf *n*	Go back *n* tape files.
eom	Skip to the end of the recorded media.

Using other software

In addition to the programs you find on your Linux CD, other software is available for backing up your server. It is usually supplied by a third party, sometimes costs money, and usually has more features and functionality than the backup software included with your Linux server. Many of these software packages are front ends to tar or cpio, so you could duplicate their functionality with scripts called by cron jobs if you needed to.

The following sections introduce you to some of the more common Linux backup programs and tell you where to find them.

Amanda

Amanda, the Advanced Maryland Automatic Network Disk Archiver, is free software designed to back up many computers on a network to a single, large-capacity tape drive. You might find Amanda on your operating system CDs, or you can download it from http://www.amanda.org.

ARKEIA

ARKEIA is a higher-end backup software for Linux and many other UNIXes plus other clients. Check out http://www.arkeia.com.

BRU

BRU is a highly rated backup program that runs in X-Window. BRU is based on tar but adds functionality for data verification and error handling. You can download BRU from http://www.bru.com. It is somewhat expensive, although it's cheaper for Linux than for some other UNIX flavors. You can also download a demo version to evaluate it.

PerfectBACKUP+

PerfectBACKUP+ is a moderately priced backup utility for Linux that runs in X-Window. You can download a 30-day demo. You can get PerfectBACKUP+ at http://www.merlinsoftech.com/.

rhbackup

Rhbackup is a utility that comes with Red Hat Linux. The configuration file for rhbackup is /etc/sysconfig/tape, while the default backup table is /etc/backuptab.

taper

Taper is another utility included with Red Hat Linux. Taper is a GUI-based backup method. To see the options available for taper, type **taper ?** as the superuser.

Configuring Your Backup System

After you choose a backup device and method, you need to set up a backup process. To formulate your process, decide how often you want to back up your Samba server, whether you will use full backups or partial backups, and how you want to store the backups.

How often?

The first question you need to answer is how often will you back up your server? Is it a printer server for which you only change the configuration once or twice a month, or is it a file server that your users access daily?

Generally, the more often your users change their data on the server, the more often you want to back it up. Backing up once a day (or night) is the most you should need for almost all circumstances.

Full or partial backups?

Decide how often to do full backups and how often to do partial backups. Full backups have the advantage of enabling you to fully restore your server in one operation, while partial backups might require several operations to restore your server.

If your server has 10GB of hard-drive space and your tape holds only 5GB, you cannot do a full backup. If a full backup takes 10 hours and you start it at midnight when the second shift goes home, you won't be very popular when the first shift comes in at 8 a.m. and the server is very slow because the backup isn't done. If you find your backup process takes a long time, you could do a full backup on weekends and partial backups during the week.

If you end up doing partial backups, you can choose from many different partial backup processes. Most partial backup processes do a full backup once a month or once a week, and then do partial, incremental backups for the rest of the month or week. Partial backups can back up only files that have changed since the last full backup. Or they can back up only the files that have changed since the last partial backup.

The downside of using partial backups is that it takes longer to completely restore your system. In this case, you need to restore using the last full backup and then use enough partial backups to restore your system as completely as possible. Depending on how you've selected files for partial backup, you might need to use every partial backup tape.

One of the more challenging parts of doing partial backups is figuring out which files have not been backed up since the last full backup. Some versions of UNIX, such as Solaris, have backup utilities like ufsdump and ufsrestore that have built-in functionality to do partial backups.

For the rest of the UNIX family, including Linux, apply the `find` command to determine which files you need to back up.

TIP

Finding files to back up with find

Find is a very useful Linux utility. With it, you can search your hard drive for files of a certain name, that match a pattern, that were modified a certain number of days ago, or that were accessed a certain number of days ago. The last two uses of find are the ones that are very suitable for use in partial backups.

The basic syntax for find is find *starting_path options*. To start searching from the current directory, type **find . *options.*** To start searching at the root directory, type **find / *options.***

You can have one or more options with the find command. The options that are particularly useful for finding files to back up are -mtime and -print. The -mtime option tells find to search for files that were modified more than *n* days ago, exactly *n* days ago, or less than *n* days ago, for the cases of -mtime +*n*, -mtime *n* and -mtime -*n*, respectively. For example, if your last full backup was 6 days ago, find / -mtime -6 would find all files

that were changed in the last 6 days, since the last backup.

Find isn't very useful unless it can tell you what files it found. The -print option tells find to print out the files that it finds. While you want to know which files need to be backed up, it's helpful to have a list in a file for tar to read by using the -T option. The following example finds all the files that have been modified in the last 6 days and then prints the filenames to the directory named files_to_backup.txt in the /tmp directory. The next line shows tar creating an archive on the tape drive with that list of files.

```
# find / -mtime -6 -print >
    /tmp/files_to_backup.txt
# tar cvf /dev/rmt0 -T /tmp/
    files_to_backup.txt
```

After you've tried these commands a few times and you're satisfied that they work, you can write a script and have cron run it every time you need it.

Making partial backups of the hard drive

If your hard drive is bigger than your backup media, you have to decide which parts of your hard drive to back up. If your drive is broken into smaller partitions, and each partition is smaller than your backup media, that makes it much easier because you can back up whole partitions. If your largest partition is bigger than your backup media, you probably have to use a backup utility with a multivolume option to have your archive backup span several backup media. One way to have your backup span several tapes (or disks) is to use tar with the -M flag.

You also probably want to do partial backups, particularly on any partitions that change frequently — for example, the partition containing your user's home directories.

Doing daily partial backups

One method of doing partial backups is to back up all the files that have changed that day. This approach works best when you have regularly scheduled full backups. Hence, the most restoration you will need in the event of a catastrophic system failure is from the last full backup and then from the daily backups since the last full backup. In this case, weekly is a good schedule for the full backup. If you did a full backup Friday night, the most you would have to do to recover would be from the full Friday night backup, then Monday, Tuesday, Wednesday, and Thursday partial backups.

Because you are only backing up the files that have changed in the last day, the daily backups should be small and the process should be quick.

To set up daily partial backups, first create a script that finds all the files that have been changed in the last day. Then write those files to a temporary file and have your archiving software read that file. The following script does just that:

```
#/bin/sh
find / -mtime -1 -print > /tmp/dailychanges.txt
tar cvf /dev/rmt0 -T /tmp/dailychanges.txt
```

After you test this script and it works, have `cron` call it daily except for the day that you do the full backup. If you do a full backup on Friday night, call this script on Monday, Tuesday, Wednesday, and Thursday nights. If the name of your script is dailybackup.sh in the /root directory, the cron record would look like the following example:

```
55 23 * * 1-4 /root/dailybackup.sh
```

Backing up files since your last full backup

A second method for partial backups is to back up all the files that have changed since your last full backup. This method does require scheduling your full backups at regular intervals.

The advantage to backing up all your files that have changed since your last full backup is that a full system backup requires only two backups: the full backup and the backup with all the changes. The disadvantage of this scheme is that each night's backup will get bigger and take longer and longer.

Backing up files since your last full backup can be harder to implement. Commercial backup software might do this easier, but if you are using the built-in utilities, it's a little trickier to implement. Here, we describe a way to do the incremental backup with several cron records.

Assume that you want to do a full backup on Friday night, and then a backup on Monday night covers what was changed on Monday. A partial backup on Tuesday night backs up everything that was changed on Monday and

Tuesday, and so on. You can do these partial backups with four different cron scripts. The one for Monday, named Monday.sh, would look like the following example:

```
#/bin/sh
find / -mtime -1 -print > /tmp/dailychanges.txt
tar cvf /dev/rmt0 -T /tmp/dailychanges.txt
```

The script for Tuesday night would look very similar:

```
#/bin/sh
find / -mtime -2 -print > /tmp/dailychanges.txt
tar cvf /dev/rmt0 -T /tmp/dailychanges.txt
```

The only difference between the two scripts is that the `mtime` value for Tuesday is -2 to cover Monday and Tuesday. Similarly, the `mtime` value for the Wednesday script would be -3, and for Thursday it would be -4.

If you name each script for the day of the week it is supposed to be run and call each by a separate cron record, the cron file looks like this when you're ready to go:

```
55 23 * * 1 /root/monday.sh
55 23 * * 2 /root/tuesday.sh
55 23 * * 3 /root/wednesday.sh
55 23 * * 4 /root/thursday.sh
55 23 * * 5 /root/fullbackup.sh
```

Again, if you need help with scripts, Appendix E gives a brief overview.

This is a fairly inelegant way of doing partial backups, but it gets the job done. Most commercial backup software has partial backup functionality built in.

Creating multilevel partial backups

A final method for doing partial backups is to use a multilevel backup scheme. A common example is to do a full backup every month, daily backups every day, and a weekly backup that backs up every file since your last full backup.

To set up this backup scheme with the Linux utilities, you need to use `cron` to run the full backup on the first day of the month (set the third field in the cron record to 1), run partial backups daily, and run weekly backups that archive everything since the last full backup (set the third field in cron to 8, 15, and 22, respectively, and use `mtime` values of -7, -14 and -21 in the scripts).

Do you need compression?

Another question you have to answer is whether you need compression techniques. You can fit a lot more data on backup media if you use compression, but some forms of compression are very sensitive to errors. One error in the data could cause the entire compressed archive to be unreadable. Others are less sensitive; only the archived file with the data error is unreadable.

Archives created with `tar` are much more vulnerable to compression problems than archives created with `cpio`.

Backup media storage

Finally, you should decide how to archive and store your backup media. Many cautious administrators store copies offsite in case of fire, Godzilla, or other natural disasters.

You can store copies of your backup media at home, a branch office, or a company that specializes in storing media. These choices depend on how sensitive or significant your data is and should be implemented into company policy.

If you use pricey backup media, you might want to reuse your older backup media. Make sure that you won't need it for a backup, be sure to test it occasionally, and label it very clearly.

Using pen and paper

Amazingly enough, there is a place for pen and paper in your backup scheme. Keep a small notebook for your server where you record your partition table, drive addresses, and any notes. The partition table is the most important; without it, the data on your hard drive can't be recognized.

Testing your backup

After you have your backup process in place (preferably before your users have come to totally depend on your server), set some time aside to try to restore your server from scratch. It's much better to find a problem in your backup and restoration process when your server is new and barely used on a quiet Saturday morning than it is to find out at 2:00 a.m., 6 hours before quarterly reports are due. See the next section for help in restoring your system.

Restoring Your System with a Backup

The best archived data in the world isn't worth much unless you know how to retrieve the data from the archive.

The order can be important

If you have a full, complete backup of your system, you don't have to worry about the order in which you restore your system. If you have a full backup and some partial backups that were created after the full one was created, you need to restore them in the correct order, which is the same order in which the archives were backed up. Restore the most recent full backup and then restore the partial backups.

You only need to recover a few files

Recovering a desperately needed file or two is probably the simplest scenario, and it's also the one most likely to get you a free lunch. In this case, just retrieve the specific files from the backup media with the proper command and options. The following example retrieves the directory /home/jerry from the tar file on the tape device /dev/rmt0:

```
# tar xvf /dev/rmt0 /home/jerry
```

Your system boots, but you need to recover one or more partitions

Say your computer crashed and your system boots, but you need to recover one or more partitions. Perhaps the partition containing the /home directory got corrupted. Follow these steps to recover a partition:

1. **Boot the system into single-user mode so you can work on the partition without interference from your users.**

   Try to let everyone know that the server will be unavailable for a while. There are two ways to boot the system into single-user mode: type **init 1** at the superuser prompt, or type **single** at the LILO prompt.

2. **Run a file-system check with** fsck **on the affected partition.**

   A small chance exists that checking the file system could even fix your problem. If not, use the Linux file-system-checking utility fsck on the affected partition. If the /home section was on the /dev/hda4 partition, the following command runs fsck on it:

   ```
   # fsck -t ext2 /dev/hda4
   ```

   You have to confirm any file fixes that fsck wants to perform on the partition.

If fsck does not fix your problem, you need to restore the partition from the backup.

Your system won't boot

A machine that won't boot can be the toughest problem to recover from, but at least you don't have to worry too much about damaging your existing file system during recovery, because it's already damaged. You need a boot disk and maybe the rescue disk, your latest backups, and possibly the paper copy of your partition table:

1. **Get the system up and running by booting with the boot disk and then supply the rescue disk when prompted.**

2. **When the system comes up, try to access the hard drive and then run** `fsck` **on each partition.**

3. **If you can't access the hard drive, you might need to repartition it with** `fdisk` **and then reformat the hard drive with** `mkfs`.

   At this point, it might just be simpler to reinstall Linux.

4. **Restore the system from the backup archive.**

Chapter 16

Securing Your Samba Server

· ·

· ·

*Y*ou could fill a bookshelf on network and server security, so we can't provide definitive treatment here. However, we can cover the general principles, direct you to some files to check, and mention some applications that you can run to increase your network security.

Passwords — The Keys to Your Server

Passwords can be your biggest security headache. Even if you have a perfect, impenetrable security setup, if your passwords are compromised, you have no security. To keep your passwords safe, you have to strike a happy balance between keeping things easy for your users and maintaining the necessary security. If your password policy is too complex, your users might end up writing down their passwords, which is much less secure than just sticking with an easier password policy.

Most modern Linux distributions have additional password security features. Linux is usually set up to use shadow passwords, with the actual encrypted password stored in a special file that only the root user can read. That prevents an intruder from encrypting passwords and then comparing them with the encrypted passwords on the Linux system. Many Linux distributions also use Pluggable Authentication Modules (Linux-PAM) to check that passwords aren't in a dictionary or easily guessed.

For a more in-depth treatment of passwords and Linux system administration, check out *Linux Administration For Dummies*.

Keeping passwords safe

To keep your passwords safe, have a password policy, and verify that users don't use very simple passwords. These two methods can work together for increased security.

Developing a sane password policy

A sane password policy depends on how you set up your Linux server and how you interact with your users. A good rapport with your users can save plenty of password trouble down the road.

With Linux, you can specify how often users must change their passwords. If you specify a long time, you lose security. If you specify a short time, people start repeating passwords, which also can decrease your security. A good rule of thumb is to force a password change every three months.

In addition to specifying how often users must change their passwords, you can recommend that your users choose good passwords. Here are a few ideas to help your users choose good passwords:

- Ask them not to use family or pet names or the name of their favorite football team.
- Suggest that they include one or two numbers or punctuation marks in the password.
- Ask that they don't use a complete word, or break the word in two.
- For an easily remembered but hard to crack password, suggest that they combine two short words with a number or punctuation mark, such as car%truck.
- Ask that they don't write down their passwords where someone can see them.

Shadow passwords

Most new Linux distributions use shadow passwords. The system keeps encrypted passwords in a file that only the root can read, usually called /etc/shadow. This helps protect against a dictionary attack, in which a password-cracker runs an entire dictionary through the encryption scheme to generate a list of encrypted passwords and then compares the encrypted passwords against those in the /etc/passwd file. If you use shadow passwords, the /etc/passwd file does not contain encrypted passwords. Instead, it has an asterisk in the password field.

If you have the choice of using shadow passwords, do it. The security is much better and the change is transparent to your users. If you can't use shadow passwords, you might want to consider updating Linux (or what ever operating system you are using).

Password checking with Linux-PAM

For even better security, you can run Linux-PAM (Pluggable Authentication Modules) on your Samba server. Linux-PAM adds security checks to common programs such as the password program. If you try to change a password, Linux invokes the password section of Linux-PAM, which prevents you from using an easily guessed password or one that is too close to a previous password.

Linux-PAM is often added by default in Linux installations, or you might need to select Linux-PAM as an option. In either case, it adds a lot of security but at the price of being more restrictive on password selection. As a result, you may have to bail out your users a little more often when you use Linux-PAM because it requires harder-to-remember passwords.

For Red Hat Linux, Linux-PAM is configured in the /etc/pam.d directory. If you want to read more about it, the documents included with Linux-PAM are very helpful.

Updating and synchronizing passwords

You can increase security by providing a seamless way to synchronize Linux and Samba passwords. *Synchronization* occurs when a user changes a password in Windows, and the corresponding password gets changed for Samba and Linux, too. You can set password synchronization with three global parameters:

- unix password sync
- passwd chat
- passwd program

Synchronizing passwords with unix password sync

If you want to synchronize your Linux passwords with your Windows/Samba passwords, set the global parameter unix password sync to yes. Then, whenever you change your Samba password, Samba attempts to change your Linux password, too. You might have to specify which password program your Samba server uses and what commands the server uses to change passwords.

Specifying which password program

If you are trying to synchronize Samba and Linux passwords, you may need to tell Samba which password program your Linux server uses. If you set the `unix password sync` parameter to yes, and a user changes a password, Samba calls the program specified in `passwd program` as the root user in an attempt to change the user's Linux password.

Talking to the password program with passwd chat

By setting the `passwd chat` Samba parameter, you can specify how Samba interacts with the password program specified in the `passwd program` parameter. The `passwd chat` parameter is useful because the password-changing process can differ for each type of UNIX operating system. The password-changing process is similar on some UNIXes (you type **passwd** as the user), but others just return `new password` for a prompt, for example. With the `passwd chat` parameter, you can customize the Samba server's password-changing routine to match your Linux server's behavior.

To build your password chat strings, you can use the following macros:

%o	old password
%n	new password
\n	line feed
\r	carriage return
\t	tab
\s	space

You can also use an asterisk (*) in the string, which matches any set of characters. If you have to use a string with a space in it, enclose the string in double quotes.

The default value for `passwd chat` is

```
passwd chat = *old*passwd* %0\n *new*password* %n\n & *new*password* %n\n
              changed
```

Some password exchanges that would work with this `passwd chat` script are

```
Please enter your old password: old_password
Please enter your new password: new_password
Please re-enter your new password: new_password
```

Or perhaps

```
Enter old password: old_password
Enter new password: new_password
Re-enter new password: new_password
```

Here is an example of a password exchange that would not work with the pre-ceding `passwd chat`:

```
Enter your current password: old_password
Enter your new password: new_password
And enter it again, to check: new_password
```

But if you replaced *old*password* with *current*password* and the second *new*password* with *enter*, the password chat would work.

Using SWAT to configure password synchronization

Now, how would you use SWAT to configure password synchronization? Because the three password synchronization parameters are global parameters, you start on the Globals page of SWAT. Then, go to the Advanced View and check under Security Options. After you configure your password para-meters, click Commit Changes and then go to the Status page of SWAT to restart the Samba daemons, nmbd and smbd.

Checking Your Users, Groups, and Permissions

To understand Linux security, you need a good understanding of permissions and how they work with users and groups. You need to be able to give the cor-rect rights to users and groups so they can get their work done, but you don't want to inadvertently give improper rights to important system directories.

Checking permissions with ls -l

If you need to review the rights of a file or directory, use the `ls` command along with the `-l` switch to display all the rights of each file or directory. You need to be in the parent directory to list a file or directory.

For the cases in which you have more than a screen full of files and directo-ries, use the pipe and `more` command to display one screen at a time. To dis-play one page of `ls -l` at a time, type **ls -l | more**. Press the spacebar each time you want to display the next page. The following example is a small list-ing of my home directory, using `ls -l`:

```
#ls -l
total 6412
drwxr-xr-x   5 george   george      4096 Feb  6 16:31 Desktop
-rw-r--r--   1 root     root      307526 Jun 23 23:16 FG7sub
-rwxr--r--   1 george   george     71680 Apr  9 23:56 SFDC14.DOC
-rw-rw-r--   1 root     root       10240 May 19 22:26 backtest
-rwxrwxr-x   1 root     root         136 May 19 22:26 backuptest.sh
```

The first column shows the rights. The first character identifies whether it's a file or a directory: a dash (-) is a file and a d is a directory. The next three letters identify the read, write, and execute rights for the owner; the next three letters give the read, write, and execute rights for the group; and the final three letters give the read, write, and execute rights for everyone on the system, including the owner and the group.

The second column from the left is the file or directory owner, and the third column is the group associated with the file or directory.

Changing permissions with chmod

To change the permissions of a file, use the chmod command. To use chmod on a file, you must be the owner of the file or have root privileges.

The easiest way to use chmod is with the options u, g, or o to indicate rights for the user, the group, or other (the world). For example, to give the user full rights (read, write, and execute) to the file named reports.sh, you would type the following command:

```
# chmod u=rwx reports.sh
```

You can combine the chmod options if you separate them with commas. For example, to give the user and group full rights to the directory named policies, while giving everyone else just read rights, you would type the following command:

```
# chmod u=rwx,g=rwx,o=r policies
```

This example adds group execute rights to the directory named accounting:

```
# chmod g+x accounting
```

This example removes write rights for the "other" user (the world) for the directory named public:

```
# chmod o-w public
```

Changing owners with chown

Use the chown command to change the owner of a file or directory. The syntax is easy; just type **chown *new_owner file_name*.**

The following example changes the owner of the weblogs file from root to apache:

```
# chown apache weblogs
```

Changing groups with chgrp

To change the group associated with a file or directory, use the chgrp command. The syntax for chgrp is very similar to the syntax for chown, except you use a group name instead of an owner's name.

The following example shows the group masters being assigned to the directory cgi-bin:

```
# chgrp masters cgi-bin
```

Checking for files with suid and sgid permissions

To give someone executing a file the same permissions as the file owner, you use two special permissions: suid and sgid. The most common example of this is the password program. Only the root user should have write rights to the /etc/passwd file, but all users need to be able to change their own passwords. Because root owns the password program, if you set the suid permission, any users who try to change their own passwords can do so, with root permissions. Sgid works similarly, but it is the group that is associated with the file instead of the owner.

Suid and sgid are dangerous with programs that allow you to start a shell from within the program. For example, in the vi editor, you can start a shell and temporarily leave the editor. If vi had the suid permission set, any shell you start would have the equivalent of root-user access.

You can see how giving someone root power on a command can be dangerous, so check which files have suid and sgid set. For an individual file, it's easy to check. Just type **ls -l** in the parent directory. Files with suid set have an s instead of an x for the owner's execution permission, while files with sgid set have an s instead of an x for the group's execute permissions.

Most security programs know enough to check for suid and sgid permissions. As an extra level of security, you may want to periodically list which files have suid and sgid permissions set. The following command finds all the programs on your system with suid and sgid set and stores their names in the file named suids in the /root directory:

```
# find / -perm +6000 -print > /root/suids
```

Checking Your Configuration Files

Your Samba server has several configuration files that you should check for security problems. These files could be targeted by people who want to break into your system, or they could open security holes.

The password files

The password files contain the list of users on your Samba server and the encrypted passwords. These files are obvious targets for a break-in attempt:

- /etc/passwd
- /etc/shadow
- The smbpasswd file

If you are not using shadow passwords, the /etc/passwd file contains the encrypted passwords. Someone with write access to the /etc/passwd file could delete an encrypted password and make an account open without a password. Make sure that only root can write to your /etc/passwd file.

If you are using shadow passwords, only root should be able to read the shadow password file, usually /etc/shadow. On the other hand, everyone should be able to read the /etc/passwd file, but only root should be able to write to this file.

If you are using encrypted passwords in Samba, you should keep the smbpasswd file as protected as the /etc/passwd file. The rights should be 0700,and if the smbpasswd file is in a private directory, the directory rights should be 0700.

The group files

The group files, /etc/group, are another set of files that you need to protect. If you add a user to the wrong group, you might give that user superuser rights. Only the root user should have write rights on the /etc/group file.

The valid services

The /etc/inetd.conf file contains a list of all the services that can be started from inetd on your Samba server. For a more secure server, you can go through this file and comment out any services that you don't need. Every service your server runs is one more service that an attacker might exploit.

Checking processes started in the /etc/rc.d directories

The processes that run automatically on most Linux servers are stored in run-level directories, such as rc3.d, in the /etc/rc.d directories. To be extra thorough, go through each directory and stop processes from starting if you don't need them. You can stop a process from starting by renaming the startup script (which beings with S) to something that does not begin with S or K. If you need to know a little bit more about processes, see Chapter 3.

Login files

Login records of your system are kept in the /var/log/utmp, /var/run/utmp, and /var/log/btmp files, if they exist. Intruders might want to tamper with these files to hide their tracks.

Logging Commands and sulog

Two commands enable you to see who last logged on to your system and who last logged on unsuccessfully: last and lastb, respectively. Log files won't prevent someone from breaking into your Samba server, but they are useful in tracking what happened if someone has broken into your Samba server.

The file/var/log/btmp has to exist for lastb to work. If it doesn't exist, you can create it with the touch command — for example, **touch /var/log/btmp**.

The SULOG variable points to the file that logs all switch-to-root-user requests. A typical place to set it is in /etc/default/su. The default place for the SULOG is /var/adm/sulog.

Security Tools

You can load various security tools on a Samba server. The program sudo gives users root-equivalent accounts for specific actions, which prevents you from having to give the root password to people. Other programs check the passwords on the system to make sure they're sufficiently hard to guess, which is a boon if you're not checking passwords with PAM.

Other tools can increase the security of network traffic. Some tools mimic an attacker, probing your system for weaknesses and letting you know about those shortcomings before a cracker takes advantage of them (with the same tools). Finally, a few programs run daily looking for signs of an intruder. If your server does get cracked, at least you can get an idea of what the intruder did.

The following sections give only one or two URLs for each tool. Because the Internet grows so fast, you can probably find 20 more sites for each of these tools. If the suggested site don't have the goods, use a search engine to find current tools.

Giving partial root access with sudo

Sudo is a nifty program that can give specific users root access for a few, specific commands. With a good use of sudo, you won't ever need to give out the root password to your users for them to perform special tasks. Sudo also has a logging feature to see what your users do with sudo, and it has a timeout feature. Sudo's home page is `http://www.courtesan.com/sudo`, and you can download it from `ftp://coast.cs.purdue.edu`.

Checking for good passwords

If your Linux server doesn't have the PAM password protection module cracklib, or you have a UNIX system without it, consider running a few password-cracking programs. These programs check the passwords for easily guessed or broken passwords and give you a report of their findings.

Crack

The crack program tries to figure out users' passwords via normal guessing algorithms. Crack takes lots of processor power to run, so run it overnight when no users will be inconvenienced. Download crack from `ftp://ftp.cert.org/pub/tools/crack` or `ftp://coast.cs.purdue.edu/pub/tols/unix/crack/`.

Obvious-pw

Obvious-pw reviews passwords and evaluates whether they seem obvious. You can download Obvious-pw from `http://ciac.llnl.gov/ciac/ToolsUnixAuth.html#Obvious`.

Improving network security

Here are a couple of programs you can run that can greatly increase the security of your network. Secure shell (also known as ssh) is used to encrypt TCP/IP traffic between two computers running SSH. TCP wrappers is a program used to allow or deny specific TCP/IP requests by network number.

Secure shell (SSH)

Secure shell, commonly known as SSH, encrypts TCP/IP communications between two computers. Both computers must be running SSH for it to work.

SSH is significant because many basic TCP/IP programs use unencrypted passwords. If you monitor network packets when someone connects with a normal telnet session, you will see that user's logon and password in unencrypted text.

If you want to know more about secure shell, visit the SSH home page at `http://www.ssh.fi`. You can also download SSH from other sites, such as `ftp://sunsite.unc.edu:/pub/packages/security/ssh` or `http://www.datafellows.com/f-secure`.

OpenSSH

A program known as OpenSSH functions as a replacement for SSH. You can download it from `http://www.openssh.com`.

TCP wrappers

The TCP wrappers program is a daemon that monitors network requests for services listed in /etc/services. It allows or disallows requests depending on how TCP wrappers is configured. TCP wrappers can filter requests based on network numbers, domain, or the requested services. TCP wrappers is usually available on your Linux (or UNIX) CD. If not, you can download it from `ftp://porcupine.org/pub/security` or `ftp://ftp.win.tue.nl/pub/security`.

Red Hat Linux and most other Linux distributions have TCP wrappers enabled by default.

Checking your system's security

Quite a few programs can probe the security of your Samba server much like a computer cracker would. However, unlike a computer cracker, they provide a nicely detailed report of any security holes they find. Be aware that these programs aren't a deep-dark secret — any adept cracker knows about them, so you should, too.

Run these programs against your Samba server to check for any security holes. If you find that your users have any of these programs, ask them why.

SATAN

SATAN is an infamous network security tool used to look for security holes in a computer or a network. However, SATAN is rather old, and it opens up several other security holes, so don't use it.

SAINT

SAINT, the Security Administrator's Integrated Network Tool, is a successor to SATAN but without the potential for opening security holes. You can use SAINT to probe a computer or an entire network for security holes. SAINT's home page is `http://www.wwdsi.com/saint/`.

COPS

COPS (Computer Oracle and Password System) is a collection of programs that checks various parts of your system for security holes. COPS checks for known problems and common security holes and reports its findings. Download COPS from `ftp://ftp.cert.org/pub/tools/cops` or `ftp://coast.cs.purdue.edu/pub/tools/unix/cops`.

Tiger

Tiger is a collection of scripts that scan a computer for potential security problems. It is like an updated version of COPS. Download Tiger from `http://wuarchive.wustl.edu/packages/security/TAMU` or `ftp://net.tamu/edu/pub/security/TAMU`.

Checking for intruders

Another group of network security tools deals with intruder detection. Tripwire checks important files for unexpected changes and can catch a cracker adding extra accounts. Gabriel and Courtney check for network probing that can indicate an attack by SATAN or SAINT.

Tripwire

Tripwire makes a database that records the size of your binary and configuration files. Then, it checks the files and compares them to the database to see if any files have changed size that shouldn't have. Computer crackers sometimes make changes to configuration files to hide their tracks. Or they might add a secret account. Or they might install binary files that do what they're supposed to, but they have a few secret back doors in them. Tripwire detects these sorts of changes.

After you set up tripwire, run it nightly from a cron script. Check Chapter 15 if you need a refresher on cron.

You can download the latest versions of tripwire from `http://www.tripwiresecurity.com`. Older versions are usually available in public ftp directories such as `http://wuarchive.wustl.edu/packages/security/tripwire`.

Watch for SATAN and SAINT with Gabriel and Courtney

SATAN and SAINT are good at probing for network holes, but they do leave an easy-to-spot trail. Easy-to-spot, that is, if you have Gabriel and Courtney, two programs that watch for excessive amounts of network probing. Gabriel's home page is `http://www.lat.com/gabe.htm`, and you can also download it from `ftp://ftp.lat.com/gabriel-1.0.tar.Z`. Download Courtney from `ftp:/ciac.llnl.gov/pub/ciac/sectools/unix` or `ftp://ftp.lat.com/courtney-1.3.tar.Z`.

Physical Security

One thing you can't overlook is the physical security of your Samba server. The level of security depends on what services your Samba server provides. A Samba server that is strictly a print server doesn't have to be nearly as secure as one that is the domain server for your whole company. If you plan to use your Samba server as a CD-ROM or Zip drive server, it needs to be more accessible than a file server that can be stored in a locked server room. Many security holes are accessible when you can reboot a server, so this section includes several ways to protect the server.

Protecting your server

The more important your Samba server, the more steps you should take to protect it. Lock it in a server room, or perhaps you can chain it to a desk.

Protecting the server's power

Depending on the nature of your Server, you might want to prevent the power switches and outlets from being turned off. If intruders can reboot a Linux server, they have a better chance of breaking into it.

Disabling booting from the floppy

You may want to disable the floppy drive of a publicly accessible Samba server if you don't want someone to be able to reboot it with a floppy. Otherwise, someone could easily take control of the Samba server. You disable the user of the floppy in the computer's BIOS when it first boots up. You might even set up a BIOS password for greater security.

Disabling rebooting with Ctrl+Alt+Delete

It isn't hard to break into a Linux box if you can stand in front of it and you know a few tricks and can reboot the Linux server. For this reason, you might want to disable rebooting the Linux server via Ctrl+Alt+Delete. (Yes, just like Windows, you can reboot a Linux server that way.) To prevent the Linux server from recognizing Ctrl+Alt+Delete as a shutdown command, edit the /etc/inittab file and comment out the line that traps CTRL+ALT+DELETE.

Part VI
The Part of Tens

The 5th Wave   By Rich Tennant

"IT'S NO USE, CAPTAIN. THE ONLY WAY WE'LL CRACK THIS CASE IS TO GET INTO PROF. TAMARA'S PERSONAL COMPUTER FILE, BUT NO ONE KNOWS THE PASSWORD. KILROY'S GOT A HUNCH IT STARTS WITH AN 'S', BUT HECK, THAT COULD BE ANYTHING."

In this part . . .

The Part of Tens is a collection of important tips in easy-to-scan lists for beginners and experienced readers alike. Chapter 17 covers common errors that administrators often make and explains how to fix them. Chapter 18 guides you through some troubleshooting steps to try if you have connectivity problems in your network. Chapter 19 lists good practices that savvy administrators should do to keep it together. Chapter 20 introduces some Samba options you might need down the road.

Chapter 17

Almost Ten Common Errors

. . . .

. . . .

*T*his chapter lists several common errors administrators often make when building Samba networks. Yes, we also explain how to correct those errors.

Editing the Wrong smb.conf File

If you make changes to Samba's configuration, and they don't seem to take effect even after you restart the smbd and nmbd daemons, you might inadvertently be editing the incorrect smb.conf file.

Use `testparm` to identify the default smb.conf file. The first line returned from `testparm` tells you what the default smb.conf is. Try this command to get the first line only:

```
# testparm -s | grep smb.conf
```

You should get a response such as:

```
Load smb config files from /etc/smb.conf
```

Write down or print out any error messages you get that look like the following example:

```
Unable to open configuration file "/etc/smb.conf"!
```

Such a message tells you that Samba searched in the /etc directory for smb.conf and could not find it. If the error reports any problems with the path or the file permissions, the error message can help you can determine what and where Samba expects the smb.conf file to be.

Some editors automatically create backup smb.conf files (such as smb.conf~). After identifying the location of the default smb.conf file and ensuring it has the settings you expect, delete any duplicates to avoid future confusion.

Using the Wrong Password Encryption Scheme

If you use encrypted passwords on your clients, which is the default for all but the earliest versions of Windows 95, you must enable encrypted passwords on the Samba server.

To verify you are using encrypted passwords on your client, check the clients by looking at the registry:

1. **Click Start⇨Run, type** regedit **in the Open field of the Run dialog box, and then click OK to start regedit.**

   In the Registry Editor window, the left panel shows the registry tree, and the right panel shows the name and value of each item.

2. **For Windows 95/98, click the plus boxes to expand HKEY_LOCAL_MACHINE, System, CurrentControlSet, Services, VxD, and then VNETSUP.**

   For Windows NT, click the plus boxes to expand HKEY_LOCAL_MACHINE, System, CurrentControlSet, Services, Rdr, and then Parameters.

   For Windows 2000, expand HKEY_LOCAL_MACHINE, System, CurrentControlSet, Services, LanManWorkstation, and then Parameters.

   If you see a key called EnablePlainTextPassword, encryption is disabled.

3. **Delete this key to return to the default of encrypted passwords.**

4. **Ensure encrypted passwords are enabled in Samba by viewing the smb.conf file. Verify the following three parameters are set. In this case, the smbpasswd file is in the /usr/local/etc/private directory:**

```
security = user
encrypt passwords = yes
smb passwd file = /usr/local/etc/private/smbpasswd
```

See Chapter 9 for more details.

Accessing the Wrong Network

Use the `smbclient` utility to identify the network to which you are connecting. When you type **smbclient -L *hostname***, the added interface returned should be the IP address of your network card. If not, you might instead see the loopback port, 127.0.0.1. In that case, you might need to add the correct network address with the `interfaces` option in the smb.conf file (see Chapter 3). For example, you would add a line similar to this to the global section of the smb.conf file:

```
Interfaces = 192.168.11.3
```

Accessing the Wrong Workgroup

Verify your Samba server is set to the same workgroup as the clients. You set the `workgroup` parameter in the global section of the smb.conf file. In SWAT, go to the Globals page, and workgroup is the first field. Click Commit Changes and restart Samba for the change to take effect.

On the Windows clients, verify the workgroup name by right-clicking the Network Neighborhood, choosing Properties, and then selecting the Identification tab.

See Chapter 11 for more information.

Using the Wrong Network Protocol for Clients

Your Windows clients might not be using the correct network protocol. Chapter 4 details the steps you take to ensure they are using NetBIOS.

Assigning the Wrong Rights

Your shared directories might have incorrect rights assigned to them. Check the rights using the `ls -l` command with the name of the directory.

The leftmost column of the output details the security rights. The first character is for the type of device: `d` indicates a directory, and a dash (-) indicates a file. The next three characters are the user rights. For example, `rwx` means the user has read, write, and execute rights. If you see a `-` there, that right is missing — for example, `r-x` means read and execute only. The next characters refer to the rights of the group that owns the share, and the final three characters show the rights for everyone else on the Linux system (the world rights).

The third column lists the file or directory owner, and the fourth column lists the group with which the file or directory is associated.

The three Linux/UNIX commands you use to change rights for files and directories are `chown`, `chgrp`, and `chmod`. `Chown` changes the owner of the file or directory, `chgrp` changes the group associated with the file or directory, and `chmod` changes the rights of the file or directory.

Then, check the read and write rights for Samba for the share with the `read only`, `read list`, and `write list` parameters. Finally, verify the list of users associated with the share, if any, by checking the `user list` parameter.

See Chapter 8 for details.

Samba Isn't Running

If you are having connectivity problems, first verify that Samba is running. It's sort of like making sure the computer is plugged in, but it happens. Type the `ps` command — for example, **ps -ae** — to show a list of currently running processes. Ensure both smbd and nmbd are listed. Or in SWAT, the Status page indicates whether smbd or nmbd are running.

Then, check your setup for how you want Samba to start (either on startup or only when requested). See Chapter 3 for more information.

Using the Wrong User Names

Make sure that client user names match the ones on the Samba server. On the Windows client, verify the spelling of the logon name. In Linux, verify the user names in the /etc/passwd file.

If you discover a misspelling, delete the misspelled user, then re-add the correctly spelled user name. For more information on adding and deleting users, review the various methods we describe in Chapter 7.

Associating Users with the Wrong Group

If your users can't access the files they need, you might not have the correct group permissions set. Check the group permissions for the file with the `ls -l` command. Also verify the groups with which the users are associated by looking at the /etc/passwd and /etc/group files.

See Chapter 7 for more information.

Chapter 18

Slightly More Than Ten Troubleshooting Steps

*T*his chapter describes several things to check when troubleshooting connectivity problems with your network. We list them in the order of simple to more complex.

Check Hub Lights

First, look at the hub lights to ensure that your network interface cards (NICs) are communicating with the hub, and the hub is working as it should. Every hub port with a connected and turned on computer should be lit up.

Check the Windows NIC with ipconfig

To view configuration information for a NIC on a Windows client, use ipconfig — a useful utility that you enter at a DOS prompt (it is not available in Windows 95).

Choose Start⇨Programs⇨MS-DOS Prompt, and then type **ipconfig /All** for a detailed output that includes the Windows computer name and the type of network interface cards installed.

See Chapter 13 for more information.

Check the Linux NIC with ifconfig

You can use ifconfig to get a picture of your Samba server's network interfaces. At a command prompt, type **ifconfig** to see whether all the network interfaces you expect are available. You can also check that the correct network addresses are being used.

See Chapter 13 for more information.

Test the Network with ping

For client connectivity problems, try using ping to see if one computer can see another over the network.

To test connectivity at the most basic level, you need to know the IP address of the computer you want to verify. For example, if you wanted to determine whether your Samba server is connected to the computer with the IP address of 192.168.11.5, you would type this command:

```
# ping 192.168.11.5
```

If the network connection is successful (that is, your server can see the computer with the IP address of 192.168.11.5), you should get back something like this:

```
PING 192.168.11.5 (192.168.11.5) from 192.168.11.3 : 56(84) bytes of data.
64 bytes from 192.168.11.5: icmp_seq=0 ttl=255 time=2.5 ms
64 bytes from 192.168.11.5: icmp_seq=1 ttl=255 time=1.4 ms
```

See Chapter 13 for more information.

Make Sure Samba Is Running

It's sort of like making sure the computer is plugged in, but it does happen. Type the `ps` command — for example, **ps -ae** — to show a list of currently running processes. Ensure that both smbd and nmbd are listed. Or in SWAT, the Status page indicates whether smbd or nmbd are running.

Chapter 14 has more details.

Identify the Correct smb.conf File with testparm

If you make changes to Samba's configuration and they don't seem to take effect even after you restart the smbd and nmbd daemons, you might inadvertently be editing the incorrect smb.conf file.

Use `testparm` to identify the default smb.conf file. The first line returned from `testparm` tells you what the default smb.conf is. Try this command to get the first line only:

```
# testparm -s | grep smb.conf
```

You should get a response such as:

```
Load smb config files from /etc/smb.conf
```

See Chapter 3 for more information.

Check Samba's Status

The Samba program `smbstatus` gives you a quick look at what connections Samba is serving. By applying different options to `smbstatus`, you can see what a specific user is doing, what files are locked, what shares are being used, or what processes Samba is running.

Just typing **smbstatus** by itself gives a summary of the connections that your Samba server is running:

See Chapter 14 for details.

Check the Server with smbclient

Smbclient was developed to give Linux or UNIX machines access to Windows or SMB shares. Because a Samba share is an SMB share, you can use smbclient to access a Samba share. In troubleshooting terms, you can connect to a Samba share from the Linux workstation that Samba is running on to check out the shares. You can use smbclient to connect to a Samba server from the same server. You don't need to go to a Windows client to check it; you can do this at the command line with smbclient.

To see what shares are available on the Samba server, you can telnet in and run smbclient as follows:

```
$ smbclient -L terrapin -N
Added interface ip=192.168.11.5 bcast=192.168.11.255 & nmask=255.255.255.0
Domain=[WORKGROUP] OS=[UNIX] Server=[Samba 2.0.3]

        Sharename      Type       Comment
        ---------      ----       -------
        samba          Disk       Samba directory
        testparm       Disk       run testparm
        test           Disk
        IPC$           IPC        IPC Service (Samba Server)
        lp             Printer    \Canon BubbleJet & BJC-4300

        Server                    Comment
        ---------                 -------
        OLORIN                    Samba 2.0.5a
        TERRAPIN                  Samba Server

        Workgroup                 Master
        ---------                 -------
        WORKGROUP                 TERRAPIN
```

You can find out a lot about the Samba server from this output. First, note that this Samba server is using the IP address 192.168.11.5, which is good — if Samba was using the loopback port 127.0.0.0, it wouldn't be communicating on the network, and therefore wouldn't make a very good server.

Next you see the workgroup or domain name, which is WORKGROUP, and the Samba version.

Below the share listing is the server and workgroup information. The Server/Comment section lists the other Samba servers in the workgroup.

See Chapter 14 for more information.

Check the Network Neighborhood with nmblookup

With nmblookup, you can verify that a Windows client is correctly set up for Samba, and you can look at all the computers on your Windows network. You can also use nmblookup to verify that your Samba server is using the correct IP addresses. Finally, nmblookup identifies the master browser for a workgroup.

If you have only one Samba server and a specific client can't connect to it, narrowing down the problem can be difficult. Try nmblookup with the -B flag (for broadcast) and the Windows client's NetBIOS name. The following example searches for the client named liberty, and successfully returns liberty's IP address:

```
terrapin# nmblookup -B liberty
Sending queries to 192.168.11.2
```

Chapter 14 has more information.

Check Connectivity from Different Clients

If you are having trouble connecting to your Samba server from one client, try it from at least one other client of the same Windows version.

If you can connect to your Samba server with one client but not the other, the problem most likely lies with the client that cannot connect successfully. On the other hand, if neither client can connect to your Samba server, the problem is likely at the Samba server.

Also, what can you see in the Network Neighborhood? If you can't see the server but you can see other clients, check the workgroup parameter and the interfaces parameter at the client. If you can't see anything in the Network Neighborhood, not even other clients, check your client's Workgroup setting and IP address.

Chapter 4 discusses this in greater length.

Connect as Different Users

You can check Samba connectivity as different users in two ways: at the Samba server using smbclient, or at the Windows client. If one user can connect but the other one can't, you've narrowed it down to a problem with the user.

At the Samba server

To connect as a different user at the Samba server, simply use the `smbclient` command, supplying the name of the desired share, and use `-U` with the user name. Provide the share name by its uniform resource location.

The following example shows an smbclient connecting to the share named alli on the server terrapin as the user alli:

```
terrapin# smbclient //terrapin/alli -U alli
Added interface ip=192.168.11.5 bcast=192.168.11.255 & nmask=255.255.255.0
Password:
Domain=[WORKGROUP] OS=[UNIX] Server=[Samba 2.0.3]
smb: \> ls
  .cshrc            H       464  Sun Aug 15 12:00:13 1999
  .login            H       559  Sun Aug 15 12:00:14 1999
  .login_conf       H       139  Sun Aug 15 12:00:15 1999
  .mailrc           H       311  Sun Aug 15 12:00:15 1999
  .profile          H       700  Sun Aug 15 12:00:16 1999
  .shrc             H       832  Sun Aug 15 12:00:17 1999
  .mail_aliases     H       351  Sun Aug 15 12:00:17 1999
  .rhosts           H       257  Sun Aug 15 12:00:18 1999

  47102 blocks of size 8192. 7104 blocks available
```

At the Windows client

The second way of testing user connectivity is to connect as different users from a Windows client. At the logon screen, just use the name of a different user that has an account on your Samba server, and enter the new user's password.

As this new user, you should then be able to access the Samba server and the user's appropriate shares.

If a specific user can't connect

If a specific user can't connect, verify that the user name is spelled correctly in the /etc/passwd and smbpasswd files (if you are using encrypted passwords). If the user's name isn't spelled right, you need to delete the user and add the correctly spelled one. It is easier to do this at the Samba server than at the Windows client.

If the user name is spelled correctly, you can reset the passwords as the superuser. To reset the password in the /etc/passwd file, type **passwd** **user_name** and then enter the password twice. If you are using encrypted passwords, you need to reset the password in the smbpasswd file by typing **smbpasswd** **user_name** and then enter the new password twice.

For Further Help

You can find help out there, or in some cases, in there. Samba comes with man pages and documentation files that you install(ed) with Samba. If you can't find the answer on your computer, the Samba community probably has the answer.

Check the man pages

UNIX software is typically packed full of helpful hints on all the various commands and options. This information is stored in the manual pages ("man pages"). Simply type the command man, followed by the name of command of which you need to know. For example, to find out what the command smbclient does, type this at a command prompt:

```
# man smbclient
```

where:

> # is the prompt.
>
> man is the command to open the man pages to get documentation, usage, options, and other information about the command.
>
> smbclient is the command you want to know more about.

When you've found the answer, press Ctrl+Z to close the man page and return to the command prompt.

Check the documentation files

When you install Samba, you also get a bunch of text files that document various things. To find out where these files are stored, at a command prompt type the following command:

```
# find / -name textdocs -print
/usr/local/share/doc/samba/textdocs
```

(The output from this command shows that my FreeBSD Samba server keeps the Samba documentation in the /usr/local/share/doc/samba/textdocs document.)

After you locate the Samba documentation, move to the correct directory, list the files with ls, and then view the files you are interested in with the more or cat command.

Check the Samba Web pages

Go online to `http://www.samba.org` and you will find

- ✔ Details about the latest release
- ✔ Announcements and news
- ✔ Mailing list discussion archives
- ✔ Real documentation
- ✔ Books to reference
- ✔ Support contacts
- ✔ Information about GUI interfaces
- ✔ An introduction to Samba
- ✔ Samba vendor information
- ✔ And more!

Chapter 19

Ten Good Practices

*T*his chapter outlines several concepts and practices that can help you to avoid some headaches in the long run.

Keep Up to Date

The best way to keep up to date in the constantly changing software world is to regularly read Web sites such as these for starters:

▶ http://www.samba.org

▶ http://www.linux.com

▶ http://slashdot.org

See Appendix C for a complete list of resources.

Plan For Growth

If you are starting from scratch, try to think about the future when you design your network. For example, if you think you might be adding more computers later, consider a higher-capacity hub.

If you're tearing into walls to run cable, think about doubling your efforts so you don't have to do that dirty work twice. It costs only a little bit more to add extra network wiring at the initial installation, but it costs a lot to go back and add it later.

If you are buying a new server or server hardware, estimate your memory requirements (RAM and hard-drive space) and double it. Six months down the road, you'll be glad you did.

Plan Your Server Changes

Before you make any drastic changes to your Samba server, estimate how long it will take to make the change. Also, determine any necessary hardware changes. If it's going to take a while, you might need to implement the modifications over a long weekend. And it will probably take longer than you expect.

Whenever you expect the server might be inaccessible as a result of a modification or upgrade, give your users a few days notice so that Joe Engineer doesn't plan on coming in over the weekend to finish an important project, only to find the server unavailable. Use posted notices, e-mail, or sticky notes — whatever best gets the message across.

Last but not least, have an alternate plan in case your changes don't work.

Keep a Backup smb.conf File

The smb.conf file is the repository for all your important Samba settings. And you often find yourself making changes to it. If you're new at that, consider making a good copy of the smb.conf file and storing it in a safe place with a name you'll remember. Then, if you mangle the real smb.conf file beyond recognition, you can replace it with the known good one.

Keep a Paper Logbook of Your Server

Although it might seem tedious at first, keep a log or journal of all your settings, configuration changes, reported problems, and other activities regarding your Samba network. You should also log the settings for your partition table and the IRQ and DMA settings for devices on your server.

After you start changing things, it's amazing how quickly you can forget what you did. If you encounter a problem or crash, you can check your logs to see what the settings were, or you can retrace your steps back to a stable configuration.

Why paper? If your server crashes and you can't bring it back up, at least you can get to your logs to try to reconstruct the events leading up to the crash.

Join Your Local Linux Users Group

Sometimes you just have to talk to somebody. If you need help and support for the ins and outs of Linux, you can turn to one of the dozens of Linux user groups out there. Typically, the group meets informally for dinner and discusses whatever topics the members choose, sometimes with a guest speaker.

Meeting with a brainy and experienced group of gurus can answer lots of questions fast. It can also be reassuring to find that there are others just like you (at whatever level you find yourself).

Visit this site to find the Linux user group in your area: `http://www.linuxlinks.com/UserGroups/`.

Educate Your Users

When you have the opportunity, explain to your users what you are doing. The computer-adept ones may quickly pick it up, and may be able to solve the problem next time without bothering you.

If any of your users display an interest in Linux, you may want to give them older versions of Linux that you have. The version may be six months out of date, but it's enough to get their feet wet, and you're not breaking any licensing laws.

Who knows? You may find a protégé who you can train to take over your job, when you are ready for bigger and better things.

Back Up Your Samba Server

You've heard it before, and you know it's true: back up, back up, back up. You know it; just make sure you do it. Remember to test your backup strategy a few times. The time to find out that your backup strategy doesn't work is *before* you really need it.

Chapter 15 has all the details for doing backups.

Have a Redundant Server

It might seem extravagant, but if you can afford to have a redundant (backup) server, you can recover from a disaster that much faster. It doesn't necessarily have to be as fast or have as much RAM as your primary server, but it should be able to replace your primary server in a pinch. As a bonus, you can use a backup server to test new Samba configurations without modifying your primary server.

Check Your Security

Unfortunately, ensuring security is a fundamental but thankless part of a network administrator's job. You need to stay on top of it. Determine how secure your server needs to be, then follow the recommendations in Chapter 16.

Also, keep up to date on security issues by regularly checking the Samba Web site.

Chapter 20

More Than Ten Samba Options You Might Need Down the Road

Samba is a complex piece of networking software, and there are lots of Samba options that we don't cover or mention only in passing in this book. You probably only need these options for special situations, but in the interest of completeness, we include them here. Some Samba parameters should never be changed or should only be used by developers, so we don't mention those.

Using Samba Variables

You can include a variable in the smb.conf file that expands to a user name, a printer name, a client name, or some other useful value. A very useful variable is %U, which expands to the name of the user who is connected. For example, your smb.conf file could contain the following entry:

```
/home/%U
```

For the user lisa, this entry expands to

```
/home/lisa
```

Table 20-1 explains the meaning of numerous useful Samba variables.

Table 20-1	Samba Variables
Variable	*What It Means*
%S	The name of the current service; can only be used in a share definition
%P	The root directory of the current service; can only be used in a share definition
%u	The user name of the current service; can only be used in a share definition
%g	The primary group of %u; can only be used in a share definition
%U	The session user name
%G	The primary group of %U
%H	The home directory of the user given by %u; can only be used in a share definition
%v	The version of Samba
%h	The host name of the Samba server
%m	The NetBIOS name of the client machine
%L	The NetBIOS name of the server
%M	The DNS name of the client machine
%N	The name of your NIS home directory server
%p	The path of the service's home directory for NIS
%R	The selected SMB protocol level after protocol negotiations
%d	The process ID of the current server process
%a	The operating system of the client machine
%I	The IP address of the client machine
%T	The current date and time

Handling Failed User Logons with map to guest

The `map to guest` parameter tells your Samba server how to handle a bad user/password combination.

The default is `map to guest = never` — if a user/password combination fails, the user is rejected.

The other useful parameter is `map to guest = bad user`. If the user name is good but the password is bad, the user is rejected. If the user name is wrong, the user gets redirected to the guest account specified by the `guest account` parameter. This is one way of setting up guest accounts for your users.

In SWAT, you find the `map to guest` option in the Advanced View of the Globals page.

Setting User and Password Options

Here are several Samba options that deal with users and passwords.

Password level

By setting the `password level` parameter, you specify how many characters in the password can be uppercase. Modern clients (Windows 95 clients and later) handle mixed-case passwords fine, so you don't need to use the `password level` parameter for those clients. Older clients such as Windows for Workgroups have trouble with mixed-case passwords.

A `password level = 4` tells Samba to try matching the password with up to four of its characters being uppercase. With a password level of 4 and a password of `eleven`, the following passwords would all be considered equivalent: `eleven`, `EleVen`, `ELEVen`, `elEVEN`, and so on.

Setting `password level` too high can slow down your server as it spends time trying various permutations of the password. It also decreases your server's security.

In SWAT, you set the `password level` option in the Advanced View of the Globals page.

Username level

The `username level` parameter is very similar to the `password level` parameter: It tells your Samba server how many uppercase characters a user name can contain. As with the password level, this is really only necessary with older clients (pre Windows 95). Also, setting the `username level` too high can slow your server's performance and increase your security risk.

In SWAT, you set the `username level` option in the Advanced View of the Globals page.

Add user script

You use the `add user script` parameter to specify a script that adds the attaching user to the Linux server on which Samba is running. The `add user script` parameter only works when `security = domain` or `security = server`.

When a client logon succeeds, Samba attempts to find the user in the /etc/passwd file. If the user isn't there and you have the `add user script` set, Samba runs the script specified as the root user to add the user using the Samba variable %u.

To access the `add user script` option in SWAT, go to the Advanced View of the Globals page and look under Logon Options.

Delete user script

The `delete user script` works to delete any dynamically created users on the Linux server that were created by the `add user script`. The `delete user script` feature only works with `security = domain`. Unlike the `add user script`, the `delete user script` doesn't work with `security = server`.

To access the `delete user script` option in SWAT, go to the Advanced View of the Globals page and look under Logon Options.

Setting File and Directory Options

Here are several file and directory options for Samba:

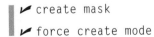

- ✔ `create mask`
- ✔ `force create mode`

✔ directory mask

✔ force directory mode

✔ max disk size

✔ dont descend

✔ map system

✔ map hidden

✔ map archive

The first four deal with the rights for files and directories created in the Samba shared directories. The fifth option, max disk size, enables you to specify an apparent disk size for a share. The sixth option, dont descend, enables you to limit access to directories from Samba. The remaining options specify how you map DOS attributes to UNIX attributes, which may be needed for compatibility with some DOS/Windows software.

Create mask

The create mask Samba option specifies, in octal, what rights newly created files in the directory have. The default create mask is 744, which gives full rights to the owner and read-only rights for the group and the world. You can set create mask for each share, or set it in the Global section of the Samba configuration file.

In SWAT, the create mask option is available in the Advanced View for that particular share.

Force create mode

The force create mode is very similar to the create mask option, but it applies only to files that Samba creates.

In SWAT, the force create mode option is available in the Advanced View for that particular share.

Directory mask

The directory mask Samba parameter is very similar to create mask except it applies to directories instead of files. The default directory mask is 755, which gives read, write, and execute permissions to the directory owner but only read and execute permissions to the group and world.

In SWAT, the directory mask option is available in the Advanced View for that particular share.

Force directory mode

The `force directory mode` Samba parameter is similar to the `directory mask` parameter, though the `force directory mode` parameter applies only to the directories that Samba creates.

In SWAT, the `force directory mode` option is available through the Advanced View for that particular share.

Max disk size

You can set the `max disk size` Samba option so that, to a client, disk size appears to be a maximum of the limit you choose (in MB). For example, if you have Windows software that thinks drives above a certain size are illegal, you can set the `max disk size` parameter to make the size appear "reasonable" to the application.

In SWAT, set the `max disk size` option in the Advanced View of the Globals page under Tuning Options.

Dont descend

You can use the `dont descend` Samba parameter to keep certain directories from appearing in your user's shares. (Yes, it is spelled without the apostrophe.) The `dont descend` Samba parameter is a convenience to make your users' shares seem less cluttered. It's not a security feature — users can still access those directories if they have the correct rights.

In SWAT, the `dont descend` option is in the Advanced view for each share, under Miscellaneous Options.

Map system

The `map system` Samba parameter determines whether DOS-style system files should be mapped to the execute bit in Linux. If you intend to use the `map system` option, the `create mask` option must have group execute permissions.

In SWAT, set the `map system` option in the Advanced View of the particular share, under Filename Handling.

Map hidden

The `map hidden` option in Samba determines whether files in DOS flagged with the hidden attribute should be mapped to the world execute bit in Linux. For the `map hidden` option to work, the `create mask` option must have world execute permissions.

In SWAT, set the `map hidden` option in the Advanced View of the particular share, under Filename Handling.

Map archive

The `map archive` option in Samba enables you to map the DOS archive attribute to the owner execute bit in Linux. For the `map archive` option to work, the `create mask` option must be set to allow owner execute permissions.

In SWAT, you set the `map archive` option on the Advanced View of the particular share, under Filename Handling.

Finding Network Resources with name resolve order

You use the `name resolve order` option to determine the order in which Samba uses its network-naming tools to find a network resource. This option should have a list of up to four of the following values:

- ✔ **lmhosts:** Do a hostname-to-IP address conversion using the Samba server's lmhosts table.

- ✔ **hosts:** Do a hostname-to-IP address conversion using whatever the Linux server's default method.

- ✔ **wins:** Use the WINS server to convert host names to IP addresses.

- ✔ **bcast:** Send a broadcast on each available network interface. This is the least reliable method.

The default order is lmhosts, hosts, wins, and bcast.

To change the `name resolve order` option in SWAT, go to the Advanced View of the Globals page. The `name resolve order` option is near the bottom, under the title Protocol Options.

Filename Handling

Many Samba options are designed for filename handling. Many of these are only needed for older clients such as in Windows for Workgroups.

Strip dot

The `strip dot` Samba parameter determines whether Samba removes the trailing dots from Linux filenames. You often use this with CDs that have filenames ending in a single dot.

In SWAT, the `strip dot` option is available in the Advanced View on the Globals page, under Filename Handling.

Case sensitive

Setting the `case sensitive` Samba option to yes makes filenames case sensitive when you are trying to match them. The default setting is no.

In SWAT, the `case sensitive` option is available in the Advanced View for that particular share, under Filename Handling.

Preserve case

The `preserve case` Samba parameter specifies whether new filenames will be created with the case that the client specifies. If `preserve case` is set to no, the new filenames are set to the default case. The default is yes.

In SWAT, the `preserve case` option isavailable in the Advanced View for that particular share, under Filename Handling.

Short preserve case

The `short preserve case` Samba option specifies whether new files created with an uppercase name and less than or equal to 8.3 characters in length are kept in uppercase or forced to the default case.

In SWAT, the `short preserve case` option is available in the Advanced View for that particular share, under Filename Handling.

Mangle case

The mangle case parameter specifies whether names that have characters that aren't the default case are mangled to make them match the default case.

In SWAT, the mangle case option is available in the Advanced View for that particular share, under Filename Handling.

Mangling char

The mangling char option determines which character to use when you mangle a filename — that is, shorten it to fit the 8.3 length that older clients expect. The default mangling char is ~.

In SWAT, set the mangling char option in the Advanced View for that particular share, under Filename Handling.

Hide dot files

The hide dot files Samba parameter determines whether files that start with a dot are hidden files. A home directory usually contains several dot files (such as .profile and .bash-profile) that are used by the Linux system, and they do not need to be available to Windows users.

In SWAT, the hide dot files option is available in the Advanced View for that particular share, under Filename Handling.

Veto files

The veto files parameter is a list of files and directories that are invisible and inaccessible to the clients. However, if a directory contains nothing but files on the veto file list, then it will be deleted if the user has the Linux permission to do that.

Each entry in the veto files list should be separated by a /. The following example keeps files ending in .tmp and files or directories with root in them hidden and inaccessible:

```
veto files = /*.tmp/*root*/
```

A veto file list can slow down your Samba server's performance because the server has to check each file and directory to see if it matches the veto list.

In SWAT, set the `veto files` option on the Advanced View of the particular share, under Filename Handling.

Delete veto files

The `delete veto files` option tells Samba what to do when a user attempts to delete a directory containing one or more vetoed directories. With `delete veto files` set to no, if a vetoed directory contains any non-vetoed files or directories, the directory will not be deleted. This is Samba's default behavior, and it's probably the safest.

In SWAT, set the `delete veto files` option in the Advanced View of the particular share, under Filename Handling.

Hide files

The `hide files` option gives a list of files and directories that are hidden from a user or users but are still accessible. Like the `veto files` option, the hidden file list must be slash (/) separated, and it can cause performance issues.

In SWAT, set the `hide files` option in the Advanced View of the particular share, under Filename Handling.

Mangled names

The `mangled names` option determines how your clients see Linux files. With `mangled names` set to yes, any Linux files or directories with incompatible names are mapped to DOS-compatible names.

In SWAT, set the `mangled names` option in the Advanced View of the particular share, under Filename Handling.

Mangled map

The `mangled map` option provides a map of UNIX filenames that are not DOS compatible to DOS-compatible names. The most common example is to use `mangled map` to change UNIX HTML files ending in .html to DOS HTML files ending in .htm, as in the following example:

```
mangled map = (*.html *.htm)
```

In SWAT, set the `mangled map` option in the Advanced View of the particular share, under Filename Handling.

Handling WinPopup Messages with the message command Parameter

Your Samba server can deal with WinPopup messages by using the `message command` Samba parameter. The command specified in the `message command` field handles the message sent by WinPopup tools.

The WinPopup tool is a way of exchanging short messages with other users on the network. More importantly, SMB servers sometime send WinPopup messages, and you can have your Samba server send them to the console.

The `message command` field takes the standard substitutions, except for %u, and has three additional substitutions:

- 🖝 `%s`: The filename containing the message
- 🖝 `%t`: The destination to which the message was sent
- 🖝 `%f`: Who the message is from

In SWAT, set the `message command` option in the Advanced View of the Globals page, under Miscellaneous Options.

Using Samba in a NIS Environment

If you are running your Samba server in a NIS environment, you can set a few Samba options to make your Samba server a better NIS citizen.

Homedir map

The `homedir map` option specifies the NIS map that the server uses to locate a user's home directory. For the `homedir map` option to work, Samba must be configured as a login server and the `nis homedir` parameter must be set to yes.

In SWAT, set `homedir map` in the Advanced View of the Globals page, under Miscellaneous Options.

NIS homedir

The NIS homedir option determines whether Samba uses NIS home directories. For the NIS homedir option to work, the Samba server must be configured as a login server. For the best performance, the NIS server should also be configured as a Samba server.

In SWAT, set NIS homedir in the Advanced View of the Globals page, under Miscellaneous Options.

Part VII

Appendixes

The 5th Wave   By Rich Tennant

WHAT DO YOU MEAN THERE'S A UNIX OPERATING SYSTEM IN THE LOBBY?

In this part . . .

Appendixes are carefully reserved for actually useful information that is just barely outside the scope of the book. Hence, some of these appendixes are for beginners and some are for experienced types. The following appendixes contain a bounty of handy and esoteric information:

- ✔ Appendix A offers a handy introduction to buying and configuring hardware, in case you are setting up a new network — for example, to interconnect the computers in your home.

- ✔ Appendix B is a guide for upgrading Samba down the road when you decide — after 18 version increments or so — that it's probably about time.

- ✔ Appendix C provides a great list of all the essential Samba and Linux Web sites, mailing lists, and other Internet resources so that you can try to keep up with all this stuff.

- ✔ Appendix D presents the ever-essential GNU General Public License. It's a lot more interesting than most of the other licenses out there, really.

- ✔ Appendix E provides an introduction to writing scripts so you can automate some of the more tedious or repetitive tasks and thus take longer coffee breaks.

- ✔ Appendix F tells you everything you need to know about how to get at the good stuff on the CD (free software you can actually use).

Appendix A

Installing Network Hardware

● ●

In This Appendix

▶ Installing and configuring network interface cards (NICs)

▶ Cabling

▶ Hubs

▶ Repeaters, bridges, routers, and brouters

● ●

*I*nstalling all the necessary hardware can be an intimidating part of the process of setting up your Samba network. If you already have all the network cards and connections in place, you might never even need to open a computer's case. You can also get away with using external (such as a laptop) or built-in (such as a USB port) helpers. Even so, the odds are good that you will have to get familiar with the inside of your computer(s) at some level.

This appendix explains how to set up the hardware for a new or remodeled network, from choosing a wiring scheme to installing network cards, cabling, and hubs. We also introduce typical components that make up larger, more complex networks, such as routers and bridges. However, installation and configuration for these devices is beyond the scope of this book.

Network Interface Cards

Each computer requires a network interface card (NIC) so that it can communicate with other computers. They are also called Ethernet cards, network adapters, or simply adapters. Anyone can install a card in a computer. But first, you need to look at the two primary types of network interface cards: ISA and PCI.

ISA or PCI?

ISA cards are the older of the two. They even work in old 286s. You can identify an ISA card by looking at the base (where the gold contacts are) because
it is a little over 5 inches long. PCI cards have a base about 3-½ inches long.
Also, ISA cards have much wider contacts than PCI cards.

Most 486s have only ISA slots, while Pentiums and faster computers usually
have both ISA and PCI slots. If you have a choice between the two, PCI cards
are easier to install and set up, and they are faster, all things being equal.

For older cards (generally ISA), you might need to manually set the parameters of the network card by setting jumper switches, the interrupts (IRQ), and
memory location values. If you don't have the documentation and the configuration software that came with the card, you should first check the manufacturer's Web page for the documentation. Otherwise, you might need to
experiment by setting each switch or jumper on the card to one value, booting the PC, and checking for conflicts in the Device Manager. If a conflict
arises, try another value and work by process of elimination. This can be a
tedious process, so you are ahead of the game if you use or buy network
cards that include full documentation and drivers.

Card speed

The cheapest cards are rated for 10 Mbps (megabits per second). This speed
is just fine for a Samba network. You can also get 100-Mbps cards, but they are
really only necessary for high-speed networks with real-time video applications. Unless you're planning on setting up a computer graphics or animation
shop, your computers will become obsolete before your 10-Mbps cards
become obsolete. Of course, if you find little price difference between the
10-Mbps card and the 100-Mbps card, you might as well get the 100-Mbps card.

Installing cards

To install a network card, complete the following steps:

1. **Power down *and unplug* the computer.**

   You can get a shock if you don't disconnect the power cord from the
   computer.

2. **Remove the computer cover.**

3. **Neutralize any static electricity from your body that could damage the
   new board or any other sensitive components.**

The best method is to place a grounding strap on your wrist and then attach the strap to a metal part of the chassis before you touch any cards or other components.

4. **Find an empty slot that matches the type of your card.**

   Identifying the installation slots is easy. They are lined up near the back of the machine so you can connect all cables in one place. ISA sockets are usually black, and PCI sockets are usually white. Some motherboards have an ISA and PCI socket for each card opening (the opening at the back of the computer where you plug the external cable into the card).

5. **Remove the metal plate that covers the back of the slot by removing the screw.**

6. **Carefully orient the card so the cable socket(s) point toward the rear, and firmly push it in.**

   Getting the card properly seated might require a little pressure. You know it's in when the screw hole on the card lines up with the one on the case.

7. **Reinstall the screw and the computer cover.**

8. **Plug the network cable into the card.**

9. **Reconnect the power cable.**

If you need more information on adding hardware to PCs, check out *Building A PC For Dummies,* 2nd Edition, by Mark L. Chambers.

What happens next depends on whether this computer will be your Samba server or a client. If it's a client, the configuration depends on what version of Windows it is running.

Configuring NICs for Linux servers

If at all possible, install the network interface card (NIC) on your Linux server before you begin the Linux installation. Linux does a good job of detecting the network card during installation and automatically installs the correct driver.

If you have to install the network card after installing Linux, watch the kernel messages as the Linux server boots up. You should see a message that Linux has found the network card. Here's an example:

```
eth0: Intel EtherExpress Pro 10/100 at 0xff40, & 00:A0:C9:04:DC:E1, IRQ 11.
  Board assembly 352509-003, Physical connectors & present: RJ45
```

This message indicates that the NIC is using IRQ 11, and it's connected with an RJ-45 connector.

If you don't see the NIC detected at boot time, you can reinsert it, change any jumper settings, or try another NIC.

Configuring NICs on Windows clients

After you install the network interface card (NIC) in your Windows client, boot the computer so Windows can detect and install the new hardware and the appropriate driver(s). Windows 95, 98, and 2000 do this installation with relative ease, but Windows NT requires a few more steps.

Windows 95/98

After a new hardware installation, Windows 95/98 first applies the Plug-and-Play scheme to identify and install the new hardware. After you install a Plug-and-Play card, Windows recognizes it on startup and starts an installation routine. Windows should automatically assign the correct resources, but it might need help installing the correct drivers. In such cases, you need to tell Windows where to find the drivers — for example, on the floppy disk that came with your card.

If you did not install a Plug-and-Play NIC, and Windows does not appear to recognize the card when you start up, open the Add New Hardware control panel. Follow the steps as guided by the wizard, and be sure to direct Windows to the correct drivers. If you don't have them, most NIC manufacturers make current drivers for their cards available for download from the Web.

Windows NT

Windows NT does not support Plug and Play, But Microsoft tests various network cards and publishes a hardware compatibility list (HCL) of hardware that works with NT. Be sure to check this list before you purchase any network cards. The hardware compatibility list is located at `http://www.microsoft.com/hcl/`.

Windows 2000

The good news is that Windows 2000 supports Plug-and-Play network cards. The bad news is that it doesn't support them all. Check the hardware compatibility list to see which cards Windows 2000 supports. The Windows hardware compatibility list is located at `http://www.microsoft.com/hcl/`.

After a new hardware installation, Windows first applies the Plug-and-Play scheme to identify and install the new hardware. After you install a Plug-and-Play card, Windows recognizes it on startup and starts an installation routine. Windows should automatically assign the correct resources, but it might need help installing the correct drivers. In such cases, you need to tell Windows where to find the drivers — for example, on the floppy disk that came with your card or on the Windows 2000 CD.

If you did not install a Plug-and-Play NIC and Windows does not appear to recognize the card when you start up, open the Add/Remove Hardware control panel. Follow the steps as guided by the wizard, and be sure to direct Windows to the correct drivers. If you don't have them, most NIC manufacturers make current drivers for their cards available for download from the Web.

Network Cabling

A few years ago, choosing the wiring for your network was full of tradeoffs based on cost, ease of installation, and reliability. Fortunately, for 95 percent of the networks out there now, the best choice is unshielded twisted pair (UTP) cable, also known as 10-baseT.

Unshielded twisted pair looks a lot like telephone wire. The connectors (called RJ-45) look like telephone jacks (called RJ-11) but are slightly wider because they have eight wires instead of four.

The best kind of UTP available today is called *Cat-5* (short for category 5). Cat-5 is rated for 100 Mbps (megabits per second), and it costs only a little more than standard UTP, which is rated for 10 Mbps. (In fact, it's hard to find anything but cat-5 cable.) After you've pulled wire through a few dusty crawl-spaces and walls, you'll appreciate being able to use Cat-5, knowing you won't have to upgrade the wire for a long time.

If you're stringing wire, add extra cables while you have your walls torn apart. It only costs a bit more, and the odds are you'll probably need the extra cables down the road.

Crossover cables

A crossover cable is a useful piece of equipment for a UTP network. It's UTP wire, but the input/output wires are crossed internally. Hence, you can directly connect two computers together without having to use a hub (more on hubs follows). This arrangement can also come in handy for troubleshooting. You can directly connect two computers together, avoiding any complications brought on by a hub or network traffic.

Also, when connecting certain types of hubs to one another, you might need a crossover cable to do so, depending on which ports are available.

A word of caution

Not too many years ago, many administrators used thin coaxial cables, called *thinnet*, for networks. Thinnet is slightly cheaper than UTP, but it has the disadvantage of bringing the entire network down if one of the wires is bad. Avoid this kind of network cabling if you can.

Hubs

If you have multiple computers (more than two), you probably want to network them together with a hub. Hubs typically have anywhere from 4 to 16 ports, plus a mechanism for linking hubs to one another.

Carry a small, good hub in your troubleshooting bag. Troubles with a hub can be hard to diagnose, so it's often easier to simply replace a hub to test it. Also, an extra hub is an easy way to quickly add more ports to a room.

Hub speed

Like network cards, the cheapest hubs run at 10 Mbps, but you can get them rated for 100 Mbps. Also like network cards, 10-Mbps hubs are adequate for most Samba networks. Unless you are doing computer animation or video editing, the increase in performance in having a 100-Mbps network probably isn't worth the increase in cost. But if your network performance is suffering and you're seeing lots of collisions, you might want to try replacing your busiest hubs with 100-Mbps hubs, and replacing the NICs on the PCs attached to that hub with 100-Mbps NICs.

Hub LEDs

Looking at a hub, you see 4 to 16 network ports (they look like telephone jacks, but wider) as well as an assortment of LEDs. Because there are so many kinds of hubs, we generalize here, but the hub should have an LED for each port, a power LED, a receiving LED, and a collision LED. The LEDs over each port should be on when a computer is connected and turned on with a good network cable. If the computer is on but the LED is off, check the network cable.

The receiving LED should blink every time the hub receives data. If it doesn't blink, check the uplink cable and port. The collision LED blinks every time a packet collision occurs. Too many collisions means your network traffic is too high, so you can monitor the collision LED as a crude way of gauging your network's traffic levels.

Connecting two hubs

At some point, you'll have more computers to connect than you have free ports on your hub. Hence, you need another hub, and you need to connect it to the first one. Again, we have to be vague because every hub works slightly differently, so be sure to check the documentation for your hubs.

Usually, one port on the hub is designated as the uplink port. These ports often have a switch for designating it as a normal port or an uplink port. Usually with an uplink port, you can connect it to another port on a second hub with a normal cat-5 cable. But be careful; sometimes, you need to use a crossover cable instead of a normal cable to connect your hubs. Check the documentation. If you don't have it, check the manufacturer's Web site.

Switched hubs

A switched hub (also called just a switch) is a special kind of hub that can greatly increase network performance. The switched hub has some intelligence in it because it looks at each packet it receives and only sends the packet through a port if the packet is destined for the port. As a result, the number of packets on the network decreases, and network throughput increases.

Switched hubs are much more expensive than plain hubs. But if your network performance is suffering and you're seeing lots of collisions, and you have replaced or upgraded the busiest section of your network to 100 Mbps (both hubs and NICs), you might want to try replacing your busiest hubs with switches.

Advanced Network Hardware

When you get more than 10 computers on a network, you're probably going to want to separate them into subnetworks for better network performance and easier network administration. Or you might have such a large network that you need special devices to keep it together. Some of the specialized network hardware devices that you might come across in larger networks are repeaters, bridges, routers, and brouters.

Repeaters

A repeater is a fairly simple network device used to connect two network segments. Think of a repeater as an amplifier that enables you to amplify network signals so that you can connect two networks that are too far apart to be connected normally.

Bridges

Bridges connect two network segments together. They have some intelligence because they look at packets and only forward those that are destined for the other network. Bridges check where a packet is supposed to go at a very low network level by looking at the actual machine address of the network interface card (not the IP address). Bridges can decrease network traffic and increase performance.

Routers

A router is like a bridge in that it connects two networks, but it does so at a higher level of sophistication. A router examines the IP addresses of the packets but only forwards the ones it needs to. A router also builds an internal software table that defines how it forwards packets. Some network utilities enable you to check these routing tables.

Brouters

A brouter is a combination of a bridge and a router. Most hardware routers are really brouters because they have built-in bridge functions.

Appendix B

Upgrading Samba

● ●

In This Appendix

▶ Planning ahead and telling your users

▶ Backing up your configuration

▶ Stopping Samba

▶ Upgrading with a packaged version

▶ Upgrading by compiling Samba

▶ Migrating Samba to a new server

▶ Verifying that the upgrade worked

● ●

Sooner or later, you're going to want or need to upgrade the Samba software on your server. You might need functionality that has been introduced in a later version of Samba, or it might have a bug fix that you need. This appendix describes how to upgrade an existing version of Samba that is already installed on your server.

Planning Ahead and Telling Your Users

The Samba upgrade process renders the server and all its shares unavailable. With luck, the upgrade might take only a half hour, but it could take several hours. Warn your users that the server will be unavailable three to four days in advance. If you tell them too early, they'll forget. If you don't give them enough warning, they won't have time to redirect their work flow to accommodate the downtime.

It's harder on you (but easier on your users) if you plan the upgrade during off hours after your users have gone home. Sometimes, you must make these sacrifices to keep your users happy. (And remember, you do want them happy.)

Backing up Your Configuration

Before you do anything, back up all your Samba configuration files as well as any system configuration files you have modified. You should have been doing regular backups of your Samba server if you are using it for anything but a print server, but it's still a good idea to duplicate the configuration files now. At a minimum, back up your smb.conf and smbpasswd files. You don't necessarily need to back up these files to removable media; storing them in the /root directory is sufficient. (Just remember where you put them.)

Stopping Samba

You can't have Samba running when you're upgrading it. Red Hat Linux, Solaris, and most other System V UNIXes have a script with which you can stop Samba. For the BSD family of UNIX, you need to find each process and kill it. (For more information about stopping Samba, see Chapter 3.)

System V servers

Most Linux distributions, including Red Hat and Caldera OpenLinux, have a script to stop Samba. Solaris and other System V UNIXes also have such a script.

For Red Hat Linux, simply type the following command:

```
# /etc/rc.d/init.d/smb stop
```

Here's an example for Solaris:

```
# /etc/init.d/smb stop
```

For other versions of UNIX, look in the /etc/rc.d/init.d or /etc/init.d directory for the script that starts and stops Samba.

BSD servers

With the BSD family of UNIX, Samba launches from a run control file, so you do not have a script to start and stop Samba. To stop Samba, use the ps command to find each process ID for the Samba daemons, smbd and nmbd, and then send each daemon the kill signal.

For FreeBSD, type the following `ps` command to list all the smbd processes running:

```
# ps -x | grep smbd
32623  ??  S      0:01.29 /usr/local/sbin/smbd -D
67863  ??  Is     0:08.65 /usr/local/sbin/smbd -D
32656  p0  R+     0:00.03 grep smbd
```

The first column of the output shows the process number. Two smbd processes are running: process IDs 32623 and 67863. To stop the smbd process with ID 32623, type this command:

```
# kill -9 32623
```

Repeat this command for every other smbd daemon running.

After you kill all the smbd daemons, use `ps` to find any running nmbd daemons and then kill them.

After you kill all the smbd and nmbd daemons, Samba is stopped.

Upgrading with a Packaged Version

One of the easier ways to upgrade Samba is with a packaged version of Samba such as with an RPM (Red Hat Package Manager) or tar file.

Unzip the Samba package

Depending on how your Samba package was created, you might need to unzip it before you can use it. If the filename ends in .gz, it's a gzipped file. To open a gzipped file, type **gzip -cd *file_name***, as in the following example:

```
# gzip -cd samba-2.0.6_tar.gz
```

Installing the package

After unzipping your Samba package, install it with `tar` or RPM.

It's almost always easier to upgrade files using RPM instead of `tar`.

Chapter 2 goes into much greater detail on unzipping, untarring, and installing Samba.

With rpm

Red Hat Linux and several other Linux makers distribute their software formatted with RPM. The following command installs the Samba 2.0.6 rpm package (the -I option is for *install*):

```
# rpm -I samba-2.0.6.i386.rpm
```

With tar

To install Samba from a tar file, you need to extract it. The command for extracting the files in a tar archive is tar -xvf archive_name. The following command extracts the files for Samba 2.0.6 from the Samba tar archive:

```
# tar -xvf samba-2.0.6_tar
```

After you extract the Samba tar file, you probably need to run a few scripts to install Samba. Check for a Readme file in the Samba directory that tells you what scripts to run for your particular UNIX version.

Upgrading by Compiling Samba

A sure way of upgrading Samba is to compile the latest available version. You do need to have the GCC C compiler on your Linux or UNIX system. Most Linux systems come with the GCC C compiler or have one available on the installation CD-ROM. For other UNIX versions, you might need to download the GCC compiler from the GNU home page (http://www.gnu.org).

You can choose to compile the Samba-latest code, or use CVS to grab the very latest Samba code. The Samba-latest code has been tested longer and will be a little more stable than the CVS code.

After you get the Samba code, specify any custom compile options and then compile the code.

Getting the source code

You can get the latest Samba source code in two ways:

- ✔ Download the Samba-latest_tar.gz file.
- ✔ Use the CVS software to get the latest daily updated Samba software.

Samba-latest is available from the Samba Web site

You can find the most recent source code for Samba at the Samba Web site, http://www.samba.org. The Samba source code is in the Download section and is called Samba-latest_tar.gz.

After you download the source code, proceed to gunzip and untar the source code into a temporary directory.

CVS Samba

If you have a working CVS client, you can use the following command to retrieve the Samba CVS code:

```
# cvs -d :pserver:CVS@samba.org:/CVSroot login
```

When you are prompted for a password, type **cvs**.

After you download the Samba source code with CVS, you need to expand it into a target directory. The following command expands the source code into the directory that contains the existing Samba source code:

```
# cvs -d :pserver:CVS@samba.org:/CVSroot co Samba
```

Next, merge the newest additions to the existing code with the following command:

```
# cvs update -d -p
```

Chapter 12 goes into greater detail on using the CVS client with Samba.

Specifying compile options

To do a custom compilation of Samba, type **./configure –help** in the Samba temporary directory to see what options you can change at compile time.

Next, type **./configure** in the Samba temporary directory to start the compilation process. If you wanted to add any options during compile time, you would add them after typing ./configure — that is, **./configure –options**.

Compiling Samba

To actually compile the binaries, type **make** in the Samba temporary directory. Then install the binaries by typing **make install** in the Samba temporary directory.

Reverting back

If your compilation was successful, the old Samba binaries should now be renamed with a .old extension. If you ever need to go back to the older version of Samba, type **make revert** to undo the upgrade and return to your previous version of Samba.

Migrating Samba to a New Server

While upgrading your Samba server, you might also want to simultaneously migrate it to a new (perhaps larger) server. (This process is similar to restoring the server after a crash.) Complete the following steps:

1. **Back up all your user data. Also, back up copies of your /etc/passwd and /etc/shadow password files and keep them for reference.**

   Chapter 15 goes into detail on doing backups.

2. **Back up your Samba configuration files onto removable media.**

   The most important files to back up are the smb.conf file, the smbpasswd file, and any custom scripts you are using.

3. **Install the new server, being sure to choose Samba during the installation process (if the choice is available).**

   See Chapter 2 for details.

4. **Add your users to the new server.**

   You will find the copy of your old /etc/passwd file useful for this step. Chapter 7 goes into detail on how to add users. If you're feeling particularly wizardly, you can try adding the users with a script.

   It's probably easiest to reset everyone's UNIX passwords. Copying the old /etc/shadow file over the new one could cause problems on the new server.

5. **Restore the user data onto the new server. (See Chapter 15.)**

Verifying that the Upgrade Worked

After you upgrade your Samba server, regardless of the method you used, you need to reconfigure Samba to ensure that it connects to the correct Samba configuration file and users. (See Chapter 14 for more information on how to test Samba using Samba utilities such as `testparm` and `smbclient`.)

Running testparm to locate smb.conf

After installing Samba, type **testparm** to identify where Samba will look for the smb.conf file. This was defined when your Samba package was compiled, so it might be in a different location than before.

Moving the backed-up configuration files to the right places

After you determine where Samba will be looking for the smb.conf file, copy the backed-up version to that directory. Then, if you are using encrypted passwords, copy the smbpasswd file to the location specified by the smb.conf file.

Starting Samba and testing it

Finally, start Samba from the command line and test it with smbstatus and smbclient. Chapter 3 tells all about how to test a new Samba installation.

Testing with smbstatus

The smbstatus command should display all the shares on your server. (Just type **smbstatus** at the command prompt.)

Testing with smbclient

By using the smbclient command with the -U switch, you can locally connect to the new Samba server as a specified user. For example, to connect to the homes section of the user trinity on the new Samba server named matrix, you would type this command:

```
# smbclient //matrix/homes -U trinity
```

You will be prompted for a password. After giving the correct password, you can browse trinity's home directory.

Appendix C

Internet Resources

*O*ne of the bigger advantages of Samba and other open-source software is the speed in which fixes are generated. After a problem is identified, the fix might be written and a patch released overnight, or at least in a few days. Because of this speed, the only way to stay current on fixes, problems, and security issues is to use the Internet.

This appendix lists helpful resources such as Web pages and mailing lists that are essential for a Samba administrator to monitor for current developments. Many sites also include a wealth of interesting articles, opinions, guidelines, and help.

Samba Sites

The main Samba Web page is http://www.samba.org.

The three mirrored US sites are

```
http://us1.samba.org/samba/samba.html
http://us2.samba.org/samba/samba.html
http://us3.samba.org/samba/samba.html
```

You can go to these pages to download the latest version of Samba (2.0.6 as of this writing).

Chapter 2 discusses installation, and Appendix B describes how to upgrade Samba.

The CD that accompanies this book includes several flavors of Samba version 2.0.6. See Appendix F for details.

Samba mailing lists

For the absolute latest information on Samba, including bug reports and security problems as well as a variety of questions and answers about using Samba (some are even from the developers), use the appropriate mailing list. You can access them from one of the Samba Web pages (click the support link), or subscribe to them via e-mail.

Some of the mailing lists are

- ✔ samba@samba.org: The main Samba list
- ✔ samba-announce@samba.org: The announcement mailing list
- ✔ samba-ntdom@samba.org: The mailing list for NT domain controller support
- ✔ samba-technical@samba.org: A technical mailing list for Samba developers
- ✔ samba-cvs@samba.org: A mailing list for people interested in running the current developing version (to get prereleased versions of Samba)

There is a complete list at http://lists.samba.org/. To subscribe to one of the lists, send e-mail to listproc@samba.org with no subject and a body of subscribe listname Your Full Name. You should receive a welcome message within a few minutes.

Samba newsgroup

The comp newsgroup related to smb networking is comp.protocols.smb.

Sun Solaris Sites

Solaris is a Sun product, so the first place to look for help with Solaris is the Sun homepage, http://www.sun.com.

Patches for Solaris and an informational database are kept at Sunsolve, `http://sunsolve.sun.com`. Full access requires a contract, but recommended patches and security patches are free at `http://sunsolve.sun.com/pubpatch`.

Documentation for Sun products is available at the Sun documentation Web page, `http://docs.sun.com`.

Solaris Central

Solaris Central, `http://www.solariscentral.org/`, is a Web page for Solaris users and administrators but is not affiliated with Sun. Solaris Central focuses on Solaris and UNIX news.

Sunfreeware

Sunfreeware, `http://www.sunfreeware.com/`, is a site sponsored by Sun that collects and distributes free software for Sun machines, both Intel and Sparc. You might find an essential utility here, as well as the latest Samba version.

Solaris newsgroups

Two of the Usenet newsgroups related to Solaris are `comp.unix.solaris` and `comp.sys.sun.admin`.

GNU/Linux Sites

There are thousands of sites devoted to Linux. The following are just a few that stand out, and any good search engine will bring up hundreds more.

Linux.com

Linux.com, `http://www.linux.com`, is a Web page with a good collection of links to other Linux articles on the Web.

Red Hat

One of the more common distributions of GNU/Linux is Red Hat. At Red Hat's home page, `http://www.RedHat.com`, you can find that company's latest version of Linux, download it for free, read all the documentation available, and browse through tech support files and discussion areas.

Caldera

Caldera is another GNU/Linux distribution that is geared toward business use. At Caldera's home page, `http://www.calderasystems.com`, you can also find the company's latest version of Linux, download it for free, read all the documentation available, and browse through tech support files and discussion areas.

Linuxtoday

Linuxtoday, `http://www.linuxtoday.com`, is a page frequently updated with links to Linux articles in online magazines. It's geared toward an industry/business viewpoint and can be very helpful in increasing a Samba/Linux presence in an office.

Tunelinux

Tunelinux, `http://www.tunelinux.com`, is a Web page devoted to increasing performance for Linux machines.

Linux Gazette

Linux Gazette, `http://www.linuxgazette.com`, is a monthly online journal devoted to teaching people about Linux. The articles range from newbie to experienced Linux administrator with emphasis on the practical.

Linux Journal

This home page, `http://linuxjournal.com`, is an online version of the magazine *Linux Journal.*

LinuxLinks

LinuxLinks, `http://www.linuxlinks.com/`, is a big collection of links to Linux home pages and is well organized by categories.

GNU/Linux newsgroups

There are many Linux newsgroups in the `comp.os.linux` hierarchy. Some of the following can be useful:

- ✔ `comp.os.linux.announce`: A moderated newsgroup with the latest announcements
- ✔ `comp.os.linux.apps`: A newsgroup for Linux applications
- ✔ `comp.os.linux.networking`: A newsgroup for Linux networking questions

FreeBSD Sites

The main FreeBSD page is at `http://www.freebsd.org`. Here you will find all sorts of links for FreeBSD information, including online man pages and tutorials.

FreeBSD Rocks

FreeBSD Rocks, `http://www.freebsdrocks.com`, is a Web page with links to FreeBSD articles on the Web.

FreeBSDzine

FreeBSDzine, `http://www.freebsdzine.org`, is an online magazine devoted to FreeBSD, with articles for all experience levels, ranging from newbie to experienced network administrator.

DaemonNews

DaemonNews, `http://www.daemonnews.org`, is a monthly online magazine focusing on the BSD family of software: FreeBSD, NetBSD, and OpenBSD.

FreeBSD mailing lists

Mailing lists are the primary means of communication in the FreeBSD community. Here's a selected set of the FreeBSD mailing lists:

- ✔ `freebsd-announce`: **Important events and project milestones**
- ✔ `freebsd-bugs`: **Bug reports**
- ✔ `freebsd-newbies`: **New FreeBSD users activities and discussions**
- ✔ `freebsd-questions`: **User questions and technical support**

To post to a specific list, just send mail to `listname@FreeBSD.org`. It will then be redistributed to mailing list members worldwide.

To subscribe to a list, send mail to `majordomo@FreeBSD.org` and include `subscribe listname optional address` in the body of the message.

You can also search the archives of the mailing lists at `http://www.freebsd.org`.

FreeBSD newsgroups

Mailing lists are the preferred method of communication in the FreeBSD community, but two recommended newsgroups are `comp.unix.freebsd.misc` and `comp.unix.freebsd.announce`.

NetBSD Sites

The main home page for NetBSD is `http://www.netbsd.org`. Here you will find all sorts of links for NetBSD information, including online man pages and tutorials.

DaemonNews

Daemonnews, `http://www.daemonnews.org`, is a monthly online magazine focusing on the BSD family of software: FreeBSD, NetBSD, and OpenBSD.

NetBSD mailing lists

The NetBSD mailing lists include

- ✔ netbsd-announce
- ✔ netbsd-bugs
- ✔ netbsd-help

NetBSD newsgroup

The NetBSD newsgroup is comp.unix.bsd.freebsd.

Open-Source Sites

Here are some important sites to frequently review for news and utilities for open-source software development.

GNU

GNU is a product of the Free Software Foundation. The GNU Web site, http://www.gnu.org, has many benchmark utilities for UNIX/Linux/BSD, including the GNU compiler (gcc), the GNU compression utility (gzip), and many others.

Slashdot

Slashdot's Web page, "News for Nerds" is at http://slashdot.org. It has many links to articles of a computer/technical/science/social nature posted daily with a very lively forum to respond to the article. Many of the posters do have a strong pro-Linux/anti-Microsoft bias, but don't let that keep you from finding useful information.

Freshmeat

Freshmeat, at http://www.freshmeat.org/, is a Web page devoted to open-source software, including downloads. You can find useful or fun packages here.

General UNIX Links

Here are a few useful links for help on UNIX networking.

Caida network tools

The Caida network tools page, `http://www.caida.org/`, is a good resource to help you troubleshoot network problems.

DNS Resources directory

Information about DNS is available at the DNS Resources page, `http://www.dns.net/dnsrd/`.

Appendix D

GNU General Public License

* *

*V*ersion 2, June 1991

Copyright (C) 1989, 1991 Free Software Foundation, Inc.
59 Temple Place - Suite 330, Boston, MA 02111-1307, USA

Everyone is permitted to copy and distribute verbatim copies of this license document, but changing it is not allowed.

Preamble

The licenses for most software are designed to take away your freedom to share and change it. By contrast, the GNU General Public License is intended to guarantee your freedom to share and change free software — to make sure the software is free for all its users. This General Public License applies to most of the Free Software Foundation's software and to any other program whose authors commit to using it. (Some other Free Software Foundation software is covered by the GNU Library General Public License instead.) You can apply it to your programs, too.

When we speak of free software, we are referring to freedom, not price. Our General Public Licenses are designed to make sure that you have the freedom to distribute copies of free software (and charge for this service if you wish), that you receive source code or can get it if you want it, that you can change the software or use pieces of it in new free programs; and that you know you can do these things.

To protect your rights, we need to make restrictions that forbid anyone to deny you these rights or to ask you to surrender the rights. These restrictions translate to certain responsibilities for you if you distribute copies of the software, or if you modify it.

For example, if you distribute copies of such a program, whether gratis or for a fee, you must give the recipients all the rights that you have. You must make sure that they, too, receive or can get the source code. And you must show them these terms so they know their rights.

We protect your rights with two steps: (1) copyright the software, and (2) offer you this license which gives you legal permission to copy, distribute and/or modify the software.

Also, for each author's protection and ours, we want to make certain that everyone understands that there is no warranty for this free software. If the software is modified by someone else and passed on, we want its recipients to know that what they have is not the original, so that any problems introduced by others will not reflect on the original authors' reputations.

Finally, any free program is threatened constantly by software patents. We wish to avoid the danger that redistributors of a free program will individually obtain patent licenses, in effect making the program proprietary. To prevent this, we have made it clear that any patent must be licensed for everyone's free use or not licensed at all.

The precise terms and conditions for copying, distribution and modification follow.

TERMS AND CONDITIONS FOR COPYING, DISTRIBUTION AND MODIFICATION

0. This License applies to any program or other work which contains a notice placed by the copyright holder saying it may be distributed under the terms of this General Public License. The "Program", below, refers to any such program or work, and a "work based on the Program" means either the Program or any derivative work under copyright law: that is to say, a work containing the Program or a portion of it, either verbatim or with modifications and/or translated into another language. (Hereinafter, translation is included without limitation in the term "modification".) Each licensee is addressed as "you".

   Activities other than copying, distribution and modification are not covered by this License; they are outside its scope. The act of running the Program is not restricted, and the output from the Program is covered only if its contents constitute a work based on the Program (independent of having been made by running the Program). Whether that is true depends on what the Program does.

1. You may copy and distribute verbatim copies of the Program's source code as you receive it, in any medium, provided that you conspicuously and appropriately publish on each copy an appropriate copyright notice and disclaimer of warranty; keep intact all the notices that refer to this License and to the absence of any warranty; and give any other recipients of the Program a copy of this License along with the Program.

   You may charge a fee for the physical act of transferring a copy, and you may at your option offer warranty protection in exchange for a fee.

2. You may modify your copy or copies of the Program or any portion of it, thus forming a work based on the Program, and copy and distribute such modifications or work under the terms of Section 1 above, provided that you also meet all of these conditions:

   a) You must cause the modified files to carry prominent notices stating that you changed the files and the date of any change.

   b) You must cause any work that you distribute or publish, that in whole or in part contains or is derived from the Program or any part thereof, to be licensed as a whole at no charge to all third parties under the terms of this License.

   c) If the modified program normally reads commands interactively when run, you must cause it, when started running for such interactive use in the most ordinary way, to print or display an announcement including an appropriate copyright notice and a notice that there is no warranty (or else, saying that you provide a warranty) and that users may redistribute the program under these conditions, and telling the user how to view a copy of this License. (Exception: if the Program itself is interactive but does not normally print such an announcement, your work based on the Program is not required to print an announcement.)

   These requirements apply to the modified work as a whole. If identifiable sections of that work are not derived from the Program, and can be reasonably considered independent and separate works in themselves, then this License, and its terms, do not apply to those sections when you distribute them as separate works. But when you distribute the same sections as part of a whole which is a work based on the Program, the distribution of the whole must be on the terms of this License, whose permissions for other licensees extend to the entire whole, and thus to each and every part regardless of who wrote it.

   Thus, it is not the intent of this section to claim rights or contest your rights to work written entirely by you; rather, the intent is to exercise the right to control the distribution of derivative or collective works based on the Program.

   In addition, mere aggregation of another work not based on the Program with the Program (or with a work based on the Program) on a volume of a storage or distribution medium does not bring the other work under the scope of this License.

3. You may copy and distribute the Program (or a work based on it, under Section 2) in object code or executable form under the terms of Sections 1 and 2 above provided that you also do one of the following:

   a) Accompany it with the complete corresponding machine-readable source code, which must be distributed under the terms of Sections 1 and 2 above on a medium customarily used for software interchange; or,

b) Accompany it with a written offer, valid for at least three years, to give any third party, for a charge no more than your cost of physically performing source distribution, a complete machine-readable copy of the corresponding source code, to be distributed under the terms of Sections 1 and 2 above on a medium customarily used for software interchange; or,

c) Accompany it with the information you received as to the offer to distribute corresponding source code. (This alternative is allowed only for noncommercial distribution and only if you received the program in object code or executable form with such an offer, in accord with Subsection b above.)

The source code for a work means the preferred form of the work for making modifications to it. For an executable work, complete source code means all the source code for all modules it contains, plus any associated interface definition files, plus the scripts used to control compilation and installation of the executable. However, as a special exception, the source code distributed need not include anything that is normally distributed (in either source or binary form) with the major components (compiler, kernel, and so on) of the operating system on which the executable runs, unless that component itself accompanies the executable.

If distribution of executable or object code is made by offering access to copy from a designated place, then offering equivalent access to copy the source code from the same place counts as distribution of the source code, even though third parties are not compelled to copy the source along with the object code.

4. You may not copy, modify, sublicense, or distribute the Program except as expressly provided under this License. Any attempt otherwise to copy, modify, sublicense or distribute the Program is void, and will automatically terminate your rights under this License. However, parties who have received copies, or rights, from you under this License will not have their licenses terminated so long as such parties remain in full compliance.

5. You are not required to accept this License, since you have not signed it. However, nothing else grants you permission to modify or distribute the Program or its derivative works. These actions are prohibited by law if you do not accept this License. Therefore, by modifying or distributing the Program (or any work based on the Program), you indicate your acceptance of this License to do so, and all its terms and conditions for copying, distributing or modifying the Program or works based on it.

6. Each time you redistribute the Program (or any work based on the Program), the recipient automatically receives a license from the original licensor to copy, distribute or modify the Program subject to these terms and conditions. You may not impose any further restrictions on the recipients' exercise of the rights granted herein. You are not responsible for enforcing compliance by third parties to this License.

7. If, as a consequence of a court judgment or allegation of patent infringement or for any other reason (not limited to patent issues), conditions are imposed on you (whether by court order, agreement or otherwise) that contradict the conditions of this License, they do not excuse you from the conditions of this License. If you cannot distribute so as to satisfy simultaneously your obligations under this License and any other pertinent obligations, then as a consequence you may not distribute the Program at all. For example, if a patent license would not permit royalty-free redistribution of the Program by all those who receive copies directly or indirectly through you, then the only way you could satisfy both it and this License would be to refrain entirely from distribution of the Program.

If any portion of this section is held invalid or unenforceable under any particular circumstance, the balance of the section is intended to apply and the section as a whole is intended to apply in other circumstances.

It is not the purpose of this section to induce you to infringe any patents or other property right claims or to contest validity of any such claims; this section has the sole purpose of protecting the integrity of the free software distribution system, which is implemented by public license practices. Many people have made generous contributions to the wide range of software distributed through that system in reliance on consistent application of that system; it is up to the author/donor to decide if he or she is willing to distribute software through any other system and a licensee cannot impose that choice.

This section is intended to make thoroughly clear what is believed to be a consequence of the rest of this License.

8. If the distribution and/or use of the Program is restricted in certain countries either by patents or by copyrighted interfaces, the original copyright holder who places the Program under this License may add an explicit geographical distribution limitation excluding those countries, so that distribution is permitted only in or among countries not thus excluded. In such case, this License incorporates the limitation as if written in the body of this License.

9. The Free Software Foundation may publish revised and/or new versions of the General Public License from time to time. Such new versions will be similar in spirit to the present version, but may differ in detail to address new problems or concerns.

Each version is given a distinguishing version number. If the Program specifies a version number of this License which applies to it and "any later version", you have the option of following the terms and conditions either of that version or of any later version published by the Free Software Foundation. If the Program does not specify a version number of this License, you may choose any version ever published by the Free Software Foundation.

10. If you wish to incorporate parts of the Program into other free programs whose distribution conditions are different, write to the author to ask for permission. For software which is copyrighted by the Free Software Foundation, write to the Free Software Foundation; we sometimes make exceptions for this. Our decision will be guided by the two goals of preserving the free status of all derivatives of our free software and of promoting the sharing and reuse of software generally.

NO WARRANTY

11. BECAUSE THE PROGRAM IS LICENSED FREE OF CHARGE, THERE IS NO WARRANTY FOR THE PROGRAM, TO THE EXTENT PERMITTED BY APPLICABLE LAW. EXCEPT WHEN OTHERWISE STATED IN WRITING THE COPYRIGHT HOLDERS AND/OR OTHER PARTIES PROVIDE THE PROGRAM "AS IS" WITHOUT WARRANTY OF ANY KIND, EITHER EXPRESSED OR IMPLIED, INCLUDING, BUT NOT LIMITED TO, THE IMPLIED WARRANTIES OF MERCHANTABILITY AND FITNESS FOR A PARTICULAR PURPOSE. THE ENTIRE RISK AS TO THE QUALITY AND PERFORMANCE OF THE PROGRAM IS WITH YOU. SHOULD THE PROGRAM PROVE DEFECTIVE, YOU ASSUME THE COST OF ALL NECESSARY SERVICING, REPAIR OR CORRECTION.

12. IN NO EVENT UNLESS REQUIRED BY APPLICABLE LAW OR AGREED TO IN WRITING WILL ANY COPYRIGHT HOLDER, OR ANY OTHER PARTY WHO MAY MODIFY AND/OR REDISTRIBUTE THE PROGRAM AS PERMITTED ABOVE, BE LIABLE TO YOU FOR DAMAGES, INCLUDING ANY GENERAL, SPECIAL, INCIDENTAL OR CONSEQUENTIAL DAMAGES ARISING OUT OF THE USE OR INABILITY TO USE THE PROGRAM (INCLUDING BUT NOT LIMITED TO LOSS OF DATA OR DATA BEING RENDERED INACCURATE OR LOSSES SUSTAINED BY YOU OR THIRD PARTIES OR A FAILURE OF THE PROGRAM TO OPERATE WITH ANY OTHER PROGRAMS), EVEN IF SUCH HOLDER OR OTHER PARTY HAS BEEN ADVISED OF THE POSSIBILITY OF SUCH DAMAGES.

END OF TERMS AND CONDITIONS

How to Apply These Terms to Your New Programs

If you develop a new program, and you want it to be of the greatest possible use to the public, the best way to achieve this is to make it free software which everyone can redistribute and change under these terms.

To do so, attach the following notices to the program. It is safest to attach them to the start of each source file to most effectively convey the exclusion of warranty; and each file should have at least the "copyright" line and a pointer to where the full notice is found.

```
one line to give the program's name and an idea of what it does.
                Copyright (C) yyyy  name of author

This program is free software; you can redistribute it and/or
modify it under the terms of the GNU General Public License
as published by the Free Software Foundation; either version 2
of the License, or (at your option) any later version.

This program is distributed in the hope that it will be useful,
but WITHOUT ANY WARRANTY; without even the implied warranty of
MERCHANTABILITY or FITNESS FOR A PARTICULAR PURPOSE.  See the
GNU General Public License for more details.

You should have received a copy of the GNU General Public License
along with this program; if not, write to the Free Software
Foundation, Inc., 59 Temple Place - Suite 330, Boston, MA  02111-1307, USA.
Also add information on how to contact you by electronic and paper mail.
If the program is interactive, make it output a short notice like this when it
                starts in an interactive mode:
Gnomovision version 69, Copyright (C) yyyy name of author
Gnomovision comes with ABSOLUTELY NO WARRANTY; for details
type `show w'.  This is free software, and you are welcome
to redistribute it under certain conditions; type `show c'
for details.
```

The hypothetical commands show w and show c should show the appropriate parts of the General Public License. Of course, the commands you use may be called something other than show w and show c; they could even be mouse-clicks or menu items — whatever suits your program.

You should also get your employer (if you work as a programmer) or your school, if any, to sign a "copyright disclaimer" for the program, if necessary. Here is a sample; alter the names:

```
Yoyodyne, Inc., hereby disclaims all copyright
interest in the program `Gnomovision'
(which makes passes at compilers) written
by James Hacker.

signature of Ty Coon, 1 April 1989
Ty Coon, President of Vice
```

This General Public License does not permit incorporating your program into proprietary programs. If your program is a subroutine library, you may consider it more useful to permit linking proprietary applications with the library. If this is what you want to do, use the GNU Library General Public License instead of this License.

Appendix E

Writing Scripts

*W*riting scripts is one of the more useful skills that a Linux system administrator can have. One recommendation suggests that if you repeat a complicated command more than twice, consider making a script for it. Writing a script for ls or cd might be a bit silly, but if you frequently string several complex commands together, definitely consider writing a script to simplify your life a little.

A script is basically a text file with a list of UNIX commands. Although a list of commands might be handy in and of itself, a script can do much more. You can pass a script variables, and you can have it perform loops (repeating functions). For just about anything you can do at a command line, you can write a script to carry it out for you.

We could easily fill several chapters or even a book on writing scripts, but this appendix only touches on the basics of script writing.

A Basic Script

The following example is a basic script named coresearch.sh. It was created with the vi text editor. The script searches for core files and stores them in the /root directory in a nicely formatted file named coresearch.txt:

```
#!/bin/sh
echo "Searching for core" > /root/coresearch.txt
echo >> /root/coresearch.txt
date >> /root/coresearch.txt
echo >> /root/coresearch.txt
find / -name core -print >> /root/coresearch.txt
echo >> /root/coresearch.txt
```

A little bit about shells

Linux is unusual in that you don't really interact directly with the operating system. Instead, you interact with a shell, and the shell communicates with the operating system. As you might expect with Linux and UNIX, there are many different kinds of shells. Often enough, a developer might have liked a shell but wanted a few more features, so he created a new shell. Some of the more common shells are the C shell, the Bourne shell, the Korn shell, and the Bourne Again shell. The shell most commonly used on Linux systems is the Bourne Again shell, or bash. A user's preferred shell is specified in the /etc/passwd file in the seventh field.

You don't need to know all the available shells, but be aware that they exist. Most Linux

commands run the same in any shell, but some vary depending on the shell. Some shells treat variables differently than others, which means that a complex script might run perfectly in the bash shell but fail miserably in the C shell. You can, however, force a script to use a specific shell by making the first line of your script refer to the desired shell preceded by #!. If the following line was the first line of a script, the script would always use the bash shell:

```
#!/bin/bash
```

As you can guess, shells get a lot more complex. You can look through the man pages for the specific shell to get an idea of how complex they can get, or check your Linux documentation.

Except for the first line, each line looks like a standard Linux command. The `echo` lines nicely format the file, the `date` line tells you when the script ran, and the `find` line searches for core files. All the lines except the first line redirect their output to the end of the coresearch.txt file (with the > operator to create a new file and then with the >> operator to add to that file).

The result should be the file named coresearch.txt that contains the following output:

```
Searching for core

Wed May 31 13:58:18 EDT 2000

/proc/sys/net/core
/home/george/core
/root/core
```

Making it executable

After you create your script, you need to make the file executable. If you try to run a script and it's not executable, you get a `permission denied` type of error. To make a script executable, at a command prompt, type **chmod +x** *script_name*. For the sample coresearch script, the following command makes it executable:

```
# chmod +x coresearch.sh
```

Putting your script on the right path or calling it directly

After you write a script and make it executable, Linux has to find the script to be able to run it. More accurately, the user who is going to need the script (usually the root user, but it could be an end user), has to be able to find it.

Each user has a search path, which is a list of directories in which to look for files. If the user is not going to call the script directly, it needs to be in the search path. You can also amend the search path list by adding directories.

The exact syntax for manipulating the search path is shell dependent; we refer to the bash shell in these examples.

What's your search path?

To display the search path for a user who is using the bash shell, type **echo $PATH**. The following example displays george's search path on the Linux server:

```
[george@olorin george]$ echo $PATH
PATH=/usr/local/bin:/bin:/usr/bin:/usr/X11R6/bin:/home/george/bin
```

For the user george to be able to run a script, it would need to be in one of the following directories: /usr/local/bin, /bin, /usr/bin, /usr/X11R6/bin, or /home/george/bin.

Adding to your search path

To permanently add a new directory to the search path for a user who is using the bash shell, open the .bash_profile file in the user's home directory and change the line that starts with PATH. The PATH line for the user george looks like the following:

```
PATH=$PATH:$HOME/bin
```

To add a new directory to the search path, just add a colon and the new path name to that line. So to add the directory /usr/samba/scripts to the user george's search path, type:

```
PATH=$PATH:$HOME/bin:/usr/samba/scripts
```

Calling the script directly

All things considered, it might be easier to place your scripts in well-known directories, such as /usr/samba/scripts, and then call the scripts with the full pathname — that is, /usr/samba/scripts/backup.sh (instead of just backup.sh). That way, you don't have to edit the user's individual files, and you are sure exactly which script file you are running.

Passing an Argument to a Script

You might want to pass one or more arguments to your scripts. Perhaps you like the script that finds core files, but you want it to find a different file called annual_review.txt. You could write an entirely new script, or you could modify the core-finding script to accept annual_review.txt as an argument.

First, change the `find` line in the script named coresearch.sh to include a variable for the passed argument. Because we are only passing one filename, call the variable `$1`. The new find line looks like this:

```
find / -name $1 -print >> /root/coresearch.txt
```

Now you can call the script with the name of the file after the script name. So to find the file annual_report, type:

```
# /root/coresearch.sh annual_report
```

To avoid confusion, you would want to rename this script to something like filesearch.sh, and rename the output file from coresearch.txt to filesearch.txt.

You can pass as many arguments as you want along to your script this way. The second argument would be named `$2`, the third `$3`, and so forth.

Variables

Examples of variables discussed thus far include the arguments passed to a script, such as $1 or $2 and the $PATH variable. To set a specific variable in a script, use the syntax *variable_name = variable_value*, and refer to the variable as *$variable_name* in the script. For example, to set the variable `sambaconfig` to `/etc/smb.conf`, use the following line in your script:

```
sambaconfig=/etc/smb.conf
```

So when you are ready to use `sambaconfig`, call it as `$sambaconfig`. To tar the Samba configuration file to a floppy, try the following command:

```
# tar cvf /dev/fd0 $sambaconfig
```

Conditions

Just like a programming language, you can add `if/then/else` statements to a script. The basic syntax is as follows:

```
if condition1 is true
then do_something
else do_something different
fi
```

The following sample script generates an error if the `tar` command cannot back up the /home directory:

```
if tar cvf /dev/rmt0 /home
then echo /home backed up
else echo tar unable to back up /home
fi
```

Another command that works well with `if` is the `test` command. Use the `test` command with `-f filename` to see if the file exists, or with `-d directoryname` to see if the directory exists.

Comments

You use the # character to identify comments. If a line starts with a #, the Linux shell ignores the rest of the line. You use the comment character to set off any comments you want to write about your shell script — what it does, what the variables mean, and anything tricky that you do in the script. For example, in the filesearch.sh script that I describe in previous sections, you would see comments like these:

```
#!/bin/sh
# filesearch.sh - a shell script to find files and write them to a file
#
# Format the file with the title and spaces.
#
echo "Searching for file" > /root/filesearch.txt
echo >> /root/coresearch.txt
#
# Write the date the command was written.
#
date >> /root/coresearch.txt
echo >> /root/coresearch.txt
#
# Find the file given by the variable $1
#
find / -name $1 -print >> /root/coresearch.txt
echo >> /root/coresearch.txt
```

This example is very heavily commented, but you get the idea.

Uses for Scripts

Now that you have a understanding of scripts, how would you use them in the context of administering a Samba server?

Backups

Backup commands are usually esoteric and complex, and you rarely use them more than once a week. Try your backup commands once or twice manually and then put them in a script file.

The following small sample script uses some of the aforementioned features. The script backs up a valid user's home directory to the Zip drive. The script name is userzip.sh. After you type it in and make it executable, run it by typing **userzip.sh** *username*.

```
#!/bin/sh
if grep $1 /etc/passwd
then
mount -t msdos /dev/hdb4 /mnt/zip
cp /home/$1 /mnt/zip
umount /mnt/zip
else
echo Not a user on the system
fi
```

The `if` command uses `grep` and the `username` variable to validate the user (the user exists in the /etc/passwd file). If valid, the contents of the user's home directory are copied to the Zip drive (after the Zip drive is mounted). If the user is not in the /etc/passwd file, you see the error message `Not a user on the system`.

System maintenance

You can use scripts, called by `cron`, to occasionally search for core files, log files, and other large files that you want to delete frequently. Any administrator task that takes more than a few lines should probably be automated in a script.

Appendix F

About the CD

- -

On the CD-ROM

▶ Multiple formats of Samba version 2.0.6

▶ Smbedit

▶ Linuxconf

▶ Webmin

- -

*T*his appendix describes the software programs on the CD that comes with this book.

What's On It?

All the software products on the CD are licensed under the GNU General Public License, which you can see, in all its glory, in Appendix D.

Samba 2.0.6

The CD contains the following versions of Samba 2.0.6:

✔ Source code

✔ RPM for Red Hat Linux, Caldera OpenLinux, and SuSE 6.1 Linux

✔ Tarred for Slackware, Sparc Solaris 2.6 and 2.7, and FreeBSD 3.2

Webmin

Webmin, a multi-purpose administration tool, is basically a simple Web server with CGI scripts that modify the Samba server's configuration files. Chapter 5 contains more information and resources.

Linuxconf

Linuxconf is a GNU program that makes configuring your Linux box easier for network and printer connections. See Chapter 6 for more about Linuxconf.

Smbedit

Smbedit is a graphical tool for administering a Samba server that runs on Windows. See Chapter 6 for more about Smbedit.

System Requirements

You would be wise to observe these software and hardware minimums.

Software

For your server, we recommend that you install some fairly recent version of Linux or any UNIX operating system that reads ISO9660-formatted CD-ROMs.

For clients, you need Microsoft Windows 95 or later installed.

Hardware

The following minimum hardware requirements apply to both your server and client computers:

- ✔ PCs with a 486 or faster processor
- ✔ CD-ROM drive
- ✔ Monitor
- ✔ At least 16MB of RAM
- ✔ At least 150MB of hard-drive space available to install the appropriate version of Samba for your operating system and the other software from this CD

If you need more information on the basics, check out *PCs For Dummies,* 6th Edition, by Dan Gookin; *UNIX For Dummies,* 4th Edition, by John R. Levine and Margaret Levine Young; and *Linux For Dummies,* by John Hall and Paul Sery.

How to Use the CD

All the programs on the CD are for installation on a Linux system except Smbedit, which is a Windows program.

For your Linux server

Follow these steps to view the CD contents and install the desired program(s) on your server. You can install any of the flavors of Samba, Webmin, and Linuxconf.

Commands might vary depending on which UNIX flavor you have installed.

1. **Insert the CD into your computer's CD-ROM drive.**

2. **When the light on your CD-ROM drive goes out, go to the command prompt and type the following command:**

   ```
   # mount -t iso9660 /dev/cdrom /mnt/cdrom
   ```

3. **Then type:**

   ```
   # cd /mnt/cdrom
   ```

4. **To list the files in the CD's contents, type the following command:**

   ```
   # ls
   ```

5. **To view the licenses in their respective directories, type vi and the filename of the license (either gpl.txt or IDG_EULA.txt).**

   This file contains the end-user license to which you agree by using the CD. In Linux, the most convenient way to read this file is to use the vi editor. When you are done reading the license, exit the program by pressing Esc and then typing **:q!**.

6. **Copy the desired program from the /cdrom directory to the directory where you want to store it.**

   For example, to copy Webmin from /cdrom to your /usr directory, type this command:

   ```
   # cp webmin /usr
   ```

7. **Change to the directory where you copied the program:**

   ```
   # cd /usr
   ```

8. **Type the name of the program and press Enter.**

   On some systems, Linux might claim that it can't find the program. It's just being fussy. Type a period and a slash in front of the program name and then press Enter. That tells Linux you want *this* specific program.

For your Windows client

Follow these steps to install Smbedit on a Windows PC:

1. **Insert the CD into your computer's CD-ROM drive.**

2. **When the light on your CD-ROM drive goes out, double-click the My Computer icon and then double-click the drive with the CD icon on it (usually D:).**

3. **Locate and copy the smbedit(version number) WinZip file to your hard drive.**

4. **Right-click the WinZip file, choose Extract to..., and then specify where to copy the files.**

5. **Open the folder where you copied the files and open the readme file.**

   This file contains instructions about installing the software and how to find more information about Smbedit.

Problems?

If you encounter installation problems, consider these possibilities:

- ✔ You don't have enough memory (RAM) for the programs you want to use.
- ✔ Other running programs are slowing down the installation or operation of the program.

If you get error messages like `Not enough memory` or `Setup cannot continue,` try one or more of these methods and then try again:

- ✔ **Turn off any antivirus software.** Installers sometimes mimic virus activity and can make your computer incorrectly believe that it is being infected by a virus.

- ✔ **Close all running programs.** The more programs you're running, the less memory that is available to other programs. Installers also typically update files and programs, so if you keep other programs running, installation might not work properly.

- ✔ **Add more RAM to your computer.** Adding more memory speeds your computer and allows more programs to run at the same time.

If you still have trouble with installing the items from the CD, please call the IDG Books Worldwide Customer Service phone number: 800-762-2974 (outside the U.S.: 317-596-5430).

Index

• **D** •

• S •

• *U* •

• X •

X button, 77
X terminal, 93, 96
   Linuxconf, 103
   LISA, 107

• Y •

Yahoo!, 14

• Z •

Zip drive
   access, limiting, 139
   access for everyone, 139
   backup device, use as, 247
   configuring internal or SCSI drive, 137
   configuring parallel port drive, 138–139
   mounting, 137–138, 247
   sharing, 16
   sharing in Samba, 140
   types, 247
zombie processes, 166

Installation Instructions

All the programs on the CD are for installation on a Linux system except Smbedit, which is a Windows program. For complete details about installing and using the software on this CD, see the "About the CD" appendix.

Limited Warranty

IDG BOOKS WORLDWIDE BOOK REGISTRATION

We want to hear from you!

Register This Book and Win!

Visit **http://my2cents.dummies.com** to register this book and tell us how you liked it!

- ✔ Get entered in our monthly prize giveaway.

- ✔ Give us feedback about this book — tell us what you like best, what you like least, or maybe what you'd like to ask the author and us to change!

- ✔ Let us know any other *For Dummies®* topics that interest you.

Your feedback helps us determine what books to publish, tells us what coverage to add as we revise our books, and lets us know whether we're meeting your needs as a *For Dummies* reader. You're our most valuable resource, and what you have to say is important to us!

Not on the Web yet? It's easy to get started with *Dummies 101®: The Internet For Windows® 98* or *The Internet For Dummies®* at local retailers everywhere.

Or let us know what you think by sending us a letter at the following address:

For Dummies Book Registration
Dummies Press
10475 Crosspoint Blvd.
Indianapolis, IN 46256

FOR DUMMIES™

BESTSELLING
BOOK SERIES